To Linda,
Thank you so
much for sharing
my long journey
to publication with
all your help and
suggestions.

Memoir of a Reluctant Atheist

My Journey Back to Stardust

Judith Heaney Rousseau

First Edition: July 2017

Printed in the United States of America

ISBN: 978-1-939237-49-1

Library of Congress Cataloging-In-Publication Data
Library of Congress Control Number: 2017914595

Published by Suncoast Digital Press, Inc.
Sarasota, Florida, USA

For my forebears,
husband, Conrad, and
our descendants
with all my love...forever

Contents

PROLOGUE

To the outside observer, I grew up to fulfill all expectations—college, marriage, and motherhood—in that prescribed orthodox order. As a little girl, teenager, and young mother, I followed all the criteria spelled out for devout, practicing Catholics.

The book begins with my ancestry. The first two chapters depict six generations on my maternal side and four generations on my paternal side. Numerous posed daguerreotypes and informal snapshots dot the pages.

Chapters Three through Fourteen portray my life from birth through age thirty-two with photos from my family albums. I was born on a chicken farm in New Hampshire in the thirties, lived through ration stamps and blackouts in the forties amid World War II, came of age in the post-war fifties of the Cold War and Eisenhower era, and encountered my own insecurities mixed together with the tumultuous happenings of that free-thinking period.

Then, at age thirty-two, circumstances divined an alternative path. I no longer believed in God. I was still the same woman raised by traditional parents to pursue the traditional life expected of the Silent Generation. I didn't proclaim my new identity. I continued to live my life with all the same morals and values. As atheists say, I believed in one less God than theists do.

I only shared this affirmation with my immediate family. When others asked my religious affiliation, I said that I was non-religious, or a non-practicing Catholic. Our family no longer attended church. Our third child was not baptized. Our second child did not receive his First Communion. None were confirmed in the Catholic Church. But all three children were taught morals, values, and respect for all life. The children behaved because it was the right way to act, not because an omniscient God was watching and judging them.

I lived my life from age thirty-two to seventy as a typical American housewife, mother, and part-time career woman—summed up in Chapter Fifteen. Then, at the dawning of the new century, as I entered my seventh decade, I decided to embark on the fulfillment of my dream to author a book and to validate atheism as a way of life. Why not combine the two? Why did I lack faith? Was I wrong? I began by researching the religions of the world and the Darwinian theory of evolution. Where, when, why, how and what do we come from?

During this intense studying period, a chance email from my college roommate afforded me the opportunity to visit Israel and Jordan with her and members of her Catholic Church. Chapters Sixteen through Twenty-Seven convey the account of my trip to the Holy Land in search of the true origin of life on Earth or beyond. Would this visit to the historical site of all Abrahamic religions coupled with the sincere faith of my fellow pilgrims and the exceptional kindness of our tour guide Father Don Senior restore my belief in God? After all, I described myself as a "reluctant" atheist.

In the final two chapters, I compare faith and belief in God to the preponderance of evolutionary evidence for the explanation of our existence. After I returned home, I continued researching organic life, all the way back to the first appearance of our own species, *Homo sapiens*.

I am not a theologian or a biologist, but I am a thinking, curious being. I read the myths, stories, and historical facts featured in the Bible and other Holy Books and contrasted them to the theories and peer-reviewed data advanced in scientific journals and text books. I assembled the most salient points in an easy-to-read format and compiled a comprehensive bibliography at the end of the book for readers interested in further exploration and information.

I loved researching this book. I guarantee you will learn, as I did, astonishing and obscure facts. Read this book with an open and inquiring mind. Enjoy the evidence of my sincere struggle to either reclaim faith or to continue to embrace atheism.

Chapter One

My Maternal Ancestry

This is a story about a little girl named Judy.

One of her earliest memories is of a nightly ritual. As she lay in bed awaiting sleep, she tried to understand the meaning of the word "forever." She knew when she died she would go to heaven or hell for forever. She tried to picture, imagine, and reach for the end of forever. But forever was forever. It did not end. It kept being there. It would not finish. It tumbled over and over into eternity, a word she did not know. She kept pushing for an end. But there was no end. How could there be an end to forever? Trying to find forever was a feat she never accomplished. Her quest ended in sleep.

The book is also a story of the grown-up quest of the little girl. If there were no end, was there a beginning? When and what and where and why and how was the beginning? The nuns in Sunday School taught her God was the answer. In childhood that simple explanation was enough.

Now, as an adult, she searched for the answer to the questions of the beginning, the end, and forever.

*****

From a study of early hominins I learned the very first generic ancestor or *Homo sapiens* became anatomically indistinguishable from archaic man about 200,000 years ago. My very first known-to-me, actual ancestor was my maternal great-great-great-great grandmother Norse, born about 199,800 years later. I don't know her Christian name, but I have her picture taken in 1866 when she was 100 years old, and the chair she sat in at the time of her portrait. She died in 1868 at the age of 102. From these dates I calculated Grandmother Norse was born in 1766, nine years prior to the start of the American Revolution.

She was the mother of Elizabeth (Norse) Webber, who died at age ninety-five and was the mother of Emily (Webber) Jones, who was the mother of Emma (Jones) Nutter, who was the mother of Willa Bessie (Nutter) Bryant, who was my grandmother and the mother of Emma Marion (Bryant) Heaney, my mother.

My great-great-great-great-grandmother Norse at age 100, taken in 1866

Another favorite picture from my ancestral album is the Jones family portrait. Lyman Jones, the father of four daughters, was a prominent furniture-maker in the state of Vermont. In the picture his wife, Emily, wore a reversible gold brooch with inlaid flowers on one side and his picture encased on the other side. I inherited this pin from my mother and gave it to my only granddaughter, Elena, on her twenty-first birthday, December 19, 2014.

During her long life of ninety-six years, my mother saved every picture, every letter, every card, every newspaper clipping, and every certificate relating to her or her family. She stashed her memorabilia in boxes under her bed or in the four drawers of her prized highboy secretary desk. Although an unorganized jumble, she had written names, dates, and places in a clear, legible script on the backs of most of the photos. Her foresight made this memoir possible.

From the faded, stylized sepia photographs to the shiny black and white, casual snapshots, I traced my mother's life from birth to death. The pictures add spice and veracity to my tale and help me understand her legacy to me. My mother was a feminist before the term was coined. Maybe the lessons she learned from her flare and willfulness caused her to monitor and restrain my actions. Many times she nixed my burgeoning adolescent dreams.

"No, Judith, that dream is impossible. You cannot be a doctor and also a wife and mother."

Left to right: Erva, Lyman with Mary on lap,
Emily, Clara, and Emma, my great-grandmother
Note the brooch on Emily, the mother.

"No, Judith, that dream is impossible. You cannot be a ballerina unless you began ballet training at age two."

"No, Judith, that dream is impossible. You cannot be a fashion model because you are not tall enough."

I don't know how much of her negativity stemmed from her parents denying her her dream to study in New York City to become a fashion designer.

My mother's parents married very young. Although my mother never said it directly, I think my grandmother's family thought Willa married beneath herself when she wed an Irishman whose family had changed its name from O'Brien to Bryant. On the back of one of the photos I learned my grandfather's middle name was Starr, a family name my mother considered giving me as a middle name and then rejected the thought. As a result I never had a middle name. I think my mother didn't want to burden me with a pretentious name like Starr, or maybe she feared I might choose it over my Christian name as she had done. At an early age she insisted on being called "Marion," her middle name, instead of her given name of "Emma" that she detested.

At the turn of the twentieth century, my mother and her younger sister Rachel grew up in Portsmouth, New Hampshire, always in rented houses, but always with indoor plumbing. My grandfather was a master carpenter. To my surprise, even at their economic level, my grandmother had domestic help. When my grandmother died in her early forties, my grandfather married Hazel, the housekeeper. I don't think my mother ever forgave him.

My mother and her sister were opposites and rivals, like Lady Mary and Lady Edith in the PBS television drama, *Downton Abbey*. My mother, a tomboy, played baseball with the boys, owned a boy doll instead of a baby doll, and stole her sister's boyfriends. She slept in on Saturday mornings while her sister rose early. This habit caused bickering between them over their assigned chores. Rising early, Rachel washed the previous night's dishes and stacked them to drain in a tipsy pyramid for my mother to dry and put away later in the morning, at her peril.

A photo gallery of Marion and Rachel from ages six to eighteen appears below. Similar to current custom, their mother dressed them in identical outfits for their formal pictures.

From left, Marion, seven, and Rachel, six

From left, Marion, ten, and Rachel, nine

*From left, Marion, thirteen, and
Rachel, twelve
On the back of the picture,
my mother wrote,
"I was mad and wouldn't fix my hair."*

*From left, Marion, eleven,
and Rachel, ten*

Because my mother repeated the fifth grade due to a long winter at home with measles and rheumatic fever, the sisters graduated together from Portsmouth High School in the class of 1915.

*Marion Bryant,
Portsmouth High
School Class of 1915*

*Rachel Bryant,
Portsmouth High School
Class of 1915*

Unusual for the time, both girls attended college. My aunt Rachel went to the University of New Hampshire where she joined Chi Omega Sorority, my Greek choice many years later. My mother attended and graduated from Farmington Maine Normal School, a two-year teachers' college. The career path for young ladies of that era was either nursing or teaching. One of my mother's aunts was a nurse and strongly recommended teaching over nursing.

My aunt Rachel left college early for marriage and motherhood. I never met my aunt Rachel, her husband, or her baby boy due to a tragedy and hushed-up, shameful scandal.

I heard the story once when I was six years old. I overheard my mother and great-aunt talking about the incident. When I questioned them, they explained the situation with facts suitable for my age. It was never mentioned again. I never asked about it again. I sometimes dreamed about it. I never was sure if the story were true or a dream. I often thought I had imagined it. Until in her nineties in bouts of youthful recollections related to dementia, my mother retold the story to me.

My aunt Rachel accidentally killed herself with a coat hanger, trying to abort an unwanted second child. I do not know any more facts than that. She was married. Was her husband leaving her? Did they not have enough money? Was the child the result of an affair? Why would she not want a second child? I do not know the circumstances. As far I know, after Rachel's death, my mother had no further contact with her brother-in-law or nephew. Also my grandmother, the grandmother of Rachel's only child, died soon after Rachel's death. This tragedy happened while my mother was living a life of adventure traveling across the country in her Model-T Ford—twenty years before she married and settled down.

After matriculation at Farmington Maine Normal School, the state of Maine required the graduates to teach school for two years within state. So, in 1917 and 1918, my mother's first teaching job was in Gardiner, Maine, at the ages of twenty-one and twenty-two. When she fulfilled her obligation, she explored teaching options in other states and accepted a position in Sioux City, Iowa.

After two years in Iowa, she moved on to Casper, Wyoming. The Department of Education of Wyoming certified her teaching credentials as valid for life, not just for a stipulated number of years. Attached to the certificate was verification from the

My mother in a cornfield in Iowa
She self-titled the photo:
"Sweetheart of the Corn."

superintendent that my mother had read the required professional books: *Juvenile Story Writing* and *Nutrition and Growth in Children.*

My mother's eighth grade class in Casper, Wyoming
My mother, sixth from left, back row

My mother mentioned a boyfriend from her time in Wyoming. She indicated on the back of his photo that the Hughes, the couple who owned the boarding house where she lived, introduced them. As a young girl I was fascinated with the picture of my mother's cowboy boyfriend.

Today I think it looks like a "come-on" he handed out to all his women friends.

After three years in Wyoming, my mother moved on to her defining adventure, an achievement any present day feminist would admire and envy. This was the Roaring Twenties—a decade devoted to modernity—showcasing the flapper-style for women, jazz music, industrial growth, and Art Deco.

My mother wrote to the Territory of Hawaii to request a teaching position. They wrote back saying they never accepted applications from the States because most times the girls did not come. So, with no promised employment, like any fearless, flamboyant feminist of the day, she booked passage on an

My mother's boyfriend in Casper, Wyoming

ocean liner to Hawaii and appeared at their doorstep. She was welcomed and immediately granted a certificate to teach.

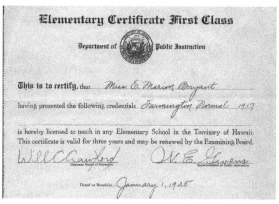

My mother's Certificate to Teach in the
Territory of Hawaii (1925)

Her two-year tenure on the Islands satisfied her desire for immediate excitement and at the same time would lead to a late-in-life love affair. She loved the children and the children loved her. Her memories were vivid. The children were Hawaiian, Japanese, Chinese, and Filipino. Also, a few white children from the extensive ranch holdings in the area attended the school. My mother noted that all the ethnic races intermarried except for the Japanese. She often told this anecdote: When she first arrived, all the Asian children looked alike and she couldn't tell one from another. After a few weeks she prided herself that she could even pick out brothers and sisters from their familial features.

The school at Kealakekua in Kona Hawaii
where my mother taught in the 1920s
The children lined up for a flag salute in the morning
and at dismissal.

My mother's long, reddish hair captivated the children. When she cut it in the flapper-style bob of the day, they wailed in despair, "Why? Why Miss Bryant cut hair?"

Admittedly, my mother was pretty but also the ratio of white women to white men was quite low. She received many marriage proposals. She turned them all down. However, the one suitor she wanted to marry did not propose. J. O. Kilmartin, a surveyor from the National Geographic Society, returned to the States by himself with no commitment to my mother.

Twelve Japanese girls in my mother's Sunday School class

Almost ten years later, my mother married my father in 1935. After my father's death in 1962, a mutual friend informed J.O. of the news. Although still married, J.O. wrote to my mother and they began a correspondence that lasted many years until his death in the 1980s.

My mother told me about the letters from J.O., the only given name I have for him. She admitted writing to him a few times a year. He asked her to send her letters to his club address at the National Geographical Society in Washington, D.C. She realized this subterfuge was to prevent his wife from learning of their secret correspondence. Although, it wasn't quite a secret—when he died, his wife wrote to my mother to tell her the sad news.

I was completely unaware of the extent and passion of this "by paper" love affair. After my mother died, I found boxes and boxes of letters from J.O. Kilmartin among her keepsakes. Many, many more than the five to six letters per year she occasionally alluded to.

My mother's boyfriend, J. O. Kilmartin, Kona, Hawaii 1924

On the back of this picture my mother wrote: "J.O. took this of me on our all-day picnic on December 26, 1924. Oh, glorious day!"

I guess that after J.O. returned to the States my mother decided to return home, too. She accepted a position to teach in Attleboro, Massachusetts, in 1926 at the salary of $1,500 per year. An attachment to the contract stated: "It shall be a condition of the election, reelection, or permanent tenure of a woman teacher that subsequent marriage shall automatically constitute a resignation of her position."

My mother on a picnic in Hawaii, taken by J.O.

After teaching four years in Attleboro, my mother accepted a teaching position in Swampscott, Massachusetts in 1930 at a salary of $1,750 per annum. She taught at the Hadley Junior High in Swampscott for five years. In 1935, she married my father, Donald Morrison Heaney, and resigned her teaching position.

My mother, Marion Emma Bryant, before her marriage in 1935

Chapter Two

My Paternal Ancestry

My documentation of my father's lineage dates back to 1777, not quite as far back as 1766 as on my mother's side, but close.

My uncle George, my father's older brother, researched the family tree and sent the findings to his siblings. The oldest lineage dates back to my great-great-grandfather, Samuel Morrison, on my father's maternal side. Samuel, probably born in Scotland, was a "high private" (my uncle's quotes) in the Napoleonic wars. He married Catherine Travers, born in 1777. Their only child, Samuel Travers Morrison, was born on November 1, 1815, in the army barracks at Carlisle, England. Later they lived in Ireland. After his mother's death in 1848, Samuel immigrated to the United States on October 17, 1848, two weeks before his thirty-third birthday.

My uncle's data does not indicate Samuel's occupation, but he married twice. First, he wed Sarah McLaughlin in 1850. Four years later, she and their three children died in an epidemic.

In 1854, he married Elizabeth Donaldson who bore him ten children. Her last child, Katherine Ann, born in 1874, was my paternal grandmother. She died in April of 1937, six months before I was born.

The dates tell the story of the longevity of my ancestors. Samuel sired his first child at age thirty-five and welcomed his thirteenth, my grandmother, at age fifty-nine. If not for Samuel's child number thirteen, I would not be here! He lived another thirty-one years and died at age ninety in 1905. From the genealogy, I noticed that I shared his birth date, November first, with mine being one hundred and twenty-two years later.

Paternal great-grandfather,
Samuel T. Morrison (1815-1905),
on the maternal side

The lineage on my father's paternal side dates back to Richard Heaney. The information on him is incomplete. He was born in either Ireland or Salem, Massachusetts. His son, Patrick Heaney, was born in Ireland or Massachusetts in 1839. He was my paternal great-grandfather. It appears both of these great-grandfathers on my father's side lived in the era of the bushy beard.

Patrick Heaney married Annie Donohoe. They had four children; the youngest was my father's father, George Francis Heaney, born on October 7, 1872, in Lynn, Massachusetts. He graduated from Lynn English High School in 1890. At that time, Lynn was the largest shoe-manufacturing city in the world. George went to work in the shoe factory as a cutter. Unsatisfied with factory work, he opened his own bicycle shop at the height of this new craze.

During the Spanish-American War, my grandfather enlisted in the Army Medical Corps and served at Huntsville, Alabama. He was discharged a short time later due to eye trouble. The war itself was very short-lived, lasting three months, two weeks, and four days from April 25, 1898, until August 12, 1898.

At the Treaty of Paris, Spain relinquished its sovereignty over Cuba, Puerto Rico, the Philippines, and Guam for the sum of twenty million dollars.

Paternal great-grandfather,
Patrick Heaney (1839-1905),
on the paternal side

Upon discharge, he entered the Civil Service as a clerk in the General Storekeeper's Office at the Boston Navy Yard. He worked there until his retirement in 1927, due to eye trouble, diagnosed as arteriosclerosis of the retina.

He married Katherine Ann Morrison, the aforementioned thirteenth child of Samuel Morrison, on January 29, 1900. They had five children: George Jr., Donald (my father), Elbridge, Virginia, and Janette. Following the lead of their father's patriotism, all three sons joined the army at some point in their careers. After high school, George Jr. went to West Point and retired as a Colonel. The next year, my father was appointed alternate to the Academy, but the first nominee accepted the opening so my father did not matriculate. Later, after various occupations, he joined the army and retired as a Lieutenant Colonel. Elbridge also served in the army and retired as a Major.

According to my uncle's biography, his father, George, and his partner invented a muffler for the new sensation, the automobile. The first one was installed in a car being built for the Czar of Russia. The partner absconded with the patent rights and their garage closed with no financial gain for my grandfather.

Later in life, my grandfather spent his time listening to news broadcasts as he was unable to read due to his poor eyesight. After Katherine died in 1937 from liver cancer, he married his wife's niece,

My grandfather,
George Francis Heaney,
in uniform as enlistee in the
Spanish-American War

My grandmother, Katherine
Anne Morrison,
at time of her marriage, 1900

My favorite photo of my father's family:
from left, my father Donald, Elbridge in front,
grandmother, George Jr., Janette, grandfather, and Virginia

Elizabeth Morrison, daughter of Katherine's older brother, John Morrison. My grandfather died in the Veteran's Hospital in St. Petersburg, Florida, in 1952 at age eighty from colon cancer.

I knew a lot about my mother's childhood from long mother-daughter chats. My father and I did not talk much about his youth. So my uncle's biography about his mother and her upbringing helped me imagine my father's younger days. Remember her father, Samuel Travers Morrison, was the great-grandfather who immigrated here at age thirty-three and married his first wife at age thirty-five. After her death and the death of their three children in an epidemic, he married my grandmother's mother at age thirty-nine and fathered ten children in twenty years. One might suppose he was Irish Catholic. Not the case.

He was raised as a Scottish Presbyterian. After studying various Christian religions on his own, he converted to Catholicism. He raised his ten children as strict Catholics with Scottish discipline. The children went to parochial schools. Katherine detested these schools and refused to send her five children to Catholic schools. She married my grandfather at age twenty-six, considered a late age for marriage for women in the nineteenth century.

She shunned social life and devoted her energy to her children. She had five children in seven years and monitored the playmates of her brood. She expected and demanded proper behavior and language. I believe this strict, Scottish and Catholic upbringing shaped my father's demeanor. My father did not smoke, drink, or swear. My mother respected and loved him, but often remarked to me, "It's difficult living with a saint."

I do not know much about his childhood or young adult activities, adventures, or jobs until he married my mother on New Year's Eve, 1935, at the age of thirty-three. His halo must have slipped a bit because their first child, my brother, was born seven months later.

From my few conversations with him about his youth, I knew he enjoyed swimming. He and his gang often swam to Egg Rock Lighthouse Station, a large crop of rocks situated about three miles out in the Atlantic Ocean, off of Lynn Beach, near his home.

I do know he was a good-looking man. At nine years old in the fourth grade, one of my friends seeing my father for the first time as he picked me up from school gushed, "Judy, I didn't know your father was so handsome!"

This revelation unnerved me. To me, he was my father, not a man to admire as handsome, or not. Today, I agree with her; my father was a very handsome man.

My father at Lynn Beach
in the 1920s

*My father in his army dress uniform in the
Panama Canal Zone at age thirty-nine*

The following chapters begin my personal story. The influence of my mother's and father's values on my life is apparent. My father was instrumental in my Catholic upbringing and also, surprisingly, in my contemplation of atheism.

Chapter Three

Infancy through Age Five

By a snug two-hour leeway, I was born on the first of November, 1937, at the small cottage hospital in Exeter, New Hampshire. My mother often remarked that I sported a full-head of red hair so arresting that the nurses paraded me through all the wards.

Front of original birth certificate

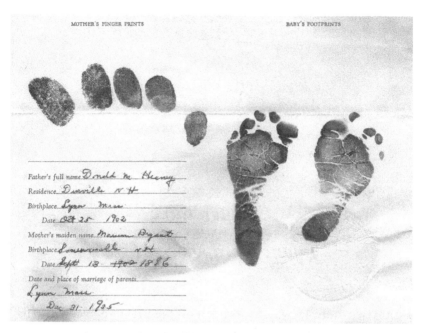

Back of original birth certificate

This side is more difficult to read, but look carefully and you can see where the year of my mother's birth was changed from 1902 to 1896. The correct year is 1896. I guess that my father supplied the information to the administrator, giving my mother's birth year the same as his because he was embarrassed his wife was six years older than he. Later, my mother must have crossed it out. She never lied about her age; instead, she boasted that she looked younger than her years. My mother was forty-one and my father was thirty-five at my birth.

My parents lived on a chicken farm in Danville, New Hampshire, a town about thirteen miles from Exeter. Danville's population in the 2010 census was 4,387, so it would be safe to assume in 1937 the number of residents was much less. Originally, in 1760, the town was chartered as Hawke, after Sir Admiral Edward Hawke. In 1836, the residents renamed the town Danville, due to at least three settlers named Daniel.

Marion Emma Bryant, my mother, a junior high history teacher in Swampscott, Massachusetts, met my father, Donald Morrison Heaney, through her uncle Charlie. I am hazy as to my father's occupation at the time of their introduction. I think he might have worked at her uncle's auto garage. My father dreamed of owning his own business. After their marriage on December 31, 1935, they cashed in my mother's teacher's retirement fund to purchase a chicken farm in Danville, New Hampshire. After her death in 1992 (at age ninety-six), I found this real estate listing among my mother's pictures and clippings:

Judy & Don—Where we lived when you were born

The properties described herein are located around this and nearby surrounding towns.

No. 525   **50 ACRES**   **$3500**

Beautiful Old Colonial Home; Farm For Garden Truck and 2400 Hens; Good Terms.

This place is said to be one of the best bargains in southern New Hampshire. Improved with splendid 2-story 10-room Colonial house, about 157 years old, in good repair throughout, has electric lights, bath, 4 fireplaces, brick oven, other quaint features, well water piped to copper tank with pressure system, is newly painted and shingled, large porch, 2 cellars, water at sink; good barn 38x58, has been remodeled into house for 2400 hens, running water to shed outside barn, electric lights. Only 3 miles to village, depot, short drive to city; RFD. store deliveries at farm, milk taken at door, short walk to bathing and fishing water. About 20 acres for hay, corn, potatoes, garden truck; remainder brook-watered pasture and woodland; fruit includes 15 apples, 3 cherries, 3 pears, grapes, berries, rhubarb, nuts. A real bargain, and less than half down.

No. 513   **121 ACRES**   **$4500**

The family chicken farm

With the information from this advertisement, I hoped to locate the old homestead. I had amateur shots of the farm house from my father's extensive collection of photographs, but no real identifying location of the farm. Now I felt I could more easily pinpoint the location from courthouse deeds.

In the fall of 2012, on a trip to visit our sons in Marblehead, Massachusetts, my husband and I drove to Danville, New Hampshire. We went to the town hall and inquired about the property. The clerks were very helpful and knew the owners and location of the farm. They gave us directions and suggested we drive out there. We did, knocked on the door, were invited in, and treated to a tour and oral history of the house.

My father and mother at the farm after their wedding, Dec. 31, 1935

My husband, Conrad, and me on the side porch, October 2012

Front view of the homestead, October 2012

The out buildings were gone and the acreage downsized, but the original exterior of the house was not remodeled, except for the removal of the overhead from the side porch and a new paint job.

I have no childhood recollections of my life on the farm. Pictures are my only "memories" from that period, as well as the information my mother and father told me. My brother was also born at the Exeter Hospital, on August 13, 1936, fifteen months before me.

My parents did not make a success of the operation. My father had no experience or knowledge about chicken farming. After a fire in the barn, the baby chicks were housed in the attic of the farmhouse. My mother wiped the droppings from their bottoms—a time consuming and unpleasant job. In 1939 after four years of trying, they abandoned the idea of poultry farming, returned to the North Shore area, rented a small house in Salem, Massachusetts, and eventually paid off the substantial debts they had incurred. My mother bragged that they settled every cent of the grain bills, but not until the mid 1940s.

My father with the chickens on the farm

21

My mother with baby chicks on the farm

My father, brother, Donnie, mother, and Granddad Heaney on the farm, 1936

My brother Donnie and me at the farm, two and one

Me at the farm, eight months

True to the dictates of the Roman Catholic Church I was baptized soon after my birth. My father was a Roman Catholic (baptized in infancy); my mother was a Congregationalist who joined her church when she was in her early twenties. Before marrying my father, my mother promised to raise any children in the Catholic faith, although she herself did not convert to Catholicism.

My mother always honored her promises. She often told this story of an early morning escapade. In her teens, one spring day, she skipped classes to watch the unloading of the circus train in Portsmouth, New

Hampshire. Later, she and her mother were called to the principal's office to explain the truancy. The principal expected to extract a promise from my mother to "never play hooky again." She promptly answered that she could not promise that. She knew she might be tempted again. According to my mother, the principal admired her honesty and excused this absence and presumably any future follies.

In 1939, when my family arrived in Salem, Massachusetts, my father did not have a job. His brother, George, a graduate of West Point, gave us five dollars a week to help with food and rent. I guess my father found various odd jobs but nothing satisfactory. Finally, in 1940, my father joined the army as an officer. Remember, he had

My Baptismal Certificate

been appointed an alternate to West Point the year after his older brother, George, had entered the Academy, but my father had not matriculated. Again we moved, this time to Fort Ethan Allen, Vermont. The installation, near Colchester, Vermont, was named after Ethan Allen, an American Revolutionary War hero. Begun as a cavalry post in 1894, it was deactivated in 1944. The area is now known locally as "The Fort."

My own memories begin from this page in the narrative. I am now three years old and do not rely on photos or feedback from other people for my recollections. In my mind, our new house was large with a castle-like turret that fascinated me. I remember walking up the stairs to the tiny attic room. I also recall a vivid childhood injustice.

Psychiatrists believe most lasting memories are linked to emotions, with pleasant emotions remembered more often than unpleasant ones.

It is the emotional arousal, not the significance of the occasion that aids the memory.

The little boy next door had a wondrous teddy bear that actually ate crackers. He was a little older than I, and I adored him. The neighbor boy invited my brother, not me, to his birthday party. I was devastated. I believe I remember the slight due to the emotions of jealousy and envy that I felt toward my sibling. (My brother does not remember the boy or the fabulous bear.)

The neighborhood boy, the bear, me, and my brother

In 1941, the U.S. Army transferred my father to Panama in the Panama Canal Zone. We traveled as a family to the new assignment. The billet

did not allot us a house on base, so my father rented a Spanish-style stucco house. An iron fence surrounded the property. I remember a round, rock-walled well in the front yard that we used as a swimming pool. I have many memories from this house: running to hide under the covers of the bed when my mother yelled "scorpion," feeding deer in our back yard, splashing in the "well" pool, and experiencing sibling rivalry again. For Christmas, from our aunt Gina, my father's favorite sister, my brother received a toy (a wooden tug boat) while I received clothes (a blue chenille bathrobe). My emotion: outrage!

Donnie and me peering through the iron fence

On December 7, 1941, the Japanese bombed Pearl Harbor. Soon after Christmas that year, the U.S. Army shipped all the dependents of the troops home to the States. My mother, with my brother and me, sailed on a banana boat back to America. My mother decided to settle in Swampscott, Massachusetts, where she had friends from her teaching

My mother feeding a deer
in the backyard

Me and Donnie sitting on
the well in the front yard

years. We rented the top floor of a two-story house on Thorndike Terrace, near an elementary school and St. John's Catholic Church.

Swampscott is where my religious memories begin. As mentioned previously, my mother promised my father to bring the children up Catholic. Donnie and I were five and four when we arrived in Swampscott. That summer of 1942, my brother turned six. My mother enrolled him in the first grade at Hadley Public School where she had taught in the attached junior high. She also registered Donnie and me in Sunday school at St. John's Catholic Church. The parochial school was across the street from us; the public school was at the end of the street. Since my father had not gone to Catholic schools, he did not want his children to attend parochial schools either. He did expect us to attend Sunday school for religious training. Traditionally, Catholics observe the rite of First Holy Communion at age seven. Many may be familiar with the prosaic adage, attributed to the Jesuit Order, "Give me a child before age seven, and I will give you a Catholic for life."

Kindergarten did not exist in Massachusetts at that time, so I couldn't enter public school. However, the nuns allowed my mother to enroll me in Sunday school with my brother at the first grade level. I don't remember any of the dogma but I do remember an emotional moment. At the end of the year, Sister asked all the children ready for second grade and the Holy Communion Class to stand. Of course, I stood up and urged my brother to stand too. He would not. To my surprise, Sister told me to sit and my brother to stand. She explained to me that I was too young to be promoted to second grade. Crying, I, alone, sat down and watched my brother stand with the rest of the class. Emotion: humiliation.

During those years of World War II, my mother snapped lots of pictures of my brother and me with her small, black box-camera to send to my father, fighting in the Far East in the Japanese Theater. Many were taken on Sunday morning, going to or coming from church. Other snapshots were of us playing in the courtyard outside of our house.

On my research trip to Massachusetts in the winter of 2012, I returned to Thorndike Terrace to photograph my first home in Swampscott. The only visible difference in the structure from the forties was the upper and lower side porches were now enclosed, and a garage had been added on the left. Even the exterior paint was the same, a muted-gray color.

My mother, Donnie, and me returning with groceries to our house on Thorndike Terrace

My former house on Thorndike Terrace, winter 2012

The gang dismantling crates of household goods,
shipped to us from Panama

Easter Sunday 1942

Christmas morning 1942,
my father's picture on the mantel,
me in the chenille bathrobe

From four and five years of age (1942-1943), I have many genuine memories of my two years living at Thorndike Terrace. My memories are not drawn from reviewing pictures but from connections to an emotion. I remember an older boy, age eight, from the "Terrace Gang" who chose to give me an ink fountain pen, a prize all the gang coveted. My emotion: pride. I remember squatting and peeing through my underpants in a rain puddle because I was too lazy to walk up the stairs to our bathroom. My emotion: shame. I remember a surprising find my brother and I made one December afternoon. Emotions: shock and disappointment.

On a freezing day in late December, my mother left Donnie and me alone in the house for an hour while she went to the food store. She cautioned us not to answer the phone, not to open the door, not to squabble with each other, and not to go into the passageway that led to the third floor, because it was not heated and was very cold. We did not heed her last admonition and ran through the hallway in a game of chase. There, on the stairs to the attic was a pile of unwrapped toys and games, many from our Santa Claus list. Even at our young ages, we immediately realized the implication of our sudden discovery. Santa Claus was a fairy tale. Mommy bought the presents. We agreed not to tell and to act surprised on Christmas morning.

After this disillusionment, I learned to question other popular childhood fables. The Easter Bunny presented no concerns. I never believed a little woodland creature delivered chocolate candy from a wicker basket on Easter morning. Too implausible. (Not like the stuffed bear I saw crunch crackers with my own eyes.) I thought I had empirical evidence that the tooth fairy existed. My mother or father could never rummage under my pillow to exchange a coin for a baby tooth without waking me up. That left the stork delivering little ones in a large white diaper. I didn't believe that one either. I knew babies grew in their mummy's tummy. However, at this stage in my Catholic upbringing, I never doubted the existence of God.

Chapter Four

My First Holy Communion

In 1943, when I was six and my brother was seven, my mother bought a house at 9 Redington Street, Swampscott, around the corner from Thorndike Terrace and across the street from the Hadley Elementary School. The house sat in back of another house that actually faced onto Redington Street and beside an alley that ran behind the stores of the main commercial street, Humphrey Street. This main artery, in approximately 500 yards, changed in name and aura to Lynn Shore Drive, an elegant thoroughfare with the ocean and boardwalk on one side and large, expensive houses on the other side. We strolled to the beach; skipped across the street to school; walked up Humphrey Street to St. John's Church, the dry cleaners, the hairdresser, and grocery stores; caught a bus to Lynn (closest city) at the nearby stop; and walked in the opposite direction to the library and to the train station for Boston. A house perfectly situated for a family with no car. This was European village-living in the United States. I knew nothing else. I still brag that today you can literally walk from Swampscott to Boston on sidewalks—a distance of twelve miles.

My mother paid $3,500 for the modest house of three rooms downstairs and three bedrooms/one bath upstairs. In 1946, after World War II was over and my father returned, they sold the house for $7,000. In 2012, although the real estate was not for sale, Zillow.com listed the three bedroom, one bath property at a value of $295,000. The selling feature was an enclosed upstairs porch with a view of Boston and the Atlantic Ocean.

On my winter trek to Massachusetts in 2012, I snapped a picture of the outside. The property was rundown, very much in need of a make-over. Fall flower pots and debris littered the front porch. However, the house looked the same from the outside as I remembered from my childhood.

I also photographed the Swampscott skyline, looking back from the Lynn Shore Drive promenade—St. John's Catholic Church to the right and the Hadley Elementary School to the left. You can spot my former house sandwiched between the two structures.

The house at 9 Redington Street, winter 2012, St. John's spire in background

Hadley School on left, St. John's Church on right, my house between the two

I grew up during the war years (1942 to 1945) in this small seaside town of Swampscott. The Native Americans called the area, *M'sqiompsk,* or red rock, due to the visible red granite along the shore. From first grade through third grade, I attended the Hadley Elementary School across the street from my house. The class composition was seven girls and twenty-three boys. None of the girls, and only a few of the boys, were Catholic. It seems the majority of the school district's Roman Catholic children were educated at nearby St. John's Parochial School where my brother and I attended on Sundays for our religious training.

My mother fulfilled her promise to my father by bringing us to the nine o'clock Mass on Sunday mornings. After the service, Donnie and I filed through a corridor from the church to the classrooms where the sisters taught us the Catholic prayers, beliefs, and rituals. They instructed us from the official *Saint Joseph Baltimore Catechism*, purchased for a dime. We were not exposed to Bible stories, only the question and answer format of the catechism. We memorized the material at home and parroted it back the next Sunday. This knowledge prepared us for the sacrament of First Holy Communion at the end of second grade, at age seven.

The nuns taught us the obligatory prayers memorized by all Roman Catholics: The Sign of the Cross, The Lord's Prayer, The Hail Mary, The Apostles' Creed (Roman Catholic version of The Nicene Creed), and The Blessing before Meals, and The Act of Contrition. From *The Catechism* we learned the formal rites of the Catholic faith. I suddenly realized in writing this memoir that I have a strange unexplained loss of memory. I can remember the name and face of every elementary school teacher I encountered from first grade to sixth grade, but I cannot recapture one sister's face or name from my years of religious study at St. John's Parrish.

As a child, I did not understand the meanings and rituals of the Catholic Mass. Until The Second Vatican Council, 1962-1965, the Mass was conducted in Latin. I did not follow any of the liturgies intoned by the priests or any of the responses rendered by the congregation in the classical language. Maybe the parochial students learned the Latin meanings in their daily lessons. I do remember one of my diversions to counter the boredom at Mass. On Sundays, I tried to sit in the front row in order to caress the fur coats of the ladies leaning back against the pew, as they waited to receive Holy Communion.

The Catechism is the initial introduction to all Catholic religious training. The following is a summary of the Eleven Lessons from this compact sixty-four page booklet, written for the beginner reader with easy words and many pictures. For my non-Catholic readers, this overview is a simplification of the tenets of the Church.

Lesson One "God Made Us" (The Purpose of Man's Existence)

1. Who made you?

   God made me.

2. Did God make all things?

   Yes, God made all things.

   The answer continues with a list of everything God created in Genesis such as Earth, sky, sun, moon, stars, night, day, oceans, trees, fish, birds, animals, angels, spirits and Adam and Eve.

3. Why did God make you?

   God made me to show His goodness and to make me happy with Him in heaven.

4. What must you do to be happy with God in heaven?

   To be happy with God in heaven I must know Him, love Him, and serve Him in this world.

Lesson Two "God is Great" (God and His Perfections)

5. Where is God?

   God is everywhere.

6. Does God know all things?

   Yes, God knows all things.

7. Can God do all things?

   Yes, God can do all things.

8. Did God have a beginning?

   No, God had no beginning. He always was.

9. Will God always be?

   Yes, God will always be.

Lesson Three "The Blessed Trinity" (The Unity and Trinity of God)

10. Is there only one God?

    Yes, there is only one God.

11. How many persons are there in God?

    In God, there are three Persons—the Father, the Son, and the Holy Spirit.

12. What do we call the three Persons in one God?

    We call the three Persons in one God, the Blessed Trinity.

13. How do we know that there are three Persons in one God?

    We know there are three Persons in one God because we have God's word for it.

Lesson Four "The First Sins" (Sin: Original Sin)

14. What is sin?

    Sin is disobedience of God's laws.

15. Who committed the first sin?

    The bad angels committed the first sin.

16. Who committed the first sin on earth?

    Our first parents, Adam and Eve, committed the first sin on earth.

17. Is this sin passed on to us from Adam?

    Yes, this sin is passed on to us from Adam.

18. What is this sin in us called?

    This sin in us is called original sin.

19. Was anyone ever free from original sin?

    The Blessed Virgin Mary was free from original sin.

Lesson Five "Our Own Sins" (Actual Sin)

20. Is original sin the only kind of sin?

    No, there is another kind of sin, called actual sin. (Note: I don't remember ever hearing of actual sin.)

21. What is actual sin?

    Actual sin is any sin which we ourselves commit.

22. How many kinds of actual sin are there?

    There are two kinds of actual sin: mortal sin and venial sin.

23. What is mortal sin?

    Mortal sin is a deadly sin.

24. What does mortal sin do to us?

    Mortal sin makes us enemies of God and robs our souls of his Grace.

25. What happens to those who die in mortal sin?

    Those who die in mortal sin are punished forever in the fire of hell.

Here, I mention again, my childhood ritual. Before going to sleep at night I remember trying to unlock the concept of "forever." It was impossible because when I thought I had imagined the end, I realized there never could be an end. This depressing thought circled around and around and could not be erased from my mind. Today I understand from reading a book by Richard Feynman, an American theoretical physicist, that our brains developed in a world of large, slow things, so understanding quantum theory or infinity is probably not compatible with how the human mind evolved. How sad and shameful to frighten children with thoughts of burning in hell forever.

26. What is venial sin?

    Venial sin is a lesser sin.

27. Does venial sin make us enemies of God or rob our souls of His grace?

No, venial sin does not make us enemies of God or rob our souls of His grace.

28. Does venial sin displease God?

Yes, venial sin does displease God.

Lesson Six "The Son of God Becomes Man" (The Incarnation)

29. Does one of the Persons of the Blessed Trinity become man?

Yes, the Second Person, the Son of God became man.

30. What is the name of the Son of God made man?

The name of the Son of God made man is Jesus Christ.

31. When was Jesus born?

Jesus was born on the first Christmas Day, more than nineteen hundred years ago.

32. Who is the Mother of Jesus?

The Mother of Jesus is the Blessed Virgin Mary.

33. Is Jesus Christ both God and man?

Yes, Jesus Christ is both God and man.

Lesson Seven "Jesus Opens Heaven for Us" (The Redemption—The Church)

34. Why did God the Son become man?

God the Son became man to satisfy for the sins of all men and to help everybody to gain heaven.

35. How did Jesus satisfy for the sins of all men?

Jesus satisfied for the sins of all men by His sufferings on the cross.

36. How does Jesus help all men to gain heaven?

Jesus helps all men to gain heaven through the Catholic Church. The Church is like a ladder to heaven. Jesus gave us only ONE ladder. The Church is our only way to heaven.

In reflection, this lesson is the most powerful of all—the essence of Christian beliefs, the story of the crucifixion and resurrection of Jesus told in simple words and dramatic pictures. The closing question and answer (number thirty-six) of this chapter reveals the Catholic Church's rigid and outright claim that only its followers ascend to heaven.

However, many other religions hold the same singular ideology, including Muslims and evangelical Christians. One correspondent of mine, a born again Christian, expressed the enigma this way. She was glad not everybody arose to heaven, because as a child she worried heaven would be too crowded. My enigma is why a self-professed Christian would be happy that not all souls entered Paradise.

At Swampscott's St. John's Parrish, one specific, historical and pompous hypocrisy disillusioned my mother from any thought of converting to Catholicism. In the forties and fifties before The Second Vatican Council, the Catholic Church routinely preached that only baptized Catholics entered heaven. All Protestants, Jews, Hindus, Muslims and members of all other religions did not gain heaven.

One Sunday in April 1945, the priest preached a sermon attesting that all infidels and non-Catholics were destined to hell. Then, the very next Sunday, April 15, 1945, after President Franklin Delano Roosevelt died on Thursday April 12, the same priest rescinded the damnation for at least one Protestant. He assured the congregation, grieving over the popular President's death, that indeed their Episcopalian leader would enter heaven.

Lesson Eight "The Sacrament of Baptism"

37. How does the Catholic Church help us to gain heaven?

   The Catholic Church helps us to gain heaven especially through the sacraments.

38. What is a sacrament?

   A sacrament is an outward sign, instituted by Christ to give grace.

39. What does grace do to the soul?

   Grace makes the soul holy and pleasing to God.

40. What sacrament have you received

   I have received the sacrament of Baptism.

41.   What did Baptism do for you?

Baptism washed away original sin from my soul and made it rich in the grace of God.

42.   Are you preparing to receive other sacraments?

I am preparing to receive the sacraments of Penance and Holy Eucharist. (The Christian sacrament of Holy Communion, in which bread and wine are consecrated and consumed.)

Lesson Nine "Sacrament of Penance"

43.   What is the sacrament of Penance?

Penance is the sacrament by which sins committed after Baptism are forgiven.

44.   What must you do to receive the sacrament of Penance worthily?

To receive the sacrament of penance worthily I must:

1.   Find out my sins.

2.   Be sorry for my sins.

3.   Make up my mind not to sin again.

4.   Tell the sins to the priest.

5.   Do the penance the priest gives to me.

A controversial position of the Catholic religion is the private recital of sins to the priest in a confessional booth. It is especially troublesome when deployed with seven-year-olds. The revised 1960 era Catechism suggests that young boys and girls do not often commit a mortal sin, the deadly sin. In fact, the text stipulates God protects them in a special way. This new, softer approach of the Church toward the Sacrament of Penance is now called the Sacrament of Reconciliation. However, when I was a child in the forties, missing Mass on Sundays or Holy Days of Obligation and eating meat on Fridays embodied mortal sins, even though these tenets were Church laws, not God's commandments. We knew the grave danger of committing a mortal sin—burning in hell forever if the sin were not confessed and absolved by the priest.

In Chapter Nine, the primer lists examples of venial sins: laughing or talking in church, being disobedient, talking back, fighting, using angry or bad words, stealing something, telling lies, being mean, or teasing someone unkindly. Most of us made up some sins to have a reasonable number to divulge in the confessional booth. After all these years, I remember only one actual lie.

On a school morning my mother asked, "Judith, are you wearing your undershirt?"

"Yes," I lied.

How I hated those ugly, orange-hued, ribbed undergarments and did not intend to go back upstairs to put one on, so I lied.

Also, I must have been aware of the consequences for misbehaving. When I was nine or ten, I wrote the following story, entitled "The Little Bad Girl," to illustrate my version of a moral parable.

The Little Bad Girl

Lesson Ten "How to Make a Good Confession"

45.   How do you make your confession?

I make my confession in this way:

1.   I go into the confessional and kneel.

2.   I make the sign of the cross and say:

"Bless me, Father, for I have sinned."

3.   I say: "This is my first confession (or, "It has been one week, or one month, since my last confession.")

4.   I confess my sins.

5.   I listen to what the priest tells me.

6.   I say the act of contrition loud enough for the priest to hear me.

46.   What do you do after leaving the confessional?

After leaving the confessional, I say the penance the priest has given me and thank God for forgiving my sins.

Lesson Eleven 'The Holy Eucharist"

47.   What is the sacrament of the Holy Eucharist?

The Holy Eucharist is the sacrament of the Body and Blood of Our Lord Jesus Christ.

48.   When does Jesus Christ become present in the Holy Eucharist?

Jesus Christ becomes present in the Holy Eucharist during the Sacrifice of the Mass.

49.   Do you receive Jesus Christ in the sacrament of the Holy Eucharist?

I do receive Jesus Christ in the sacrament of the Holy Eucharist when I receive Holy Communion.

50.   Do you see Jesus Christ in the Holy Eucharist?

No, I do not see Jesus Christ in the Holy Eucharist because He is hidden under the appearances of bread and wine.

In simple but emphatic rhetoric *The Catechism* continues to stress the actual presence of Jesus in the Holy Eucharist. I believe this is because the Church knows a child tries to actually see Jesus in the bread before accepting the concept. I am reminded of a young man who told me this story. In the third grade at a parochial school, the sister asked the children to draw a picture of Jesus. All the class, except for him, sketched the iconic image of a man with long hair and beard in a flowing robe. He colored a tableau of the sky, trees, flowers, birds, and a rainbow. The teacher chose his representation of Jesus to tape on the bulletin board.

51.   What must you do to receive Holy Communion?

To receive Holy Communion I must:

1.   Have a soul free from mortal sin.

2.   Not eat or drink anything for one hour before Holy Communion. But water may be taken at any time before Holy Communion.

52.   What should you do before Holy Communion?

Before Holy Communion I should:

1.   Think of Jesus.

2.   Say the prayers I have learned.

3.   Ask Jesus to come to me.

53.   What should you do after Holy Communion?

After Holy Communion I should:

1.   Thank Jesus for coming to me.

2.   Tell Him how much I love Him.

3.   Ask Him to help me.

4.   Pray for others.

After learning the prayers, memorizing the Catechism's questions and answers, rehearsing the ceremony, and confessing my sins, I was ready to receive my First Holy Communion on the first Sunday of May, 1945. I guess I didn't have any special emotion attached to this traditional Catholic religious rite because I don't remember it firsthand. Also, I didn't question any of the untenable beliefs advanced to me. The Jesuits had me at age seven. In fact, I envisioned I might be the Second Virgin Mary or First Virgin Judith when Jesus returned to Earth again.

My experience differed from my son Terry's introduction to the beliefs of the Church. When he was seven in 1969, the Star of the Sea Catholic Church of Marblehead, Massachusetts, no longer ran a daily parochial school or Sunday school. On Monday afternoons, mothers, acting as CCD (Confraternity of Christian Doctrine) religious teachers, replaced the nuns in instructing the children in religious education. I became the leader for Terry's First Holy Communion class. Unlike me, he considered the reality of the intriguing suppositions posed in *The Catechism*. The outcome of his conclusion will be discussed in a later chapter.

Many authors write of their search to understand the power of the Church's influence on our logical thinking. Richard Dawkins, famed biologist and atheist, discussed in his book, *The God Delusion,* one possible evolutionary reason why children's brains profited by unquestionably accepting advice from a trusted parent or other adult. Youth who didn't obey an admonition such as, "Don't swim in the crocodile infested river," would not mature to reproduce. So, due to Darwinian natural selection, the young people who heeded the elders' counsel lived to bear offspring. Their tractable minds were receptive to other ideas that may or may not have been correct; such as Zeus, the most powerful of all Gods, ruled over them from Mount Olympus, or that a prophet named Jesus died to give them eternal life.

My First Holy Communion,
May 1945

Chapter Five

My Pre-Teen Years 1945-1950

My elementary Roman Catholic indoctrination was complete. I was baptized and had received my First Holy Communion. The Jesuits deemed me a Catholic for life. Presumably, I would undertake the Sacrament of Confirmation at age twelve, marry in the faith through the Sacrament of Matrimony, raise my children in the teachings of the Church, be a committed Catholic for life and rise to heaven after my death anointed by the Sacrament of Extreme Unction (Last Rites). I was not aware of these presumptions for my life.

I was aware of World War II and its effect on my childhood. The war regulations along the Eastern seaboard required sacrifices from all civilians, even children. At home, we pulled down black-out shades at night. At school, we practiced air raid drills by filing to the basement to face the wall and wait for the imaginary sirens to end. We helped finance the war one dime at a time by buying ten-cent-war-stamps to fill United States War Bond booklets to be turned in to buy War Bonds, redeemable in ten years. All citizens were issued ration books for sugar, butter, meat, and gas for when and if these items became available. I remember my mother sending me to the market to stand in line to buy sugar or butter for the household.

Also, my adored father was fighting in New Guinea and the few letters home were censored by the War Department. One letter related this sailor superstition that gave us hope: "When one goes under the Golden Gate Bridge, if the person throws a coin up to the span, he will be sure to come back under it sooner or later." My brother and I believed our daddy tossed the coin and would come back. We knew we were always in his thoughts because he named his jeeps after us: one for me and one for Donnie.

World War II ended in August 1945. To celebrate, I rode with my friend in her father's car up and down Humphrey Street. We tooted the car's horn, yelled, and waved wildly at all the townspeople on the sidewalks. My father returned in the spring of 1946. He accepted a position as an engineer at Reynolds Metal in Longview, Washington. He left ahead of us to begin his job. My mother sold the house, packed the goods, and escorted us, along with our cocker spaniel, Mike, across the country via a three-day train trip.

When we arrived, we stayed at a motel for a month because our brand new house was not complete. We played with other children in the courtyard. One evening during a card game of Go Fish, I noticed one little girl reneged on a card in her

My father standing by his jeep,
"Judith"

hand. I was shocked by her action, accused her of cheating, and refused to continue playing the game. Is my sense of fairness innate, taught by family example, or remembered from internalized religious convictions? I truthfully don't know. I never remember cheating at a card game, board game, or at school. In high school, my biology teacher accused me of copying off the boy sitting in front of me. I was incensed at the suggestion and shouted out in class, "I don't cheat, but if I did, I certainly wouldn't copy from his paper." Believe me, she believed me.

Maybe my sense of justice was fueled by the books I read. I loved reading stories about animals. I remember one poignant account of a dog in an anthology of heroic animal deeds. I was shaken by the ending and sobbed and sobbed. In the tale, the family pet was left to watch over the baby sleeping in an old-fashioned rocker-cradle resting on the ground. A wolf tried to seize the child but the faithful dog tipped the cradle over to protect and hide the baby, fought with the wolf, and chased him away. When the father returned from hunting, he saw the upside down cradle, blood on the ground, and the dog lying next to the little bed. Before checking under it, he shot the loyal German shepherd, thinking the dog had harmed the baby.

When I enrolled in the fourth grade at Longview, Washington, the school experience proved quite different from the days at Swampscott, Massachusetts. For the first time, we rode a bus to school. We lived out in the country in a sub-division of new homes. Unlike the village lifestyle, we had to drive everywhere. The long school day encompassed two recesses and a lunch period. The favorite game at recess for the girls was "crack the whip." Before going out to the field, two classmates would vie to hold my hand in the playground game. I always reserved one hand for my best friend, Barbara, and the other for "my favorite" of the day. Occasionally, I chose to hold Norma's hand, the most unpopular girl in the class. The other girls appeared surprised but accepted my decision. What compelled me to consider the feelings of the unpopular girl? Did religion instill compassion in me? Did my mother teach me by example? Or was it simply an evolutionary instinct?

Strangely, although my Catholic father lived with us now, I don't remember ever attending church or Sunday school. I checked my childhood memory with my brother, and he agreed with me. He didn't remember attending church either.

Our stay in Longview was not long. My father pined for New England. So after less than a year, in April 1947, he resigned his employment at the plant. My parents took us out of school and we drove across the country on a three-week-long trip back to New England.

My mother urged me to keep a daily log of the experience. I still have the tattered notebook with my snapshots and memoirs. We drove down the Oregon coast, across California, through Arizona and New Mexico, up to the Continental Divide and down, through the panhandle of Texas, across the states of Oklahoma, Arkansas, Tennessee, Virginia, Maryland, Pennsylvania, New Jersey, New York, Connecticut until finally arriving home to Massachusetts. I bought a souvenir in each state.

We arrived in Swampscott on Sunday, April 27, a journey of nineteen days. My mother's friend from her teaching days invited us to stay with her while we looked for a house to buy. Coincidentally, we bought the house next door to hers at 14 Shaw Road, Swampscott.

Me, my mother, Mike, and Don
with Golden Gate Bridge
in the background

Don, me, Mike, my mother
at foot of a giant Sequoia

Don watching a flock of sheep cross over the highway

My mother, Don, and me
looking down at the Grand Canyon

Mike, me, and Don in
the Painted Desert, New Mexico

Me, Mike, and Don at the
Continental Divide, New Mexico

Me and my mother at
Valley Forge, Pennsylvania

The house on Shaw Road straddled the line between our former school district, the Hadley Elementary School, and the Clark Elementary School. My mother persuaded the superintendent to let my brother and me continue at the Hadley. We liked the idea even though we had to walk a distance of about one-half mile to school. The town of Swampscott did not operate school buses.

The house at 14 Shaw Road, 2013
In 1946, the house looked the same except painted dark brown

My father found an engineering job in Lewiston, Maine. He lived in an apartment there during the week and commuted home to Swampscott on weekends. This arrangement made the weekends special time. I played with my friends on Saturdays, but Sunday was family day. My father, brother, and I attended church together while my mother stayed home and prepared a Sunday noontime feast. After dinner we went on a traditional Sunday outing, very typical behavior during the forties and fifties.

The routine was predictable. Before setting out, my father told us two kids, "go drain yourselves." Then we all piled in the car, including our dog, Mike, and took a scenic drive along Route 1A North, always stopping to buy popcorn from the old gent with the pushcart at Salem Commons. We played a guessing game with my father who planned a mystery destination for us. He gave us the initials of the "secret place" and my brother and I vied to be the first to guess the location.

These stops were not amusement parks, movies, or shopping meccas. Usually they were a beach, a fishing wharf, or a city park. My favorite was an old, rundown colonial house in the middle of the woods that we christened "The Gingerbread House." My father never ran out of fun and interesting places to visit. A saying of his at the time, although not "politically correct" now, was "Essex County (Massachusetts) is the only place for a white man to live."

One Sunday, an accident precipitated an especially harrowing two or three weeks for my mother as well as the rest of us. At Stage Fort Park, Gloucester, a large public park bordering the ocean, my brother tried a Tarzan maneuver over a gully with a flag pole rope, fell, and broke his leg. A couple of days later, I stumbled playing in the street with the gang and broke my arm. At the end of the week Don and I both came down with the measles.

Don and me one Sunday at the beach

Those years in Swampscott were my pre-teen years from age nine until eleven. My fondest memory was of my haircut. My father loved his little girl in pigtails, but I hated them. My mother parted my hair down the middle and pulled it so tight in plaiting the braids that I didn't need side-barrettes. I had very thick hair and lots of it. I begged for curls. Finally, I convinced both of them to let me have my hair cut and to have a permanent wave. I beamed with pride with my shorter, curly hair.

Today, looking through pictures of me with braids, I see a classic hairstyle and an adorable young lady. Maybe father did know best.

Don, my mother, and me on a Sunday outing

The stay in Swampscott at Shaw Road did not last long either. My father grew tired of commuting and being away from his family. In the fall of 1948, he reenlisted in the army as a Lieutenant Colonel. His initial assignment was to Fort Bragg, North Carolina.

Me before haircut

Me after haircut

A new adventure began. Life in the late forties in the South presented new horizons for me. I had no concept of racial segregation. Very few African-Americans lived in the Northeast at the time. In North Carolina I saw many "White Only" or "Black Only" signs designating which drinking fountain, movie section, or rest room was appropriate. Schools, churches, and restaurants were completely segregated.

This time my father drove with us to the army base and our assigned house, Quarters 55—a large, imposing, stucco house. Upstairs, the amenities included a master bedroom with private bath, dressing room, and sitting room, besides two other large bedrooms and bath. The first floor consisted of a large living room with attached den, dining room and butler pantry, a large kitchen, and a maid's room with bath. My mother chose furniture from the army's stocked warehouse to add to our furnishings. To me the house was elegant, although my brother's room was nearer our shared bathroom.

I loved living at Fort Bragg. It was like a gated community of today. We kids had the run of the place, unconcerned with traffic or crime. We roller skated and rode bikes freely on the streets. We played softball, invented chase and tag games, and climbed trees in the grassy center islands. Every day in the summer we swam in the Olympic-size pool, and played tennis and golf at the Officers' Club.

The United States government ran a school on the base for grades one through eight. We could ride a bus, but on nice days we usually pedaled our bikes to school. I remember my seventh grade teacher, Mrs. Dash, for three reasons. First, she brought her black and white Irish setter to school with her, and he slept quietly under or by her desk. Second, since I read quickly and extensively, I often skimmed over unfamiliar words. Mrs. Dash cured

Me, my mother, and Don in front of the new residence on a Sunday

50

me of this bad habit. She insisted we use the dictionary to check on a word's exact meaning instead of guessing by the context. And third, she gave me a life-long appreciation of and interest in birding. She required the class to keep a list of all the birds we observed and identified. I remember my thrill when spotting a huge flock of cedar waxwings migrating through North Carolina as they headed north for the winter. The winner of the contest was announced at the end of the school year at a picnic at her house. I did not win, even with a list of over 100 birds.

Also, those two years were a turning juncture in my awareness of self. Up to now I had sailed through life with few adversities. I was smart, athletic enough, popular with both boys and girls, and very confident in myself. I thought this would always be. The second or third week, after arriving at my new classroom, the gym teacher introduced a square dancing class and asked the boys to select a partner. Drawing from my past experiences, I expected to be chosen first by the boys. When I wasn't asked first, second, or even third or fourth, I consoled myself with the thought that next time I would be the first pick. Nope! I soon learned that sixth-grade boys preferred girls with bosoms. My case was hopeless and probably would be for a very long time— that is, if there were a God.

Because in my prayers to God, I had asked Him to delay my breast development (we can assume not my exact words) to at least age fourteen. I hated the little bumps appearing through girls' T-shirts as puberty blossomed. Training bras had not been invented, or at least none of the mothers knew of them. I desired to instantaneously fill out a "B" cup at age fifteen.

Another set back from this awkward period—I discovered I couldn't read the blackboard from my seat at the back of the room. I noticed a friend of mine constantly sharpening her pencil at the front of the room and stealing glances at the board. I tried the same method, but eventually I told my parents and was fitted with glasses for myopia or nearsightedness. I hated them and only wore them to read the problems or assignments on the blackboard. Wearing glasses shattered the image I had of myself. My nightly prayers to God for perfect vision went unanswered, but not my request for slow-breast endowment. He heard me on that one. I was flat-chested until well past age fifteen.

Although I struggled inwardly from my unpopularity with the boys and my perceived ugliness from the glasses, I came of age at Fort Bragg, North Carolina in the late forties. As I write this, the memories flood back.

Many accomplishments valuable for future adulthood stemmed from those years, such as learning to play the piano; taking dancing, golf, and tennis lessons; and teaching myself to shuffle playing cards. Other favorite pastimes included hours playing Canasta, the newly popular card game in the forties, reading all the books from the Nancy Drew detective series, and discovering the addictive Parker Brothers board game Clue. We hosted countless sleepovers at each other's houses. We turned out the lights and snickered as we discussed the unknown mysteries of sex. We thought it was a disgusting undertaking that had to be done to make a baby. We only half believed it. As we wondered about the actual act, we rehearsed how to suggest such an unseemly topic to a future husband.

While I was enjoying my growing up years, my mother enjoyed having a live-in maid. Lettie lived in the maid's room during the week and went home on the weekends. She worked for my mother one day a week and cleaned for neighbors the other four days. For my mother, Lettie's most important job was washing the dishes and cleaning up the kitchen after our evening meal. My mother loved to cook, but hated the washing-up chores. She paid Lettie $5.00 a week for this arrangement. On the weekends, Lettie carried home lots of food and our out-grown clothes.

I liked Lettie, but hated one remark I overheard her say to my mother, "Judith is such a pretty girl. She has such beautiful, full lips." I was embarrassed by this statement and tried to squish my lips together in her presence.

Again, I don't remember going to church and Sunday school, but I know I did. I do remember being impressed that the Bishop from Raleigh, North Carolina came to the Army Chapel to perform the Sacrament of Confirmation for the graduating class. The only memory I have of the ceremony was bowing to him and kissing his ring. My father presented me with a real gold cross necklace to mark the occasion. I gave the heirloom to my granddaughter, Ellie, on her First Communion.

Those two years were very happy because my father was with us every day. We didn't go on Sunday drives, but we took several long vacations by car. We visited Grampy, my father's father, at the St. Petersburg Veteran's Hospital in Florida. We toured Washington, D.C. and its monuments and museums. We vacationed in the Smoky Mountains of North Carolina and visited the Atlantic Shore many times.

In early 1950, my father was scheduled to be reassigned and was due for foreign duty. We hoped to go to Europe, but my father thought war was going to break out again on the Continent, so he requested assignment to Japan. His appointment was to Kobe, Honshu, Japan. My mother learned that my brother and I would have to ride a train fifty miles each way to attend an American school. Because of this, she decided not to go with my father. The three of us returned to Swampscott to wait out my father's deployment. As it happened, my father was right about the war prediction. However, it broke out in Korea, not in Europe. Chances are the army dependents in Japan would have been sent back to the States.

Again, we bought a house in Swampscott. I entered the eighth grade in the middle of the year at Hadley Junior High School. The year was 1950. I was thirteen, a teenager.

Me and a friend
at the North Carolina shore

Me in the Smoky Mountains

Chapter Six

My Turbulent Teenage Years 1950-1955

My mother, brother, and I moved back to Swampscott, Massachusetts in the fall of 1950. A few weeks prior to our return, my parents traveled to Swampscott to locate and buy a house. This house was in a different section of town from our previous homes. However, since my brother and I were now in the upper grades, the students from all areas of town attended either the Hadley Junior High (grades seven and eight) or Swampscott High School (grades nine to twelve). The distance to both schools was over one mile and under two miles. No free school transportation was provided, but we could ride the commercial bus with a student discount ticket, or walk. Depending on the weather forecast, I chose one way or the other.

Our house at 974 Humphrey Street,
Swampscott, 1950

The same house
in the fall of 2012

I entered the eighth grade at Hadley Junior High. There were five divisions, A through E. Divisions A–C were college prep, and D–E were non-college sections. The principal assigned me to Division B, even though my transcript listed all A's. (I suppose she was suspicious of the Southern grading or school system.) My best friend from elementary school was in the A section, but I knew some of the girls in my classroom.

Me, Don, Mike, and my father in Swampscott before Dad left for Japan

Again, my time in Swampscott was limited to the two and one half years my father was assigned to Japan. These years were ages thirteen through fifteen—part junior high and part high school. As a mother and grandmother myself, I now appreciate the difficulties my mother experienced raising two teenagers without the presence of a father figure.

Before my father left, anticipating our need for transportation, he bought my mother a small, black car—a Ford Prefect made in England. It was a four-door with only room to seat four comfortably. But we often squeezed six teenagers and my mother in it at a time. We named it 'erbert 'orrace 'eaney.

From my memory as the younger sister, my brother, Don, did not present many problems for my mother. He was an easy-going adolescent and did all the right things. He earned his own money as a morning

Picture of a Ford Prefect —similar to 'erbert 'orrace 'eaney

paperboy; officiated as an altar boy at St. John's Parrish (I recently questioned him about any improper behavior from the priests and he said there was none); tried hard at his schoolwork, but was not an all "A" student (I think he would have been diagnosed as dyslexic today); and cherished me as his little sister. I knew this because he bought me a pink radio which cost at least a month's earnings from his paper route. And, of course, he liked meeting and flirting with my girlfriends, one in particular.

I, on the other hand, developed warring campaigns with my mother. I begged for more and more privileges. I pleaded for a larger allowance to supplement my babysitting earnings that would allow me to buy all my own clothes by myself. I pushed to host the first boy/girl party of our gang, a cook-out at the beach. I asked to be allowed to go to the Pilgrim Seniors' Group at the Congregational Church because most of my clique went there, not the Catholic Church.

This group of teenage boys and girls met Sunday evenings in the parish basement for Bible study and recreational pursuits, such as round-robin ping pong. The church also sponsored boy and girl basketball teams before the CYO (Catholic Youth Organization) became popular in Catholic parishes. In the summers the Pilgrim Seniors sponsored many outdoor activities to amusement parks and over-nights to the White Mountains in New Hampshire. I had no desire to attend the actual church services, just the teen groups.

Before consenting to any of my many requests, my mother corresponded with my father by postal mail—no phone calls or emails. I, of course, petitioned my father on my own behalf.

The proposal to buy my own clothes lost. My father's answer:

Now look, young lady. Your proposition about your buying your own clothes is too ridiculous. You are much too young to have the experience necessary for that deal. About the time you graduate from college will be adequate time for that.

The cook-out won. I invited ten girls and ten boys on a Saturday afternoon from four until seven p.m. to Nahant Beach, a town near Swampscott. This long stretch of beach was equipped with outdoor grills for cooking hotdogs and hamburgers and plenty of soft sand for team games of softball and volleyball. My mother asked other mothers to help and to act as chaperones. The event was a success. My father wrote:

I am much interested in the cook-out at Nahant Beach that you have planned ... Let me know all about it. Twenty kids is a lot of people to manage, did Don go also? There should be a grown-up along on such a deal, you are still just a little girl, you know.

However, to my request to attend the Congregational Church with my friends, my father said "no." I implored my father to let me go to the Youth Church Group but he answered all my pleas and arguments with counter arguments. We conducted a debate by mail. I don't have my side word for word, only the transcript of my father's rebuttals to my plaintive logic. For you the reader, it will be like listening to one side of a telephone conversation. You will have to imagine my premises.

I have read with interest your long paragraphs about religion. I am very proud of your letter. I think it was very well thought out and very well presented for a gal of your age. I am sure that you will make a good debater in high school. Well done. However, I will take your letter, in whole, paragraph by paragraph and word by word and in analysis we may find flaws in your arguments.

Freedom of religion is essential of civilization, but freedom after the child has been educated, not freedom of whims by the callow youth, after you have learned more of life and morals. At the moment I have responsibility to educate you to make your own decisions later. I am sure that you will concede that I have been quite impartial and completely free of bigotry in this matter. My relations to you are special. It is my part to see that you have the training and experience in the traditional faith of your fathers. In later years you will be able to form true comparisons: you are not yet ready. You have based present request on social basis not on grounds of convictions.

You speak of the Pilgrims. They did indeed come to find freedom of religion, but they did then deny it to anyone who did not agree with them. Read about Roger Williams and Anne Hutchinson. Read about Cotton Mather, the most bigoted man who has lived in modern times.

You say that the Catholic Church tries to force people to do things; that is partly true: they use certain moral force and other efforts. There are two kinds of churches: the liturgical which includes Catholic, Episcopal, and Lutheran: and the evangelical which includes most of the other Christian sects. In the former, the church depends on the form of service to invoke a pious attitude and respect for the teachings. In the latter, the church depends on the oratorical ability of the preacher for success. In any human endeavor success is measured by the box office; that is, how many people come to see the show and how many come back. Of the many churches in the English-speaking world, only the Catholic and the Methodist are growing, all the others are losing ground. In this analysis I am going to point out the one point of similarity so that we may decide a question. I submit that these two only are strongly directed and led by the bishops.

These two are like people under a dictator; they recognize that, in matters of religion, the people are not the rulers. They must be led by LEADERS who do possess, or claim to possess the right and knowledge to lead. One of these two is old, and if you believe the Christian story, has the right from Jesus, himself; the other is less than two hundred years old and is so unsure of its own teachings that the people themselves are constantly changing sides in small internal squabbles.

You say that the Protestants are the most cultured people. I will concede that in New England the richer people are of those religions, whereas in other sections of this country and in many other countries, the Catholics are the wealthier.

But of <u>culture,</u> you are quite wrong. The more progressive countries are Protestants, true, but NOT the more CULTURED. I assure you that the culture of the modern world comes from the Catholic countries. Even in Germany, the difference is obvious: the Protestant Prussians are much more aggressive, more successful and wealthier; but the culture of Germany is in the Catholic Bavaria. There the people know how to LIVE; they have less, but they LIVE better. They produce music; the Prussians produce war and destruction. France, Spain, Italy—that is where all Western culture arose, that is where people know how to live. In those countries the people are poor, but have some love of life and happiness. In the Northern countries, the people have more, but are dour and less free and happy.

> *You are right that we live in a country where there is some discrimination against Catholics. It is not too bad, but it does exist. Character is forged under adversity. When you read of the persecutions of the Albigenses and the early Protestants, you admire the courage and character of those people. In the same way we are slightly on the short end, would you admire those who run from it or those who disdain it?*

> *The answer is still __NO__. I love you. You wrote a very, very, very good letter for a gal of your age and I am proud of you.*

I loved rereading this letter from my father written sixty years ago. I am amazed at his encyclopedic knowledge of religious history. Eventually, however, I won my father over with persistence as most "little" girls are able to do. He allowed me to go to Sunday services and Sunday school with my friends and most importantly The Pilgrim Senior Group, but I had to also attend early Catholic Mass every Sunday. He required me to keep a journal of the lessons I learned from the Protestant church and the lessons I learned from the Catholic Mass.

Although at the time I was thrilled to "win the battle," I think my father "won the war." His stipulation for me to consider the tenets of the two religions and to contrast them should be a requirement of all parents in introducing their offspring to religious beliefs. Richard Dawkins, acclaimed British biologist and atheist, considers it child abuse to call a child a Catholic child, or a Muslim child, or any religious sect. He argues that you don't call a child a Tory child, or a Democratic child, or a Republican child just because the parents are of that political party.

Although my father was doing the right thing by having me monitor the two religions, I think I was going through the motions. I had no real interest in either religion. My interests were the Boston Red Sox, my girlfriends, and my wardrobe. Every Saturday three of four of us teenagers rode the bus to Lynn, the nearby city, where there were several department stores. We spent the morning trying on the brand name clothes, nationally advertised in the magazine, *Seventeen*. A favorite purchase was a Ship and Shore blouse, adorned with real pearl buttons, for $4.00. We were the first among the girls in Swampscott to discover the new fashion, Bermuda shorts. We considered ourselves trend setters wearing them instead of jeans or long, chino pants—the then current style for both boys and girls in the fifties.

Attending the eighth, ninth, and tenth grades in Swampscott in the fifties, I enjoyed activities typical of most teens of that era. I loved babysitting the three young children next door because their family had a television set. We did not have one. The picture screen was tiny, about five inches by ten inches, but perfectly acceptable when your family didn't own one. I followed the Boston Red Sox baseball team. I never watched a televised game but listened regularly on my little, pink radio. I could quote every pitcher's ERA and knew the batting statistics for every batter. At the first Major League game I attended at Fenway Park with my mother and brother, I saw Ted Williams hit a home run. And like most teens, my bedroom was a messy jumble of girlish artifacts.

Freshmen year, I was part of a group of fifteen girls, self-named the "Quinze Belles Filles," (Fifteen Beautiful Girls). We thought ourselves a sorority with a French name instead of a Greek name. We even embroidered the epithet as an emblem on the pocket of a plain white blouse and wore it as our uniform to school on Fridays. Our naïveté must have been quite apparent, at least to the teachers, but we believed our club name was a mysterious secret, not decodable by the other students.

My messy room

Among these girls, my best friend was Peggy. I adored her. I loved her as a friend and soul mate—not in a sexual way. In fact, all we talked about was boys and which boy might like us and which boy we liked. But I was jealous of her when it came to other girls. She was my best friend and I was her best friend. My heart actually jumped when I saw her first period in Latin class. If I had known the meaning of, or even heard the word "lesbian," I might have questioned my feelings, but these concepts were not expressed or even perceived by most teenagers in the fifties. In adulthood, I learned that most young girls growing up have a crush on another girl, such as a camp counselor, older neighbor, or peer. These emotions are considered normal and teach the child how to love another human being.

In 2010, my concern about too early education on such topics surfaced when I read an op-ed column in the local *Sarasota Herald Tribune* on "How to Fight Homophobia." I wrote the following letter that was published in the "Letters from our Readers" section with the title "Fighting Homophobia":

> *Regarding Wednesday's op-ed column "How to fight Homophobia," I have a suggestion: Let's stop teaching young children, even Kindergartners about homosexuality. In this article, the thirteen-year-old who committed suicide was a very young boy when the bullying and taunting began. In my generation, we didn't know the words homosexual, lesbian, transgender, or bisexual until high school, or in my case, college. I would hope that an older teen exploring his/her sexuality could handle it better and that his/her peers would be more understanding. Although painful, scoffs of "sissy" or "tomboy" seldom evoked suicide.*

In the spring of 1953, my sophomore year, we learned my father's tour of duty in Japan was over and he was to be reassigned to Camp Breckinridge, Kentucky. I was devastated. That meant we would have to move to a small army base in the middle of nowhere. I had been practicing hard to try out for the High School Drill Team. This group of seven girls performed gymnastic routines with the band during half-time at the football games. I had a good chance of making the squad because the coach liked me, and I was able to do the splits and the required acrobatic maneuvers. Now my hopes were shattered. My best friend, Peggy, was upset too. I knew begging would get me nowhere. We moved that spring of 1953 to the small remote army base. My only consolation was that my mother promised I could visit Peggy in the summer.

In March 1953, my father, mother, brother, and I drove from Swampscott to Camp Breckinridge, Kentucky in the little black English car. Before we left, the Quinze Belles Filles hosted a going-away party for me and gave me a gift—a navy blue Samsonite make-up case. Although sad at leaving, I felt special and almost grown-up with my own cosmetic case.

I didn't know it at the time, but we were to spend only one year at Camp Breckinridge. In sharp contrast to Fort Bragg, North Carolina, this army base was temporary, built in 1942 as an inland prisoner-of-war camp for 3,000 German army soldiers. In 1949, the camp was deactivated, but during the Korean War (1950-1954) it was reopened for infantry training.

My going-away party, Peggy on the left

Approaching our new home from Route 60, I became disoriented. I didn't know which way was north, south, east, or west. All I knew was that I was somewhere in the middle of the United States, but I needed the ocean for a reference point. I felt like Dorothy set down in Oz by a car, instead of a tornado. Our assigned quarters did not make me feel any better. Instead of a large stucco residence, our home was a one-story, wooden box with five small rooms and one bath.

The house is still standing. It looked exactly the same in 1953 as it looks in the picture to the right, minus the disability entrance ramp, the peeling paint, and the sign on the door. Camp Breckinridge is now a Job Corps Training Center.

Our "quarters" in 2012

Still struggling from the disappointment with the house, my parents had to decide where to send my brother and me to school. The choices were two: St. Ann's parochial school or the local high school, both in

Morganfield, Kentucky, the nearest town to the base. Today Morganfield has a population of 3,000, much less in 1953. The one public school building (for white students only) housed all the grades, elementary through high school. My father pressed for St. Ann's, but Don and I protested. We didn't want to wear uniforms or study religion every day. In hindsight, St. Ann's would have been a much wiser choice but my father, apparently feeling guilty about our dismal quarters, yielded to our adolescent whining.

The week after arriving, my mother drove Don and me to the public school for registration. The principal welcomed us and attempted to assign us to classes corresponding to our proffered transcripts. Immediately, a problem loomed. Due to the small enrollment of the high school, 174 students, less than fifty per grade, the school had few appropriate classes for us. The curriculum was severely limited: no language courses, no Chemistry course, no Physics course, no Geometry course and no Trigonometry course. I was assigned to Biology, English, History of Kentucky, Typing, and Shorthand. Since my brother was a junior and needed credits in academic courses for college admission, my father decided to send him to Fork Union Military Academy, a boarding school in Fork Union, Virginia.

For me, the school and my father plotted a program allowing me to finish the language courses begun my sophomore year at Swampscott High School. The one teacher, versed in Latin at Morganfield High, tutored me after school. At night, I studied French on the base in a course designed for the soldier recruits. The text book was *Education Manual 588, Unified French Course*. Today, my husband uses this excellent volume for reviewing his French grammar. I dropped Geometry and World History. I continued piano lessons with a nun at St. Ann's.

Besides the lack of subject choices, the teaching style was inferior to Massachusetts' standards. In English class, similar to grade school reading circles, each student read a page or two from the sophomore literary selection, *Silas Marner* by George Eliot. Even in Biology class we read from the text book—no lab facility, no lab equipment, no lab experiments. However, I enjoyed the challenge of bettering my speed each day in the shorthand and typing classes.

Socially, I lucked out. The daughter of the Commanding General at Camp Breckinridge was a sophomore at Morganfield High. The principal called Pat to the office, introduced us, and asked her to acquaint me with the school and social activities. For the next three months, until near the end of the school year, Pat included me in all of the school and after-hours activities.

Teen life in the rural south differed from its counterpart in small town New England. First, everyone smoked. When initially offered a cigarette, I refused with a "No thanks."

Amazed, the group inquired, "Don't you smoke? Don't any of your friends smoke?"

"Some do," I lied, "and I do sometimes."

I accepted the cigarette and tried to copy their puffing without actually inhaling. I had promised my father I wouldn't smoke, and I didn't want to. I think I succeeded in "appearing" to smoke.

Second, weekends were for slumber parties; every weekend one of the girls in the clique hosted a slumber party. Of course, the boys were informed of the location. The group consisted of sophomores, juniors, and seniors, so many of the girls and boys drove. These nights were spent racing up and down the dark streets, a carload of boys and a carload of girls chasing each other, often driving backwards as fast as forwards. I never felt part of the group, but was always invited because of Pat.

Third, at this season of the year, basketball was king. I liked this aspect of rural Kentucky living. The entire town supported the team and attended all the games. Plus, I had a crush on one of the players. That year, 1953, Morganfield made the State Tournament and a caravan of cars traveled more than one hundred miles each way to watch the team play in Louisville.

While living in Kentucky, I was surprised by the strange names of the girls, such as Melba, Shelba, and Billy Joe. My best friend, Peggy, and I exchanged letters almost everyday. She kept me informed with humorous accounts and hand-drawn images of the happenings at Swampscott High. I wrote of the personalities and events at Morganfield High. After the General and his daughter, Pat, were transferred in late spring, I was dropped by the high school gang. My mother noticed my depression and lack of invitations and honored her promise for me to visit Peggy that summer.

My mother and Peggy's mother realized that the visit would work for everybody. Peggy's father had recently died and her mother had returned to work, leaving Peggy on her own for the summer. Our two mothers decided to let me live at Peggy's for six weeks in the summer of 1953. I traveled from Kentucky to Boston by train in a private, one-person sleeping compartment. Peggy turned sixteen that summer and got her driver's license. After driving her mother to work, Peggy had use of the car. We filled the magical, long summer with swimming, sailing, sunning, and playing cards with the boys in rocky, secret coves, falling in and out of love with John and Judd, and experiencing our first kisses—six weeks never to be duplicated or forgotten.

When I returned home to Kentucky in late August, in vivid contrast to the summer, my junior year at Morganfield High offered no hope of excitement. They were to be the dreariest months of my teen existence. Having distanced myself from the girls at school and with my brother away

| *Me at the beach,* | *Me in front of Peggy's house,* |
| *summer 1953* | *summer 1953* |

at Fork Union Military Academy, I had no peer-age confidant, a necessity for a teenage girl. I went through the motions. I rode the bus to school, attended the easy, uninspiring classes (this year I didn't even have Latin and French to challenge my mind), and looked forward to noontime. The focal point of the day was lunch. Not for table companionship, but for the actual food. It, at least, promised a surprise. And every day, I hoped my father would be transferred so we could move.

During those months in Morganfield, my best friend was a forty-something, childless matron named Mandy. She lived next door in a unit attached to our house. After school I rushed over to visit her and talk about my boring life. We often discussed sex, a topic never mentioned to my mother. Now from an adult perspective, I am sure Mandy shared all my insecurities and secrets with my mother, since they were neighbors and close friends. One confounding bit of information Mandy conveyed to me was not to dance too close to a boy.

"Why?"

"Don't you feel something hard when you dance close to a boy?"

Innocently and quizzically, I said, "No."

"I guess the boys are too young," she mused.

As she did not elaborate, I had no idea what she meant. I believe my memory cues for remembering this odd conversation are curiosity and bewilderment.

Early in 1954, my stay in Kentucky ended. The army decommissioned my father. Once again, he was unemployed. In February of my junior year, we returned to Swampscott.

This time I had curriculum problems of an opposite kind. I could not enroll in Chemistry so late in the year. I could not take Physics without taking Chemistry, so those two courses are missing from my high school transcript. I resumed French, but not Latin, which was OK by me.

Again we bought in Swampscott: a large Victorian house, built in 1880. It was on the corner of Elmwood Road and Monument Avenue, near our former house on Redington Street, but it edged on a much more elegant neighborhood. We were surrounded by mansions. My mother claimed everyone thought we were rich, but that was not true. My father bought the house for $14,000 in 1954 and sold it for $17,000 in 1958, because the taxes were exorbitant. Zillow.com now lists the property's market value at $515,500. I would have thought more, as the views of the Atlantic Ocean and the Boston skyline are spectacular.

Thrilled to be back at Swampscott High for the last year and a half of my high school career, I was determined to excel in academics and

94 Elmwood Road,   *94 Elmwood Road,*
Swampscott 1954   *Swampscott 2012*

popularity. Since my schedule did not include any advanced math or science courses, my grades were always A's. I qualified for the High Honor Roll every semester—one target accomplished.

As for my goal of "Miss Popularity," I had a plausible plan. When I lived in Kentucky my friend Peggy, knowing how much I hated my thick myopic glasses, read in the Boston papers about the miracle of contact lenses and sent me the information about them. This was in the fifties before most people knew of them. I was determined to beg, cry, or promise anything until my parents bought them for me.

In his typical thorough manner of investigating a subject, my father researched the options. Montgomery Frost and Company, world famous eye specialists, had an office in Boston. They sold contact lenses and had placed the ad that Peggy had seen. However, before talking with them, my father studied the report issued by The Armed Services Technical Information Agency entitled "Contact Lenses: An Evaluation Study." This 113-page document assessed four different lenses under rigorous combat conditions. The winner was the "Lacrilens," a fluidless plastic, ventilated lens which covered the entire eye. Its main drawback was it was made from a casting of the eye and required a considerable number of office visits to perfect the fit. Another disadvantage was the high price, a fee of $200, comparable to $1600 today. Finally, my father agreed to the expense and time commitment. He was the one who accompanied me on my many trips to the Boston optician.

The contact lenses revolutionized my social life. Wearing thick glasses, I had felt ugly and unsure of myself, especially around boys. Now I felt pretty and worthy of attention.

Another factor figured into my social life. The Quinze Belles Filles were dissolved. New cliques formed. My best friend, Peggy, joined a group of girls entering Swampscott High from St. John's Parochial School. My other friends were still together, but Peggy seldom socialized with them. So I had two groups of friends. Not all bad.

In May 1954, my brother graduated from Fork Union Military Academy. To repay Peggy for hosting me the summer before, my parents invited her to join us on the graduation trip to Virginia. This was a plus for Don because Peggy was one of his favorites among my girlfriends.

The two of us were hits among the cadets. One Spanish-speaking senior sent an emissary to ask me to meet him by the chapel. With Peggy as a chaperone, I agreed to meet him and a friendship developed. The next year José enrolled at Niagara University in New York on a basketball scholarship. Christmas 1954, unable to afford to return home to Puerto Rico for the holidays, he spent a week with us, enjoying sleigh rides, school basketball games, and parties.

The summer between my junior year and senior year was not as magical as my summer spent at Peggy's house, but I remember one unbelievable week. I dated a different boy each night: to a yacht club dance, to a concert with The Four Aces at Hampton Beach, New Hampshire, to a beach party, to a dance at the outdoor Starlight Ballroom, to a party at a summer cottage, and to two movies dates. I owed it all to my contact lenses. It was now official. I achieved my second goal: becoming popular.

Senior year in high school is a memorable time in the lives of most teenagers. The clubs, sports, and personal comments, listed under my graduation picture in *The Sea Gull,* the Swampscott High School Yearbook, sum up my activities and future hopes.

JUDITH HEANEY

"Just for chucks!"

To attend U. of Mass. Interests are sports; popular music, fashion magazines, writing letters, and the Bungas.

Field Hockey 1, 2, 4; Varsity Basketball 4; Intramural Basketball 1, 2, 3, 4; Volleyball 3, 4; Dramatic Club 1, 2, 3, 4; **Swampscotta** Associate Editor 4; Travel Club 4; Yearbook Staff 4; Decorating Committees 1, 2, 3, 4; National Honor Society 4.

My varied activities of sports, writing, drama, and academics earned me the title of "Most Versatile Girl" in the class poll. Peggy was voted "Most Popular Girl." The mentioned "Bungas" were a cliquish group similar to the "Quinze Beau Filles." However, my most unexpected honor was being crowned "Miss Massachusetts Homemaker of 1955." I never took a Home Economics course in my life, except for mandatory cooking and sewing in junior high.

This General Mills contest was offered to all high schools in the United States. The Betty Crocker Homemaker of Tomorrow Scholarship Program began in 1955 and ended in1977. Senior girls took a written test on homemaking attitudes and knowledge. The girl with the highest score in each school received a pin, and she was entered into the state competition for a scholarship. In 1955, the monetary award for each state winner was $1,500 and the national prize was $5,000. Besides answering the multiple choice questions, all entrants wrote a page long essay entitled, "Why is a Home More Than a House?"

I won from the state of Massachusetts and became a local celebrity.

The *Lynn Daily Item*, newspaper from the neighboring city of Lynn, Massachusetts, awarded me the "Item's Bouquet of the Week." Many other laurels followed. I was honored at an assembly at school, asked to speak at a Daughters of the American Revolution Convention held at the prestigious New Ocean House Hotel in Swampscott, met with Massachusetts Governor Christian Herter at the Boston Statehouse, was interviewed by a Boston radio station, modeled in a fashion show for the local Women's Club (again at The New Ocean House Hotel), and asked to usher at the Marblehead Summer Playhouse where I met Boris Karloff, Sarah Churchill, and Gloria Vanderbilt among others. I also won a trip to Washington, DC, Williamsburg, and Philadelphia. All the state winners appeared on a half-hour national television show with Eddie Fisher. A girl from Alabama won the national scholarship prize. The downside of my unexpected largess was I missed traveling to Washington, DC with my class on the Senior Trip. It was the same week as my prize tour.

As an aside to my readers, much of the glowing article is the result of an over-praiseworthy interviewer. Don't believe everything you read.

Chapter Seven

The Summer Before College

The decision to attend a specific college is a combination of many components. In 1955, I examined the same factors explored by my three sons in the years 1980, 1983, and 1988, as well as my granddaughter in 2012 and my grandson in 2014. However, my parents did not counsel me as thoroughly as my husband and I guided our three boys. Generation one, mine, and generation two, my sons', did not spend the same amount of time, money, and travel that our son dedicated to advising and mentoring our granddaughter and grandson regarding their college choices.

However, the particulars that we all considered were the same: affordability, campus, academic reputation, and likelihood of admission. In the mid-fifties, the elite colleges and universities were single sex. The Seven Sister Colleges (Barnard, Bryn Mawr, Mount Holyoke, Radcliffe, Smith, Vassar, and Wellesley) corresponded to the Ivy League schools as female equivalents. My father urged me to attend Mount Holyoke or Smith. I refused to consider all-women's colleges. Besides, these prestigious schools were expensive. Although my "Miss Massachusetts Homemaker of 1955 Award," a scholarship from General Mills, would cover the first year at most colleges, paying the tuition and board for the next three years would be a burden on my family. In addition, my mother, the practical one, cautioned me that most of the students would be rich with pricey clothes and substantial allowances for trips to Bermuda or Mexico over breaks and therefore, I would struggle to fit in.

In 1955 we chose three schools for consideration: Jackson College for Women at Tufts University in Melrose, Massachusetts (technically not a women's college since the women shared the same campus and attended classes with the men), the University of New Hampshire, at Durham, New Hampshire, and the University of Massachusetts at Amherst, in western Massachusetts.

My mother and I toured the campus at Jackson College. I don't remember my impressions but, enough said, I didn't choose it. I never visited the University of New Hampshire because the guidance counselor at Swampscott High advised me to pick the University of Massachusetts over the University of New Hampshire. She believed UMass had a much better scholastic standing than UNH. As I intended to take two years of Liberal Arts before declaring a major, I didn't consider the academic reputation of any of the specific departments at the University of Massachusetts.

In the spring of my senior year of high school, I visited a neighbor girl at UMass for a weekend. I stayed at her sorority house, viewed the campus and dorms, and attended a fraternity party on a fix-up date. So, I was familiar with the school. Plus, the University of Massachusetts recruited me and offered me admission without taking the SAT. Plus, the tuition was one hundred dollars a semester and board was reasonable as well at two hundred fifty dollars per semester. Plus, two of my girlfriends from Swampscott High planned to attend UMass. Plus, my scholarship of fifteen hundred dollars would cover almost all expenses for all four years. With all these pluses, before graduating from Swampscott High School in June 1955, I elected to enter the University of Massachusetts Class of 1959 in the fall.

In the summer of 1955 I needed a job to earn money to buy clothes for school. I was seventeen; my work options were limited. I wanted a job in town because I had no car. Peggy, worked as a soda jerk at the corner drugstore. I decided clerking in a local store offered my best chance for employment. I did not want to travel to either of the two nearby cities, Lynn or Salem, as I would have to take a bus or train. The problem was the limited number of stores in our bedroom community. The restaurants only hired girls age eighteen or older. Somebody suggested that I apply to waitress in the Children's Dining Room at The New Ocean House, where there would be no age requirement. This celebrated Swampscott summer hotel, overlooking the Atlantic Ocean, was about a mile walk from my house.

The history of the New Ocean House is impressive. The hotel was on Puritan Road, one of the most famous Indian trails along the North Shore. In 1955 the clapboard Victorian hotel, with 600 rooms and suites, featured numerous clay tennis courts, an indoor and an outdoor pool, a nine-hole golf course and a pebbled, white sand beach at its front door.

Recurring fires had plagued the structure. The first Ocean House built in 1835 was destroyed by fire in 1864. The inn, now named the New Ocean House, was rebuilt, but again was engulfed in flames in 1882. The hotel debuted once more in 1884 with 250 rooms. In 1902 modern improvements were added such as individual call bells in each room, telephones, and elevators. It was expanded twice more to become one of the most elegant and luxurious retreats along the North Shore of Massachusetts. Well-known guests included Sinclair Lewis, Helen Keller, Harpo Marx, Babe Ruth, Presidents Calvin Coolidge and Herbert Hoover, Reverend Billy Graham, Lucille Ball, and President John F. Kennedy. A final fire in May 1969 leveled the beloved landmark. Today condominiums stand in its place.

The New Ocean House Swampscott, Massachusetts, 1960

What were my chances of being hired to waitress in this posh palace? The cons: I had never waitressed before and I was only seventeen. The pros: I lived in town and could provide local references. Hooray! The manager hired me as staff for the Children's Dining Room. College girls and seasonal professionals worked in the Main Dining Room. They flocked to the famous hotel from all over the country.

Since I was a "townie," I did not have to be housed in the employee dorm, a large, open room on the second floor of a garage-type building with no privacy. However, I was assigned a cot in the dreary loft for use during my off hours.

The New Ocean House Hotel restaurant operated seven days a week. Guests ate on a meal plan which included breakfast, lunch, and dinner. The staff's off hours were after breakfast and before lunch, between lunch and dinner, and in the evening after dinner. The college kids loved the set-up. They were allowed to go to the beach when not on duty or rest in the cavernous dorm area. All meals were provided. They came with their friends and met new friends, including college boys who worked as busboys, bartenders, waiters, and kitchen help.

At this snooty establishment even the Children's Room oozed formality. A nanny in a starched white uniform accompanied the youngsters, often dressed in pinafores or sailor suits, to their meals. The parents escorted them to their assigned tables and seats, if the young ones were not with a nursemaid. After ordering food for the children, mom and dad left to eat in the main dining hall. A padded window seat and a small child's table and chairs served as a play area for the children to await the return of their parents. Our staff consisted of another high school girl, a high school boy as our lone busboy, and me. We watched and entertained our charges until the mothers and fathers retrieved them.

I enjoyed most aspects of my first full-time summer job. It was well-paying and undemanding. Most of the children were well-behaved. As I strode through the hallways and main dining room on the long walk from our location to the kitchen to place the food orders, I noted the heavy white linens adorning all the tables, the string of silverware on both left and right sides of the charger plates, and the guests, dressed in evening attire at night. I traveled this route many times each day because our young guests begged for plate upon plate of petit fours for dessert. We smuggled the extra portions of the mini delicacies out of the kitchen to indulge the youngsters. The families paid us generous gratuities at the end of their two-or-three-week stay. Sometimes the parents engaged me to babysit for the evening. The hotel required patrons to pay babysitters one dollar an hour, which was triple the going sitter rate at that time.

Another plus of the job was the fun atmosphere. Although I had a steady boyfriend that summer, I flirted with the busboy, Bob. He had attended St. John's Prep, a prestigious boarding school in the area, and planned to attend Holy Cross College in the fall. He too had a steady girlfriend, so we considered our coquetry platonic and innocent.

I remember two downsides to my job. First, I had to buy two light green waitress uniforms in order to have one ready, clean, and pressed every day. Second, I realized after a few days that I did not want to mix with the college crowd at the beach or in the dorm. I felt young and out of place around them. They had come together as friends from their various colleges. This meant that I sometimes walked a mile home and back as often as six times a day.

In the evenings, I dated Ken, a Swampscott boy who was to be a junior at the University of Massachusetts in the fall. Besides the typical movie dates, several special occasions stand out: a trip to Boston to watch the Harlem Globe Trotters, double dates to the Corinthian Yacht Club summer dances, and an outdoor concert on the lawn at the famed Crane Estate in Ipswich to hear Louis Armstrong and his magic trumpet.

On Tuesday evenings each week, a high school friend Sheila and I ushered at the Marblehead Summer Playhouse. Performances were held in the large auditorium at Marblehead High School. Marblehead was a town next door to Swampscott. My boyfriend, Ken, drove us there and picked us up. Three of the famous celebrities who performed that summer of 1955 were Boris Karloff, Sarah Churchill, and Gloria Vanderbilt who appeared in the play *Picnic*.

During the summer the university notified all freshmen of their dormitory assignment and roommate. My roommate's name was Ruth. She lived on a farm near Springfield, Massachusetts. We exchanged letters and she invited me to visit for a weekend before the semester started in September. Ken agreed to drive me to her house and return to pick me up. Ruth was slight but with an ample bust and a flawless complexion. I pegged her as quiet, serious, and smart. I don't remember what we did, but I remember the food. At noon we went into the fields and garden to pick fresh corn and tomatoes. Our lunch consisted of these two vegetables plus milk. For supper: corn and tomatoes again with the addition of a meat. That was the menu for Friday, Saturday, and Sunday. Breakfast? I don't remember what we ate, but surely not corn and tomatoes. Healthful and tasty meals, but they were very strange to me. I realized then that at college I would be exposed to new, unusual, and foreign situations.

Somehow, with the help of my mother, I managed to sort my clothes and gather the inventory of requisites that were necessary for a 1950s women's dorm room: typewriter, hi-fi and favorite record albums, wind-up alarm clock, the three-inch thick reference book entitled *College Edition of Webster's New World Dictionary of the American Language*, large pink, plastic hair rollers, nylon stockings, and even hats and gloves for church and faculty teas.

Due to my full scholarship and lucrative summer job, I had expendable money available to assemble my idea of a college wardrobe. I bought several pair of Bermuda shorts, including the new and popular madras plaid fabric, pleated wool skirts, a camel hair winter coat, button-down oxford shirts, ballerina flats in assorted shades, two pairs of dress shoes with Capezio heels, penny loafers, sneakers, and cashmere sweater sets in almost every color. (One former classmate, at my recent fiftieth college reunion in 2009, teased me about my collection of sweaters that I kept under my bed in a metal, coffin-like box. I countered truthfully to her that I always lent them to friends and acquaintances upon request.)

As for my religious activity during the summer of 1955, I don't remember any particulars. I know I did not attend the Congregational Church and the Pilgrim Seniors Group anymore, though I am sure I continued going to Mass at St. John's Catholic Church. Although I did not believe all the Roman Catholic theology, I followed the expected formalities of confession and communion as I had been taught since early childhood. I did not foresee that in college my Catholic faith would become stronger.

At the end of the summer I packed my clothes and personal belongings into numerous boxes and suitcases. Since my father was in Greenland on an engineering job and my brother was on a six-month stint in the Army Reserves to fulfill his military obligation, my mother, with my aunt Alice for a companion, drove me and my stuff to college in mid-September, 1955.

Today most colleges begin the semester during the second or third week of August, but in the 1950s, colleges routinely opened a week or two after Labor Day. In 1955, Freshmen Orientation began on Thursday, September 15, and classes began on Wednesday, September 21, allowing a full week for Freshmen Orientation.

For seventeen years, I dreamed and planned on experiencing three milestones common for young ladies of that era: college, marriage, and motherhood. Settled in the back seat of our gray and black Ford sedan among the cardboard boxes, my thoughts overwhelmed me. In my seventy-plus mind of today I try to recall those intense feelings on that two-and-one-half hour car ride to the University of Massachusetts. I lived inside my mind with my girlish dreams in bloom as I journeyed on that first step toward adulthood.

Is it true? Am I on my way to college? Is my dream, my hope, my first ambition for my life actually happening? At this moment in time should

I pinch myself to see if it is real? Although I always knew that I would go to college, is it possible that soon I will really be a freshmen coed?

Throughout my lifetime, I have held strong ideas about honor, morality, truth, fairness, and my place in the "ether." But in 1955, as a teenager, I could not imagine the possibilities for women that would unfold in the modern world. At that time my expectations were limited. My life was cloistered…my future foreseen…my horizons narrow. Only the prescribed life envisioned by all women awaited. No Robert Frost's "The Road Not Taken" for me, only a fated, customary path.

This path to college took us on Route 128 around Boston, to Route 2 West, a pleasant autumnal drive through the northern part of the state, to a trek along Route 202 South for about fifteen miles. Then, we turned right onto Amherst Road which began a seven-mile steep descent into Amherst. The small, picturesque New England town, complete with ubiquitous town common, is also home to Amherst College, one of the designated "Little Three Colleges," (Amherst, Williams, and Wesleyan) that are considered just one notch beneath the Ivy Colleges, as well as home to the state college, the University of Massachusetts. We turned left onto North Pleasant Street that led to the UMass campus.

Arnold Dorm, University Massachusetts April 2009
(The dorm looked the same in September 1955.)

My mother followed the line of cars all heading in the same direction. Our destination was Arnold, a large red-brick women's dorm that housed only freshmen coeds. The quadrangle of five buildings loomed into view. As we neared the front entrance to the middle dorm that I knew to be Arnold, husky upperclassmen jumped in front of our car and motioned where to park. They opened our doors, greeted us with quick smiles, and immediately began to unload the backseat and lug all the boxes and paraphernalia up the stairs. No elevators. My room was on the second floor with a faux balcony over the front door of the dorm. I had arrived.

Chapter Eight

Victory and Defeat My Freshmen Year

I was sure that thinking back over more than fifty years to recapture my college experiences would be a daunting challenge. I did not have a trove of photographs as I have for my early life, my married life, and the lives of my children and grandchildren. But in that era before emails, my mother saved every letter I sent her from college. I admit that in sorting out her archives after her death in 1992, I tossed out some of those missives, but I kept samples from each of my four years at school, as I had dated every one of them with month, day, and year. In addition, I found my old-fashioned, paper-and-paste scrapbook with the title page, "The College Life of Judy Heaney 1955 -1959," filled with mementos, but few pictures. Also, I have the yearbooks from all four years, as well as a video produced by the Fiftieth Reunion Memory Committee, highlighting the adventures and achievements of the Class of '59. Now, as I try to knit together this formative period, I worry I have too much material covering these four years, considered by many as "the best years of your life."

Let's begin by returning to Arnold House, Room 217. Since I had arrived at the dorm before my roommate, Ruth, I claimed the right to choose my side of the room. The furniture on both sides was identical: metal cot with skimpy mattress, wooden four-drawer bureau, wooden wardrobe closet, and wooden desk and chair. All the homey accoutrements had to be purchased and supplied by the occupants, except for the basic linens that I had pre-ordered from Gordon Linens. A brown paper parcel containing three large white towels and one set of thin white bed sheets lay atop each mattress. With the help of Mom and aunt Alice, I made the bed on my side of the room, stored away my clothes, and arranged my desk.

As we waited for my roommate to arrive, the Resident Assistant (RA) popped in to welcome us. An RA was an upperclassman who lived in a dorm with the freshmen to proctor and advise them. She gave me a copy of the *Massachusetts Collegian*, the college newspaper, which contained a detailed itinerary for Freshman Week.

Freshman Week Itinerary 1955

Besides the schedule, the paper printed welcome messages from the University President, the Provost, and the Student Government President. I also noticed a noteworthy statistic tucked at the bottom of page one: the composition of the freshmen class, approximately 1,000 undergraduates with 650 men and 350 women. Hooray, a ratio of almost two to one in my favor. In contrast, in 2014 the university had an enrollment of 22,000 underclassmen, 4,650 first-year students, bearing a ratio of three to one, women to men. I think this is typical of most universities in the 21st century.

Besides the program, we received Freshman Handbooks or Mug Books, as they were affectionately known. This eight-by-five inch soft-cover directory was our bible for the year. Instead of an online dating site, we had at our fingertips the names, photographs, and hometowns of all the incoming freshmen, male and female. In addition, our welcome package included a day-planner-calendar-notebook, a prototype for the Blackberry.

No one had cell phones, of course. Instead, two payphones stood outside the mail room that was off the lobby on the first floor. Each of the 200 girls in Arnold House was assigned phone duty during the year. When in charge, she answered the phone, buzzed the recipient's floor via the intercom, and announced, "Telephone for 'whomever.'" If in residence, the girl answered the intercom and said, "I'll be right there." If the individual did not rush to answer, her roommate or someone would yell, "She's not here." Then, the acting secretary filled out a message slip and placed it in the proper cubby hole. Along the back wall of the mail room, numbered small boxes corresponded to the number of each dorm room. This bank of small, square compartments was similar to rental boxes in a post office lobby, but open-ended with no door, lock, or key. This was our "voice mail."

It's certainly not an instant communication system, but how immensely satisfying to return from class and spot a note in your mailbox. Oft-used shorthand was "MCNM" for "man called, no message."

Samples of telephone messages

Before relating stories of my accomplishments and disappointments during my freshmen year, I need to historify (a real word) college life, both culturally and academically in that era. This was the fifties—a time of avuncular President Dwight Eisenhower and the morals portrayed in the *Andy Griffith Show, Father Knows Best,* and *Leave it to Beaver.* A time before the demonstrations against the Vietnam War and the free-love of the Sexual Revolution. Pundits nicknamed us The Silent Generation.

College administrations protected the young women students—not with police escort services or surveillance cameras—but with respected and expected societal rules. Each freshmen dorm had a housemother (a grandmotherly type) as well as Resident Assistants, upper classmen on each floor. No men were allowed above the first floor. They were entertained in the front lobby area or in public lounges at either end of the first level. The first semester freshmen girls' curfew was 7 p.m. on week nights and 11 p.m. on weekends, except for major dances or programs when it was extended to midnight. A basement recreation room with laundry equipment and the only television in the dorm was reserved for women's use only. In 1955 and for many years after, no one envisioned a coed dormitory.

Despite these rigid rules, in the fall of my freshmen year, a fire at a university storage barn on Tuesday night, November 8, 1955, sparked a "panty raid." The Boston and Springfield newspapers exaggerated the event and the wire services carried the news to the New York papers. One salacious headline read "Coeds Stripped by Panty Raiders" and a quote from the campus policeman Red Blasko stated, "Some of the trophies carried back to the men's dorms were stripped right off their not too unwilling owners."

The melee occurred because some of the college men congregated to watch the fire, and then drifted to the women's quad. Soon they began shouting, "We want panties." The outside reports claimed mobs of men were running through the corridors of the dorms and pounding on doors. In reality, this never happened. Boys did chant outside our windows for panties and other underwear and some girls did toss down the requested articles, but the dorms weren't breached and the ruckus was soon over. I know because I was there. An example of gross exaggeration to sell papers, or "fake news."

Academically, the requirements for a Liberal Arts degree were rigorous. During the first two years the curriculum mandated five academic courses plus four credits in Physical Education each semester. If a candidate for the Bachelor of Arts in the College of Arts and Sciences, the basic subjects for freshmen and sophomore years were four semesters of English, two semesters of a foreign language, two semesters of math, four semesters of science, four semesters of social studies, and four semesters of electives. After two years you declared your major. Then you chose sixteen courses in your selected discipline and four electives for an accumulated total of 128 credits that were required for graduation. In addition, maybe unique to the coastal state of Massachusetts, everyone had to pass a swimming test.

The Baby Boomers, the Generation X's, and the Millennials may not agree with my next analysis. Our grades were not dumbed-down or inflated as I believe they are today. These were the years of the "Gentlemen C." You earned your grade in the old-fashioned way by working hard. In the late sixties, with threat of the draft and the Vietnam War looming over the heads of the young men, some professors upped all grades to at least a B to insure the youth were not drafted. I believe the charade continues today with professorial gifts of arbitrarily high marks.

At UMass, I tentatively chose to major in Journalism and minor in French. My courses for first and second semester freshmen year:

First Semester:	**Second Semester:**
English Composition/Speech	English Composition/Speech
Mathematics, Algebra & Trig	Algebra
Modern European History	Modern European History
Introductory Zoology	Introductory Botany
Intermediate French	Intermediate French
Physical Education	Physical Education

I enjoyed all my introductory or 101 classes in the Liberal Arts Curriculum, but not Intermediate French. In my four years of French in high school, we never practiced speaking or listening to the language. We read, wrote, and studied vocabulary and grammar. In college we had a French lab each week. I struggled to understand the oral conversations. My sophomore year I dropped French as my minor and opted for a proposed double major, English/Journalism. I loved to read. What could be better than reading to earn my credits and diploma?

The fall of 1955 overflowed with academic classes, plus Dance Club, Roister Doisters (drama group), the Newman Club (Roman Catholic religious organization), reporting for the *Collegian,* football games, church, and Sorority Rush. In remembering my first semester activities, Sorority Rush was the most important to me. I definitely wanted to pledge a sorority.

The Panhellenic Council, comprised of the seven sororities on campus (Chi Omega, Kappa Alpha Theta, Kappa Kappa Gamma, Phi Delta Nu, Pi Beta Phi, Sigma Delta Tau, and Sigma Kappa) distributed a handbook to all the incoming freshmen women with rules, rush schedule, financial information, and suggestions for a successful experience. The actual rush period was crammed into a two-week period over one month from November 13 to December 13, with two weeks out for the Thanksgiving Holiday.

Perhaps, some brief explanations are needed. Round Robins meant any freshmen girl interested in pledging a sorority could visit any or all the houses. To appear on the eligibility list, a girl must have achieved a 1.8 GPA on Dean's Saturday. During Preferential Bidding, the prospective pledge listed her sorority choices in order on a preference slip. If her preferences matched the lists sent in by the sororities, she received a formal invitation to pledge all the matches.

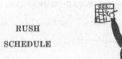

RUSH SCHEDULE

November 13—Sunday Panhellenic Tea 3-5 P.M.
November 16—Wednesday Registration in dorms 9:30-10 P.M.
November 20—Sunday Round Robins Afternoon and Evening
December 3—Saturday Eligibility Lists posted
December 4—Sunday Open House 7-9 P.M.
December 6—Tuesday Invitation Party 7-9 P.M.
December 8—Thursday Theme Party 7-9 P.M.
December 12—Monday Closed Date 6-8 P.M.
December 13—Tuesday Preferential Bidding 11-12:30
December 13—Tuesday Pledging Evening

Rush Schedule at UMass 1955

RUSHING RULES

The following are the rules which sorority members and Freshmen girls are requested to follows during the Rushing Period:

1. Sorority members are not allowed to communicate with freshmen or transfers during the silence period, 12 noon Monday, December 12 to 7 P.M. Tuesday, December 13, 1955.

2. Sorority members are not allowed to pay for rushees' food or entertainment *before* or during the formal rush period.

3. Freshmen are not allowed in any sorority house at times other than those scheduled by Panhellenic Council.

4. Sorority members are not allowed to ask any freshman or transfer to commit herself before Preferential Bidding.

5. Sorority members are not allowed to pre-arrange dates for freshmen girls.

6. The quota for each house shall be 20 freshmen for one year.

7. No upperclassmen other than transfers should be rushed during formal rushing. However, upperclassmen may also be pledged on December 13, 1955.

8. Upperclassmen other than transfers should not attend Round Robins.

9. When freshmen visit upperclassmen in their dormitories they may be received only in the social rooms.

10. Upperclassmen are not allowed in freshmen dormitories before or during the formal rush period for purposes of rushing.

The Panhellenic rushing rules were as detailed and punitive as the NCAA's rules for recruiting high school athletes for college. I can only assume, because I don't remember, that I followed all the rules because I pledged my first choice, Chi Omega.

My reasons for choosing Chi Omega were sound, but also calculating. I limited myself to four choices: Chi Omega, Kappa Kappa Gamma, Pi Beta Phi, and Kappa Alpha Theta. Any of these sororities was a possibility. I considered where my friends hoped to pledge, the esthetics of the physical house, and the friendliness of the sisters. But I had an overriding, ulterior motive in choosing Chi Omega.

My primary ambition was to become a Scroll in my sophomore year. Scrolls were the sophomore women's Honor Society, the members chosen and tapped at Honors Convocation in the spring. The Scrolls, wearing their maroon-colored slouch hats, were very visible during Freshman Orientation Week. They, along with the Sophomore Men's Honor Society, the Maroon Key, directed, counseled, and orchestrated Freshmen Week. I plotted a plan to assure my nomination as a Scroll for sophomore year.

I fashioned myself into the "perfect image" of a Scroll. Scrolls were academic achievers, campus-doers, and sorority members. My grade average was well above the 2.5 average needed for consideration. My extra-curricular activities were many. I was Secretary of the Freshmen Class, a participant in Dance Club and the Freshmen Class Play, a reporter on the *Collegian* staff, and a member of the Newmen Club. All the Scrolls belonged to sororities, and of the fifteen Scrolls, six were Chi Omegas. My premeditated assumption was that the Chi Omega Scrolls, as in evolution, would attempt to replicate themselves. So, I pledged Chi Omega.

Freshmen Class Officers 1955

All my careful planning collapsed. I was not elected a Scroll. Mrs. Churchill, the housemother of Arnold, blackballed me from achieving this honor. As a freshmen class leader, Mrs. C knew me and hoped I would serve as a model for other freshmen girls. However, one night in February, an unfortunate incident derailed my dream.

This major disappointment in my college career resulted from a misstep in my social life. I was never the "femme fatale" in high school, at least not until my senior year, when I abandoned thick glasses for contact lenses and became more sure of myself. With the aforementioned ratio of two men to one woman among the freshmen and the fact that all the upperclassmen checked over the new crop of freshmen girls, either in person or via the Mug Book, a dateless-freshmen-girl was an oxymoron. Needless to say, first-year boys did not fare as well.

Due to the Puritanical curfew hours for the freshmen girls, we dated only on Friday, Saturday, or Sunday nights, unless there was a special university event. Within two or three weeks, I filled my "Blackberry" notebook with a date every weekend night up to Christmas vacation. I had two built-in dates: my boyfriend from home, Ken, a junior at UMass, and the boy I had dated on the fix-up date the previous spring. I also met many new men in class or at the get-together dances and picnics. The perplexing irony with filling my datebook up to Christmas vacation was that if I met someone I really liked, I could not date him until after Christmas break. I met such a boy.

We three friends from Swampscott with our three roommates formed an immediate social circle, an easy, chummy group. By combining our friends we soon had an extended lively group of men and women. Through a friend of a friend, I agreed to a fix-up date with John, a freshmen football player. I didn't know him, but he wanted to meet me. Because all my weekends were booked, we finally found a free week night for a date. The University's Concert Series had scheduled a major concert at "The Cage" (the athletic field house) on a Tuesday night in early October.

That cold autumn night we walked the half-mile to The Cage to listen to the Montovani Orchestra, a well-known group with six albums in the Top Thirty. John was very tall with a blonde crew-cut. Reportedly, he liked my looks, but also the fact that I did not drink or smoke. Many Catholic youth at that time took a pledge, as he had done, not to drink until age twenty-one. I had not taken the drinking pledge, but I had promised my father never to smoke.

After the concert we walked back to Arnold House. I remember the haunting strains of such classics as "Some Enchanted Evening" and "Greensleeves" in my head and the freezing wind chafing my cheeks. Along with the cold night and the sounds of the violins, I remember the unexpected goodnight kiss. With it, I violated one of my sacred rules, one prevalent among Catholic girls in the 1950s—never kiss on the first date. Period. We neared Arnold and stood outside among the throng of couples saying good night. John grabbed me and kissed me on the lips. I flayed and pounded my fists on his heavy, winter top coat with no effect.

Soon our effect on each other was evident. We saw one another more and more. Although my weekends were booked, we studied together in the library or dorm lounges, ate breakfast, lunch and dinner together in the dining commons, and walked to and from classes together. My letters home to my mother mentioned John again and again.

> *…This Friday night I am going to the library with John. You don't have to worry about me chasing John. I like him a lot and he must like me a lot by the way he acts. I'm with him constantly.*

> *Last weekend I went out with John both Friday and Saturday nights. He asked me to the Military Ball, but I had already told Kennie I'd go with him. I see him (John) every day and I know he likes me and I like him so much. I'm really afraid I'm growing away from Kennie and I think he (Kennie) knows it too.*

> *I had a swell snowball fight with John on Tuesday. We were tossing each other into the snow banks and burying each other. <u>Great fun</u>!!!*

After two months of seeing each other almost every day, John and I did not look forward to the upcoming Christmas break. He lived in Springfield in western Massachusetts and I lived in Swampscott on the coast. We did not expect to see each other over the two-week recess.

Unlike today's college schedules, the winter holidays were not the end of the semester. Due to our late start in the middle of September, the term did not conclude until near the end of January. So, when at home, instead of enjoying a carefree holiday period, we studied for final exams and wrote research papers. I also had a job at a local department store, T. W. Rodgers, in Lynn. I sold ladies underwear—not negligees,

John and me in front of Arnold House, 1955

but rayon panties. For some reason, these items were popular Christmas gifts for wives, mothers, aunts, and grandmothers.

John promised to write. I expected maybe a few letters over the two weeks. A letter arrived from John every day and sometimes twice a day. In the fifties, first-class postage was three cents and most people sent Christmas cards. In order to deliver all the mail, postal service occurred twice a day. The mailman and my mother joked about the daily or twice-daily "love letters."

"Another letter from Springfield," the nosey postman announced as he tromped up the porch steps and greeted my mother at the front door.

Like any mother, my mom was anxious to meet John, and John and I were anxious to spend some time together over the vacation period. But our relationship was new and we made no plans for visits. When I returned to school in January, I was sure of his feelings for me due to the contents and frequency of his letters.

In rereading the letters I wrote home to my mother in January of 1956, I am experiencing nostalgic pleasures as well as humiliating discoveries. They jog my memory while they display my poor grammatical skills. I also don't know how I crammed so many activities into one day or weekend as we were in the middle of exams. My January 11, 1956, letter included this detailed and copious paragraph:

> *…Just to prove I do use my typewriter I am typing this. I just finished typing my French theme, so you see I do use it. I'm writing this just before my English class at 4 o'clock…Guess what? After classes today I have 5 things I have to do. Two of them I don't think are going to get done. At 10 minutes to 5 I have to go for a Collegian meeting. I am going to be on the sports staff. At 5 to 6 I have Modern Dance club. At 7:15 I have a class officer's meeting. At 7:30 I have tryouts for Naiads (precision*

swim team). At 8:30 I have play rehearsal. I think I am going to skip the Modern Dance Club and the Naiads. I don't think I would have made the Naiads anywhere (sic) and if I had, I would have to have (sic) 3 nights a week practising (sic) and I don't think I can spare the time...

The rest of the letter outlined my plans for the weekend. Chi Omega was having its pledge formal and I had invited John. He hitchhiked home to Springfield and came back with his father's car. We double dated with another couple. The formal was held at a fancy hotel in Northampton, Massachusetts.

My next letter dated Monday January 23, 1956, described the previous weekend in Springfield, Massachusetts. Thank heavens for these letters because I have no recollection of these goings-on. Our group of friends included three members of the men's freshmen basketball team. UMass was playing Springfield College in Springfield on Saturday night.

Again, John went home on Friday and drove back Saturday morning.

...He came for Marie (she lived in Springfield), Mike (member of the basketball team and Marie's boyfriend), and I (sic) at 11 o'clock on Saturday morning. Mike decided to go with us instead of taking the team bus. We got in Springfield around noon...We 4 (sic) had lunch at Marie's. We had fish chowder and tuna fish sandwiches and cake. Mike was staying at Marie's because John's parents had relatives staying at his house. Saturday afternoon John went home, Mike slept, and Marie and I studied. We had steak for supper, then John came and drove Mike to the field house at 5:45. Then we went to the game at 6:00. We won both games. (Freshmen and Varsity) After the game eight of us went to DeMarco's–a diner and dine place...

...All the boys except John play freshmen basketball. We had pizza at DeMarco's and then we danced to an orchestra. It was piles of fun with all the kids there. Afterwards we drove around Springfield and got in about two. Sunday morning we all went to 11:00 Mass. (Now all my friends were Catholic so I embraced my Catholicism again.) *Then we went to Marie's and read the Sunday paper.* (I smile at our next childlike activity and wonder who suggested it.) *We weren't eating until two so we decided*

to go to the zoo. We went to the monkey and lion house. It was fun. Then we had a delicious dinner at Marie's house. Roast beef with all the fixings. Marie's parents drove us back to the university. John didn't introduce me to his parents because all his relatives were there...

Somehow I survived the exams and completed my first semester with good grades. Not all A's like in high school, but a very respectable 3.2 average, more than required for selection as a Scroll. I received a transcript and a copy was mailed to my parents (unlike today where only the students receive the transcript and they may or may not share it with their parents, who usually are underwriting their education).

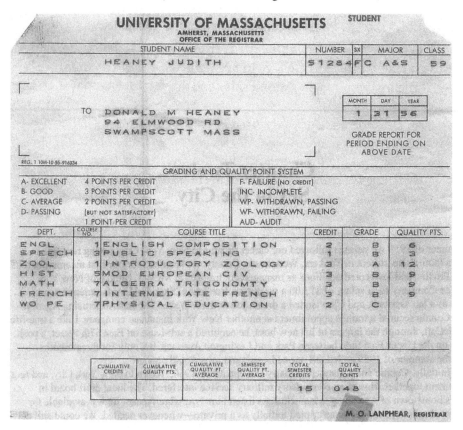

DEPT.	COURSE NO.	COURSE TITLE	CREDIT	GRADE	QUALITY PTS.
ENGL	1	ENGLISH COMPOSITION	2	B	6
SPEECH	3	PUBLIC SPEAKING	1	B	3
ZOOL	1	INTRODUCTORY ZOOLOGY	3	A	12
HIST	5	MOD EUROPEAN CIV	3	B	9
MATH	7	ALGEBRA TRIGONOMTY	3	B	9
FRENCH	7	INTERMEDIATE FRENCH	3	B	9
WO PE	7	PHYSICAL EDUCATION	2	C	

Transcript for First Semester Freshmen Year

I returned to school for second semester, ready to study, enjoy my sisters at Chi Omega, and all the college doings. However, my love life was a mess. I dated Kennie at home over the semester break, but I felt I was not being fair to him. He drove me back and forth to UMass. He tried to woo me by suggesting we drive to Princeton for a weekend to visit his friend after the Winter Carnival festivities.

Carnival Weekend was February 9 through February 12. I had agreed to go to the ball with John, a pragmatic decision because I planned to wear the same gown I had worn to my high school senior prom with Kennie.

One of the letters to my mother helped me recall all the details of the weekend. The sororities, fraternities, and dorms participated in a snow sculpture contest. Chi Omega won first place among the sororities. Friday night was the ball. Saturday afternoon was a fashion show and I was one of the models. Saturday night was an Old Timer's Party at John's fraternity, Kappa Sigma. The guys wore derbies, vests, and painted mustaches, while the gals wore vests and Gibson blouses.

"It was the best of times, it was the worst of times, it was the age of wisdom, it was the age of foolishness..." to quote from the first lines of Dickens' novel *A Tale of Two Cities.* In a ten-minute time slot, my young life was about to mimic the glory and tragedy of the ten-year French revolution.

After the Winter Carnival Ball, John and I sat in the lounge area of Arnold House to say good night. As he was kissing me, John surprised me by forcing his high school ring into my hand while saying, "I love you."

John and me at the Winter Carnival Ball

If I accepted the ring, I was agreeing to go steady. I thought of Kennie's invitation to drive to Princeton for a weekend. I was looking forward to the outing because the picture in my head of college life included trips to other campuses. Selfishly, I wanted all the experiences from my early adolescent dreams of a college coed.

"I love you, too," I said. "But I promised Kennie I would go to Princeton with him next weekend and I really want to go."

John looked at me and said, "OK. I understand—but after that let's only date each other."

"OK," I murmured and kissed him again.

It was nearing one in the morning, closing time. The R.A., Linda, was blinking the lights to clear the lobby. John and I stood up. Holding hands, we moved toward the front door. Many other couples blocked the exit. The lights dimmed again and again; the clinging couples lingered; the housemother, Mrs. Churchill, emerged from her office. She approached John and me and said, "Judy, will you please help Linda clear the area?"

"Yes, of course," I said, but I hugged and kissed John one more time.

Mrs. Churchill advanced towards us with a grim look and shoved us apart with an angry retort, "I expected you to set an example for the other girls, but you're still kissing your date."

Quickly, I uttered, "I'm sorry." John hurried out the door and I galloped up the stairs to my room.

The next morning Mrs. Churchill called me into her office. "I'm very disappointed in your behavior last night. I thought you were drunk when I looked at your eyes. But Linda told me you don't drink and she suggested your eyes were probably glassy due to your contact lens. However, I needed your help and you didn't cooperate."

Again I said, "I'm very sorry, Mrs. Churchill. It won't happen again."

Of course I didn't tell her it was a very special night for John and me. I never thought of the incident again. My apology to Mrs. C. was sincere and she knew I wasn't drunk because Linda had vouched for me. But, evidently that one misstep sealed my fate for consideration for Scrolls, as decidedly and completely as the guillotine that lopped off Marie Antoinette's head.

I didn't tell my mother about the confrontation with Mrs. Churchill but I confided in her about my decision regarding Kennie. My mother had always liked Kennie.

…Sunday I went to the library and talked everything over with Ken. We decided it would be best if I didn't go to Princeton. So Kennie and I are through and I am diffinitely (sic) going steady

with John. Maybe I am foolish, but I think I am doing the right thing…

So, unlike the ten year duration of the French Revolution, in ten minutes on the night of the Winter Carnival Ball, I experienced the best and the worst of times.

Spring semester freshmen year continued with busy days and nights. No more stringent curfew hours. John and I became an item. We campaigned together for next year's sophomore class officer positions. I was reelected secretary, unopposed. I had urged John to run and he was elected vice-president.

I ran his campaign for UMOC, an acronym for Ugliest Man on Campus, a gimmick to raise money for charity. It cost a penny every time you voted and you were encouraged to vote often. So, in reality it was a popularity contest for a good cause. My friends and I drew zipper scars on his face and molded knobby tumors with putty around his nose. John won.

On Parents' Day in April, my mother and father visited and met John for the first time. They took us to dinner at the well-known Log Cabin, an expensive steak restaurant in Holyoke, Massachusetts with a spectacular view looking down into the valley. In my next letter home, I commented, "I'm glad you like John. The better you know him the better you will like him."

A few weeks later I went to Springfield with John to meet his parents. My comments home, "I finally met his parents and his younger brother. They were very

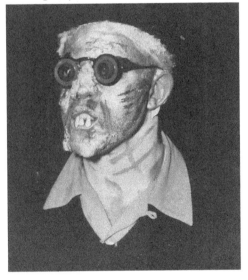

John as UMOC, 1956

nice, especially his mother. She really tried to make me feel at home."

As the weather warmed that spring, all of us were awaiting the bells announcing Spring Day. A sad fact but Spring Day bells tolled no more after 1956. The "Umie" tradition ended that year due to the drunken behavior of some of the students. I described the event in a letter home.

...First of all I'll tell you about Spring Day. One day in spring the chapel bells ring at 9:20 and it is Spring Day. Everyone gets out of class and goes down to the pond where there are games and a picnic lunch and everything. Last Wednesday was a beautiful day and everyone thought it would be Spring Day. But at 9:20, the bells didn't ring so I went off to my 10:00 class. At 10:20 the bells rang. Everyone was completely surprised, but we all went down to the pond. There we found out it was a hoax spring day. Some unidentified kids had rung the bells, but the Spring Day Committee had to go through with it, because some kids had taken off. So it wasn't a very good day compared to what it would have been if it had been on the right day...

Scenes from Spring Day 1956

For me, at least, another sad day that first spring at college was Honors Convocation. I had carefully plotted my strategy. I was positive I would be tapped as a Scroll. As a believer in prayer, I prayed every night to God, "Please, God, let me be a Scroll. That's all I want."

The all-school gathering was in the huge expanse of the athletics' cage. I sat near the end of a row so the current Scrolls circulating through the audience would have no difficulty spotting me. I was sitting with John who I was sure would be tapped for Maroon Key.

The Honor Societies wandered through the rows. John was tapped for Maroon Key. Five Chi Omegas, Cleo, Gail, Nancy, Sara, and Sylvia were tapped. Most of the audience was looking at me as the Scrolls continued to search the faces. Finally, they found their target, sitting in the balcony, an unsuspecting but very happy Kappa Alpha Theta. I was not chosen. The number of Chi Omegas represented was reduced—only five Chi Omegas, instead of six, became Scrolls.

The freshmen dorm housemothers approved the selections. Mrs. Churchill achieved her revenge on me for what she considered insubordination on Winter Carnival Ball night. To this day, more than fifty years later, the memory of the loss of that coveted honor saddens me.

However, a happy memory ended my freshmen year. In early June, just before school was over, John's fraternity pin arrived. He "pinned" me. This ritual meant "we were engaged to be engaged." The correct manner of wearing two pins, your sorority pin and your intended's fraternity pin, was to secure the main insignias side by side. Then cross and fasten the two guard chains that identified your university's Greek chapter, Iota Beta for Chi Omega and Alpha for Kappa Sigma.

Before I went home for the summer, I needed to settle two important decisions: my roommate and my courses for next year. Since my current roommate pledged a different sorority from mine, we decided not to room together again, but room with sisters from our respective sororities.

Chi Omega and Kappa Sigma pins with guard chains

…Well, I just got my roommate situation all straignted (sic) out. I'm rooming with one of my Chi O sisters, Marilyn…She is a great kid. She's Catholic, lots of fun, responsible, gay (not the current meaning of the word), pinned to a swell guy who was a Maroon Key last year. He's a sophomore. She, of course, is a freshman. She is really great and I have never known her to get drunk though she may have an occasional drink. She lives in West Springfield and has a twin sister who goes to college in Springfield besides 3 other sisters. She is really great. I know you will like her and approve of her…John approves whole heartedly of her…

I listed my tentative schedule for my parents.

First Semester	**Second Semester**
English	English
Sociology	Psychology
Bacteriology	Geology
French Literature	French Literature
Economics	English (Creative Writing)
And, of course, Phys. Ed.	

Do you approve or not? It is recommened (sic) for a journalism majar (sic) John is taking the same except for French Literature he is taking Government both semesters.

My summer plans included visits from John because in one letter, written in April, I asked again, "Remind Daddy to buy tickets for the double-header on the 4th of July between the Yankees and the Red Sox. Grandstand seats on the 1st or 3rd base line."

Chapter Nine

Pulled Apart My Sophomore Year

Summers are special and memorable when we are young. We look forward to three months of no school, tantalizing days of freedom coinciding with the best weather of the year. The summer of 1956, between my freshmen and sophomore years of college, split into contrasting halves, one inducing boredom and drudgery from Monday through Friday and the other exuding pleasure and romance on the weekends.

I worked nine to five for minimum wage ($1.00 an hour) in an insurance agency as "Jill-of-all-trades," filling in for the vacationing, regular office staffers. I typed simple forms and envelopes, filed reams of miscellaneous items, and answered the phone. To reach the office, I walked a mile to the Swampscott train station, and then rode the local Boston and Maine rail line to the neighboring city of Salem, a ten-minute trip. My take home pay, after social security and income taxes were subtracted, was $32 a week. I received one perk. The manager allowed me to leave a half hour early in order to make my train connection. In return, I deposited the office correspondence at the Salem Post Office that was on the way to the station.

I hated the job because of the mind-dulling repetition, and my mother's insistence that I wear my thick glasses in order to "rest" my eyes from the contact lenses. Ironically, this was exactly the opposite recommendation for successful contact lens wearing. I felt ugly again and insignificant. I usually ate my brown-bag lunch with Brenda, a high school age girl. She listened to my stories about college life, while regaling me with sordid exploits from her social life, replete with poor grammar and the slang word "a—hole," a vernacular expression that always stung my ear.

On most weekends, John hitchhiked or drove his father's car to visit me in Swampscott. Occasionally, I took the bus from Boston to visit him in Springfield. On those trips, as the bus pulled into the depot and I spotted John though the window, I had a rush of pride on seeing him waiting for me and felt an intense longing to be with him. During the week we wrote to each other every day. I don't have those letters for reference, because when I married Connie (aka Conrad), my mother insisted that I destroy any notes and trinkets from former boyfriends.

When John visited me, we often walked to Fishermen's Beach, the local hangout in Swampscott, played tennis at the town courts, and sometimes drove to well-known Crane's Beach in Ipswich to search out secluded spots among the dunes. Surf, sky, and sand—the preferred trappings for summer romantic trysts. We occasionally double-dated with my UMass/Swampscott high school friend, Sandra, whose boyfriend from UMass also lived in Springfield. John and he sometimes came together in one car. One Sunday night on their trip home, out of money and gas, they were stranded on the highway. They called John's father to rescue them.

On a Saturday afternoon in August, as was the summer custom, the Chi Omega sorority sisters from the North Shore of Boston hosted a "get-to-know the Chi Omegas tea" for prospective freshmen from the area, who planned to attend the University. Chi Omegas from the sophomore, junior, and senior classes gathered at my house to meet the incoming coeds … all legal under sorority rushing rules. John was there, wearing his Maroon Key hat.

On one visit to Springfield, I attended his cousin's wedding, where John was one of the ushers. To the ceremony and reception on Saturday, I remember wearing my favorite, sleeveless Lantz dress in a deep pink and white pattern trimmed in white rickrack. As John's family is Polish, their traditional wedding festivities included plenty of lively polkas.

I was staying at John's house. John's relatives, who had gathered at his house for a farewell brunch, chatted with us as we left for Mass on Sunday morning.

"Are you two going to Holy Communion?" they slyly asked.

"Yes," both John and I answered.

They looked at each other with knowing smiles. I realized they were teasing us, but I felt unprepared to respond and somehow insulted. Were they insinuating that after a Saturday night, how could we receive Holy Communion without going to confession first?

"Leave them alone," John's mother interjected. "They're good kids."

In an earlier chapter, I wrote about how many psychologists believe most genuine memories are recalled due to an accompanying, underlying emotion. I remember the scene at John's house because of embarrassment and hurt feelings, definitely not because of shame or guilt. On recollection, I accept the probability that his aunts and uncles were just kidding us, because they thought we were a nice, young couple, and they were trying to be funny or clever.

I attended another wedding that summer as a bridesmaid for my childhood friend, Paula. She was a year older than I and had completed her sophomore year at the University of Florida. Her fiancé was a senior and graduating that year. He wanted to marry and begin their life together. She promised her father to finish college and graduate at a later date. I thought it was very romantic, but it was a weekend without John.

Summer was over too soon and it was time to return to school. Sophomore year began with two disappointments. I planned to return to school wearing my pin and John's pin, as we were still very much a couple. However, at some point in the summer, one of the pearls came loose and fell off John's pin. I returned it to the factory, but it had not arrived in time for me to wear back to school. I cringed to think that our friends might infer that John and I had broken up.

When we set out for college that September morning, my father again endeared me to him with a heartfelt gesture for his heartbroken daughter. At that early hour, he stopped at the Swampscott Post Office and jiggled the door knob to try and rouse any occupants. The postmaster answered the door. My father inquired if there were a package for a "Miss Judith Heaney." No package. My father's gallant effort to help me boosted my dispirited mood.

My other disappointment was not being a part of the Scroll and Maroon Key festivities welcoming the new freshmen class. But, a second hero emerged to assuage my spirits. John insisted I wear his Maroon Key hat. I'm sure this oddity confused the new students. Was she a Scroll? Was she a Maroon Key? Who was she? At least, that was fun.

Classes began. John and I planned our schedule so we had every class together. I dropped French Literature and replaced it with American Government. My first semester sophomore classes had more arresting titles than my freshmen courses: English, Humane Letters; Sociology,

Introductory; Bacteriology, Introductory; Elements of Economics; and the already mentioned American Government.

In a letter home I told my parents: "I am studying more this year than last and am in less (sic) activities. On talking with the juniors they said sophomore year is the hardest because of all the reading courses. However, I am working hard and still hope to make the dean's list." I guess my predictions were true, because first semester sophomore year I achieved my highest grade point average of 3.4 with two A's and three B's and even a B in Phys. Ed.

Extra-curricular activities included sophomore class officer (secretary), which involved running the Soph-Senior Hop and Sophomore Banquet, a *Collegian* reporter, and member of the Newman Club (Catholic students religious group). I was also active in my sorority, Chi Omega.

In the fifties many of the social activities revolved around the fraternities and sororities. In general, the sorority houses were smaller than the fraternity houses. The women did not live in their house until senior year, while the fraternity brothers lived in beginning sophomore year. In the 2000s although Chi Omega and Kappa Sigma are still present on campus, the Greek societies are not the social force they were in the fifties. The Chi O house and the Kappa Sig house still stand but they no longer are owned by the social groups. The former is a single family residence and the latter is an administrative office of the University of Massachusetts.

Sophomore Class Officers with John and me

One early fall weekend, six of us, three guys and three girls, took the bus to my house in Swampscott. Nothing was happening on campus so we decided to vamoose. I forewarned my mother. The three men, one of course John, stayed on cots in our family room. One of the girls was also from Swampscott and slept at her own house, while the other girl stayed with me in the twin beds in my bedroom. I think my mother enjoyed the

*Chi Omega house
at UMass in the fifties*

*Kappa Sigma house
at UMass in the fifties*

confusion and I know we enjoyed the weekend. My mother indulged us with home-cooked meals.

Saturday night the six of us walked to the Swampscott train station and took the train into Boston to see the epic Academy Award winning movie, *Around the World in Eighty Days,* based on Jules Verne's novel and starring David Niven as Phineas Fogg. Reportedly, Niven said he would have acted the part for nothing. The movie, in Technicolor and award-winning cinematography, similar to surround vision, ran an unbelievable 183 minutes. Forty famous actors appeared in cameo roles, including Frank Sinatra, Buster Keaton, Marlene Dietrich, and Noel Coward.

Due to its recent release and popularity, the only seats available were in the front row. The huge screen heightened the images of the balloon ride and foreign vistas. The vivid fantasy is forever engraved in my memory. I sat among five of my good friends, held hands with John, and while ignoring my aching neck, wished the night would never end ... a perfect evening, from my nineteen-year-old prospective.

While researching, I ordered the original 1956 version from Netflix and watched it with my husband on our much smaller television screen. I did not recapture my enthrallment with the film, but the nostalgia from that night in the fall of 1956 remains a winner in my memory.

Another memorable trip was to New York City. Over semester break, John and I decided to go into the city with his roommate, Doug, and girlfriend, Mary, who went to another college. We planned to go in for the day to see the Sunday matinee of the Broadway musical *Li'l Abner.* The lead, Peter Palmer, was a former Kappa Sigma at the University of Illinois and we hoped to solicit his autograph at the stage door. When my mother learned of our plans, she suggested we stay overnight with my aunt Gina and uncle Matt in Greenwich, Connecticut. The four of us agreed. We went into New York City by train on Saturday, went to dinner and a TV show Saturday night, and then met my aunt and uncle in Grand Central station at midnight. We all rode the train back to their apartment. Mary and I stayed with them, but the guys stayed at the Greenwich YMCA.

> *...The only hitch in the New York trip was the sleeping accommodations (sic) for the boys. It was in a huge room with about 12 other beds filled with "drunken" bums. They were talking in their sleep, coughing, and one guy even got sick during the night. The man at the desk checked their wallets, because he said he didn't think it would be safe for them to keep them with them. I guess they had a pretty rugged night, but they checked it off as an experience. (sic)...Gee, thanks a lot Mum (sic) for thinking of aunt Gina and taking the initiative to write to her. As the old saying goes, I guess you're not so dumb...*

Many of my school activities revolved around the Newman Club. Father David Power was the advisor and chaplain. He came to know John and me very well, as we were very active in the group.

> *...Starting today, Lent, I'm going to go to Mass every morning with John...Next Sunday is the cummion (sic) breakfast and Governor Furcolo is going to speak. John and I are going...*

In the spring of sophomore year, the Newman Club offered all Catholic women a chance to attend a retreat at the Cenacle Retreat Center, run by the Cenacle Sisters in Lancaster, Massachusetts, seventy miles from the university. Several of us decided to go, including two of my Chi Omega sisters, Nancy and Sara, who are still close friends today. The large red-brick mansion was on a 200-acre estate with room for forty retreatants.

The Cenacle Sisters mission is threefold: prayer, community, and ministry. The Cenacle (from the Latin *cenaculum* for dining room), also known as the "Upper Room," is a room in Jerusalem traditionally held to be the site of The Last Supper. Two churches, near Mount Zion, compete for the authentic location of the original Cenacle; one, the Church of Dormition and the other, the Church of St. Mark. In Christian tradition, from the New Testament, (Acts1:13), the "upper room" was not only the site of the Last Supper, but the first Christian church. In English, cenacle means a small dining room, usually on a second floor.

We spent a weekend at the retreat. While there we did not speak to each other; complete silence prevailed. At our meals the sisters read from the Bible or holy books. Each day of the retreat, we prayed, meditated, confessed to a priest, and received Holy Communion.

I remember the silence as comforting and peaceful. I remember the meals as simple and tasty. I remember my confusion as I labored to confess meaningful sins. I was struggling for peace with my sexual urgings. My roommate, Marilyn, a devout Catholic, claimed the Catholic Church considered petting a sin, even by married people, unless the action culminated in intercourse for the purpose of procreation. I could not accept the Catholic viewpoint that a married couple were not allowed to touch each other for pleasure unless they intended to have sex. I hoped to resolve this problem at the retreat, but I was too shy to ask the appropriate questions. Nancy encountered an unforeseen complication. For some arcane reason, the sisters singled out Nancy as a prospective candidate to join their order. She continually received mail after we returned to campus, urging her to consider a vocation.

The retreat closed in 1975, because a newer, larger Cenacle retreat opened in Boston. In 1985, the property became a Maharishi Ayurvedic Health Center for rest and recharge. Ayurveda is an ancient preventive health care developed in India over 6,000 years ago.

Cenacle Retreat House in the 1950s

The spring of 1957, I experienced more disappointments. John and I ran again for junior class offices, but we were both defeated. I tried out for the Precionettes, a drill team that marched with the band at football games, but I didn't make it. I applied to be a counselor or RA (Resident Assistant) in a freshmen dorm my junior year. When my friends received their acceptance letters, I didn't get mine. I thought Mrs. Churchill blackballed me again. In my pain, I threatened to transfer to the University of New Hampshire. At least there was a Chi Omega sorority on that campus.

Luckily, it was a postal problem. The next day my letter arrived. I was assigned to Thatcher. This dorm was formerly a boy's dorm and had been John's dorm during his freshmen year. The rumor was that Mrs. Churchill did blackball me, but Mrs. Davies, the housemother of Thatcher, knew me and John and said, "I would love to have Judy as a counselor in my dorm." One disappointment remedied.

In a letter home I described two fun events the spring of 1957.

…Today is the "KNURD" that is "drunk" spelled backward. It's a big spring picnic with big juicy steaks and beer held at Sportman's Park. It is held by KΣ and ΣAE. John and I are going. Next week is his spring formal…Only 2 more weeks of classes and then finals.

The Kappa Sig formal this week-end (sic) was lots of fun. We went with Doug and Mary again. There was a steak barbecue the afternoon of the formal. John gave me orchids again for a corsage…

A sad event of the spring of 1957 was the untimely death of John's mother. She died unexpectedly of ovarian cancer. I went to the funeral in Springfield, and stayed with my Chi O sister, Marie, who also lived in Springfield and had gone to high school with John.

Now with this complication of no woman in the house, my overly proper mother forbade any further visits to John's house, despite my desperate pleas.

Doug, Mary, me, and John at the Kappa Sig formal

…John would like me to come home with him on Saturday and take me out to dinner and to the movies and to stay overnight for there is absolutely nothing going on up here. Now the only objection you have had so far is because you say it isn't proper since no woman can be there. However after talking around, we have come up with substantial proof that it is proper. In the Springfield paper in one of the etiquette columns, it stated that it was proper for a young lady to stay at a young man's house as long as one of the parents was there. Especially since John's mother is deceased it will be all right. So, please, don't you think it will be all right. It will be so dead up here, everybody's going home. So please write and give me permission, OK?

They did not give me permission, but I went anyway. I eventually confessed to my father and extracted a promise from him that he would not tell my mother. However, I am sure he told her. To her credit she never mentioned it to me. Now as an adult and wife, I understand she was protecting my father and his promise to his daughter.

Speaking of my mother and her old-fashioned ideas about dating protocol, she and I had arrived at a polemic juncture. She did not want me to tie myself down to one boy because she thought I was too young and would miss promising opportunities. My mother had quite a globe-trotting life before she married at age thirty-nine. Plus, she did not like John for an unbecoming, prejudicial reason. He was Polish. She believed and often said to me, "Polish men beat their wives. And I mean it; I won't go to your wedding if you marry him."

This pronouncement elicited powerful bouts of crying and ranting from me. My distraught father ran around the house, slamming windows shut, while muttering, "I'm raising a houseful of fish wives."

Although she was always polite to John, he felt her contentious vibes. In contrast, my father took long walks with him along the beach and discussed politics and the future.

The constant battering of me by my mother had its toll. I wanted to experience all the possibilities that college and an unknown, unfettered future offered. On the other hand, I loved John. I was sure of this. The constant haranguing from my mother and my own indecision led me to confide in Father Power, my spiritual advisor. He knew John and me very well. However, he did not know my mother. As John said, "She is a strong woman."

My discussions with Father Power resolved nothing. I explained to him how I was being torn apart by my mother's constant belittling of John and my sincere love for him. Of course, I admitted that I loved my mother, too. I confessed the awful bigoted slurs that my mother hurled at me about John's ethnicity.

Father Power was silent. He said nothing.

In distress, I questioned, "What should I do?"

Father Power was silent. He said nothing.

"Do you believe Polish men beat their wives?" I demanded.

Father Power was silent. He said nothing.

"Please, Father, what can I do to stop being pulled apart by two people I love very much? Please tell me what to do."

Father Power was silent. He said nothing.

After this unproductive session with Father Power, I came to the conclusion that he didn't like me and didn't approve of my relationship with John, or he felt an obligation not to come between a child and her mother.

I knew that I needed to resolve the situation by myself before we went home for the summer. I compromised with John and my mother. I broke up with John on a steady basis. We agreed to go out with other people over the summer. When we returned to school in the fall, we would reassess the relationship.

Chapter Ten

The Genesis of the Paisans Junior Year

Each summer I experienced a different job. The summer of 1955 I waitressed in the children's dining room at the New Ocean House in my hometown of Swampscott; the summer of 1956 I filled in as an office clerk at an insurance office in the neighboring city of Salem; the summer of 1957 I landed a government position in the capitol city of Boston.

In the spring of 1957, my father had suggested I take the civil service test and apply for a government appointment. I was offered summer employment at the Internal Revenue Service in Boston at the GS1 level. The pay was $50 a week. I was thrilled to be going into Boston every day. I loved Boston. While in high school, I often ventured there by myself to stroll the streets, shop in Filene's and Jordan's, and visit The Boston Museum of Fine Arts.

My job became the best aspect of the summer of 1957. I walked to the Swampscott train station and headed into the city, a half hour ride. Then, I took the subway to my job. This year, I defied my mother and wore my contacts. In that era, for trips into the city, summer attire required gloves and dresses, no pants, or slacks as was the current term. In fact, it wasn't until the late sixties that pants, even dressy pant suits, were allowed for women in Boston's Copley Plaza Hotel. I felt sophisticated and businesslike, wearing gloves and skirts every day.

I also learned about the business world. From the repetitive IRS task that I performed that summer, I refuted a false conception that I had harbored all my nineteen years. My job assignment, basically sorting and shuffling papers, was the first step in an IRS audit. Along with other summer hires, I leafed through returns from self-employed tax payers. At my desk, I separated them into piles, dictated by a rigid formula, either for further review or not for further review. If the return were from a retail business, net profit to gross receipts could not exceed 10 percent. If it ran over this amount, the return was tagged for additional scrutiny. The standard for professionals, such as doctors, dentists, or lawyers, adhered to a more lenient percentage code. Their net to gross profit could not surpass 25 percent. In checking the returns, I discovered that business owners made substantially more money than the academics. This fact surprised me.

One of my coworkers was a college student who attended Boston College, a Jesuit school. Our desks were adjacent to each other. We flirted and ate lunch together, but we had only one date. After Jim made the trip from his house in South Roxbury to my house in Swampscott, a distance of seventeen miles, he concluded that he didn't relish a "long-distance romance." I remember that our one date was to Revere Beach, a sleazy amusement strip along the shore between Lynn and Boston. I agreed to ride the monster roller coaster with him. This strategy allowed me to hold his hand and snuggle a bit—out of fright, of course—while still clinging true to my "no kiss on the first date" rule.

The summer was a bust from a romantic viewpoint. I spent the weekends with high school girlfriends, either at the beach or at the movies. John and I exchanged a few letters, but did not visit each other. I promised myself never to endure such a boring summer again.

I was glad to return to school in September for three reasons. First, my courses were more meaningful and challenging, now that I was into my double major of English/Journalism.

My first semester courses were:
English, Creative Writing
Journalism, Mass. Comm.
Sociology, The Family
History, English
English, Shakespeare

My second semester courses were:
Journalism, Communications
English, Contemporary Novel
Government, European
Home Ec., Meal Planning
English, Modern Drama

Second, I was one of two resident assistants on the second floor of Thatcher, a freshmen dorm. My sorority sister Sara was an RA on the third floor. Our main duty was to convey the dorm and college rules to the freshmen and answer their questions, while acting as a role model for them. Our other jobs included phone duty attendant and "light-flicking" official at the curfew hour. For this work, we received free room rent, amounting to one hundred dollars a semester.

Third, I saw John again. Although John and I didn't see each other exclusively, we began dating again. One fall weekend, because John knew I wanted to visit other college campuses, he arranged a weekend to Syracuse University in Syracuse, New York to visit one of his good friends. It was a football weekend with Holy Cross. He would room with his friend and I would stay in the Chi Omega sorority house. John commandeered his father's car and we set off on the 143 mile trip at noon on Friday.

All went smoothly until the car broke down on the highway. No cell phones in the fifties. We managed to find a highway phone booth to notify his dad who agreed to come and retrieve the car. Somehow John and I continued on to Syracuse by bus. My best memory from the weekend was John's gift of a souvenir scarf, a long, knitted muffler in Syracuse colors of orange and navy blue. The worst memories were of the unfriendly Chi O sisters and the Saturday night fraternity party where all the kids seemed to disappear into dark, but not completely hidden, corners of the frat rec room, for "make out" sessions. No dancing, socializing, or even much beer drinking. We took a bus back to UMass on Sunday … a weekend from hell. But I checked off one more "college-life" experience.

Junior year was a year of transition for me. I undertook new responsibilities and expanded my social life. I formed a strong and special relationship with four of my Chi O sisters. We called ourselves the "*paisans*" (meaning countryman/compatriot or friend/pal in Greek slang). We remain close friends to this day.

Besides my dorm counseling position, I acquired two other jobs. I worked in the agricultural office, cataloging elm trees diagnosed with "Dutch elm disease." Under my creative writing professor's tutelage, I taught remedial English to foreign students once a week. I dated many different boys as my mother had hoped, including freshmen, graduate students, men from Amherst College, John, and the special someone I married. However, my grades suffered. In November, I penned to my mother, "I don't think I'm going to get too good an average this semester. That what's (sic) happens when I'm not pinned and looking for men."

Besides earning a "Mrs." degree, as was the presupposed common goal for women in the fifties, college was for learning. After revisiting the titles of my courses junior year, I have vivid memories from some and no recollections from others.

My Friends, The Paisans: Phyllis, Nancy, Sara, and Cleo

I remember three courses from first semester: Shakespeare, Creative Writing, and a sociology class, entitled The Family. Frank Prentice Rand, a veritable legend at the school, taught Shakespeare on Tuesday, Thursday, and Saturday mornings at 8 a.m. in Old Chapel. In the class syllabus, Professor Rand assigned readings due for each class. At the beginning of the period, he quizzed us on the assignment. This "mini" test counted as one third of our grade. With this method, most of us attempted to stay current in class. The test questions weeded out anyone who had not read his or her assignment. Two sample questions: From *Romeo and Juliet*, "What was the name of Juliet's cousin?" From *The Tempest*, "How many days did Prospero allow Ariel to perform her spiriting?" These questions assured careful reading of the play!

Professor Rand taught at the university for forty-three years. He retired in 1960, so I was lucky to have had him. One of the main stages in the university's Fine Arts Center is named the Rand Theater in his honor for his years as poet, playwright, historian, theater director, and English professor at the university.

The creative writing course was also on Tuesday, Thursday, and Saturday. My good friend Nancy was in the class. I admired her writing skills and she admired my imagination, so we often collaborated using her verbal wizardry and my story ideas.

The course, The Family, was a marriage/sex course, and many students considered it a "gut" course, the jargon for an easy A or B grade. For one assignment, we listed all the qualities we wanted in a prospective spouse. I listed the usual generic characteristics such as kind, intelligent, and good-looking. I continued on to quite specific requirements. I wanted a man with 20/20 eye sight so his genes would counteract my 20/400 refraction. Also he needed to have many brothers and sisters so our children would have lots of cousins. Talking to my friends, I became more visionary. I declared I wanted to live on Park Avenue in New York City and summer on Nantucket Island. My friends teased me saying, "Judy, only Cash McCall will satisfy you." He was the protagonist in a

Professor Frank Prentice Rand

current popular book of the same name by Cameron Hawley. The novel lauded the hero as a successful business man who operated in anonymity. A 1959 movie, based on the novel, starred James Garner and Natalie Wood.

Near the end of junior year, I chanced upon a new beau. Soon the paisans began teasing me and calling this boy, Cash McCall.

I met him as Nancy, Sara, and I were walking back from church to Chi Omega for Sunday dinner. A convertible pulled up and stopped. In the front seat, we recognized Janet, one of our Chi O sisters, squeezed between two guys.

"Hi, do you want a lift back to the house?" she asked.

"Sure," we said in unison. The walk from Saint Brigid's Catholic Church in Amherst to the Chi O house was at least a mile and a half.

We piled in the back seat. "This is Ed," she said, indicating the driver, "and Connie." (For clarification, Connie's name was Conrad, but at school everyone called him Connie.)

"Hi," we said in unison again.

When we pulled up to the sorority house, Connie jumped out and opened the back door to let us out. Dressed in a tight short dress, I stepped out first as Connie helped us from the car. I noticed his eyes checking out my legs.

The next day Janet asked me, "Would you like to go out with Connie? He wants to take you to the Greek sing next Friday night." This was an annual singing competition among the sororities and fraternities.

I tried to recall where I had seen Connie before that Sunday morning. Then I remembered. I had seen him sitting atop the piano at The Drake, the downtown bar where we all hung out. I also remembered, when I was on duty one Friday night at Thatcher dorm, I had to flick the lights several times to urge him to finish up saying "good night" to one of the freshmen girls. I decided he was cute.

"Yes," I said to Janet. A spring romance began.

Connie belonged to QTV, the only remaining Latin letter fraternity in the United States. It was founded on May 12, 1869, and was the oldest fraternity on campus. Connie has been my husband for over fifty years, and I still don't know what the initials mean, although he'll admit to "Quit Teasing Virgins."

*QTV fraternity house
at UMass, 1959*

In a letter home to my mother, I described my new boyfriend:

…Yes, Connie's name is Rousseau. He is a junior (Should be a senior left school for a year) 6 ft. tall, blonde hair that is receding, green eyes, nice looking,… beautiful collegiate dresser—just love his clothes—a really good boy—treats me like a queen—took me to church last Sunday—takes me to the movies in the middle of the week—his fraternity formal should be great this week end. He lives in Amesbury and works as a life guard at Salisbury Beach in the summer for the past 4 summers. Am wearing another girl's dress to the formal….

From second semester, I remember two courses. One was Contemporary Novel. I only recall two titles from the syllabus: *Catcher in the Rye* by J.D. Salinger and *The Young Lions* by Irwin Shaw. I revered Salinger's book and went on to buy and read all his published novels, including *Nine Stories,* and *Franny and Zooey,* the first in his series about the Glass family. The salient point I remembered from these modern novels was the language, which surprised me. I had heard the "f" word spoken out loud only once in my life during high school, never in college. I had not encountered it again, either as graffiti or oral expletive, until reading it in print in these assignments. I believe it is a sad commentary on our "evolving" culture that this word is in common use in print and speech today, but that in the fifties and sixties, it was seldom seen, heard, or spoken,

Me and Connie at QTV Formal

except in the "popular" novels. This fact propounds the question: Did the novelists popularize slovenly language, or did they imitate the language of the populist?

The "gut" course for second semester was the Home Ec course: Meal Planning. Four of us Chi O's signed up for the course together and were assigned our own abutting fully-applianced kitchens. In the hour-long weekly lecture period we studied nutrition and cooking techniques, and then used this knowledge to plan a meal that we cooked in the next day's lab section.

When we entered our kitchen cubicle, all the ingredients for our meal, measured in exact quantities, were arranged on our counters. In the three-hour class we assembled, cooked, and ate our concoction. For the final exam, the four of us were required to plan and prepare a dinner party for nine, including ourselves, the instructor, and four invited guests. To the surprise of the professor, we invited men friends, not our sorority sisters. I invited Connie.

As junior year was ending, Nancy, Sara, and I began to think about applying for summer jobs together. We wanted to spend the summer waitressing on Cape Cod, another college ritual to experience. We knew we needed to apply in advance. One weekend in early May, the three of us went home to my house. We borrowed the family car, drove to the Cape, and scoured the restaurants for summer employment.

I had a major problem. I needed to be of legal age to serve alcohol. Sara and Nancy turned twenty-one in May, but I wouldn't be twenty-one until November. What to do? Marilyn, my sophomore year roommate, rescued me. She was twenty-one and loaned me her school identification card. At a quick glance, her picture looked like me. She would not need it because she was getting married in August.

Our trip to Cape Cod was successful, even though my friends still tease me about my mother's parting words as we pulled out of the driveway. "Remember *when* you have a flat tire, we have Triple A." No mishaps.

Mr. Pizakis, the owner of two restaurants, The Mayflower Café and the Mayflower Restaurant on Main Street, Hyannis, hired the three of us. He didn't even ask our ages. I guess he assumed, as we were soon to be college seniors, we were all twenty-one. We were to begin the week before Memorial Day, which was the traditional beginning of the summer season.

We returned to campus for our final exams. We also needed to choose rooms and roommates in the Chi O house for senior year. The house accommodated twenty-six women, only space for the senior class. On the second floor were three, four-person bedrooms, one bath, and the housemother's suite. On the third floor were six double rooms and one bath. The one additional double room on the fourth floor also used the third floor bathroom. Nancy and I chose to share a room together; Phyllis and Cleo shared another room; and Sara roomed with Marie—all of us on the third floor. The mystery that still haunts us Chi Os today is how twenty-six women coped with only two bathrooms. None of us can remember having a problem, either on weekday mornings or on a Saturday night. I said good-bye to Connie for the summer. We had been dating exclusively for about a month and a half. I would miss him. He would be lifeguarding at Salisbury Beach, and I would be waitressing on Cape Cod. We wished each other a safe and fun summer. Would we date again when we returned to school in the fall?

Chapter Eleven

Senior Year and Graduation

The summer of 1958 added another link to my chain of long-imagined experiences that I felt belonged in any coed's résumé. I spent the summer on Cape Cod working and living with my sorority sisters. The Cape was the summer destination for numerous college kids east of the Mississippi and north of Washington, D.C. Dirty and dusty cars with "Cape Cod or Bust" splashed on their trunks, above Ohio, Michigan, or Indiana license plates, arrived daily in May and June.

In early May, we secured our jobs during a preliminary trip to the Cape. Mr. Pizakis, proprietor of the Mayflower Café in Hyannis, hired Nancy, Sara, and me for the summer. We were to begin the week before Memorial Day. Nancy's mother and father drove the three of us to Hyannis and helped us find rooms to rent. Her parents insisted on a respectable place. We chose two upstairs rooms in a small cape-style house, owned by a young couple with a baby. Nancy's mother felt that accommodations in a family home would be safe. However, it was over a mile walk to the restaurant.

As a prerequisite for our job, we needed to supply our own white waitress uniforms and comfortable, white shoes. Independently, distaining the usual synthetic loose-fitting uniforms, Nancy and I both bought white, cotton uniforms with button-down collars. We wanted to project a preppy style, even though these garments required washing and ironing each day. Sara, sensibly, purchased two drip-dry traditional uniforms.

Soon, our choice of rooms became intolerable. Nancy could not abide the fetid, diaper-pail smell that permeated the entire house, even wafting up to our rooms. Plus, the walk to and from the restaurant and downtown, hangout bars was too long. Mr. Pizakis came to the rescue. He owned a dilapidated rooming house behind his restaurant. He offered us a three-room apartment and bath for $10.00 a week each, including Gordon linens. We shared it with two other girls from the restaurant, plus Sara's cousin, Ann, who had joined us. So, for sixty dollars a week, six employees lived in three rooms in a run-down apartment building with unreliable plumbing. (For comparison, the next year, four of us rented a furnished two-bedroom apartment for one hundred and eighty dollars a month in New York City.) The commode broke half way through the summer. We used the fill-a-pail-with-water-from-the-bathtub method to flush the toilet for the rest of the summer. But, it was a one-minute walk to work and in the middle of the nightlife.

In the late nineties, on a nostalgic trip to Cape Cod, Sara, Nancy, and I visited the restaurant and our old rooming house. The restaurant was there with a new name, but the apartment building behind the restaurant was torn down, and in its stead, a parking lot.

Sara, Nancy, and me in front of the restaurant

The summer on the Cape was fattening, fun, and financially rewarding. The restaurant was open for lunch and dinner. We ate all our meals at the restaurant, except breakfast, which we skipped. We made up for it with ice cream sundaes in the restaurant and beer at night in the bars. One of the friendly, old cooks noticed how much weight I was gaining and threatened to weigh me on the meat scale. At the end of the summer, at Marilyn's wedding, Father Power claimed he didn't recognize me walking down the aisle because of my round face.

The social scene was fun, as we had hoped and expected. The socializing began after midnight when the restaurants closed and the college kids went out to the bars and dance clubs. At night I needed and used Marilyn's I.D. "Marilyn" visited many drinking establishments on the Cape that summer. The four of us friends stayed together. We knew enough not to go out alone with a guy until we really knew him. I also tried to follow my rule of "no kissing on the first date," but on my first individual date, I broke the rule in order to get some sleep.

I had a mini summer romance with a boy who had just graduated from a college in New England. I met Ben at the restaurant. He came in with a friend and I waited on them. He invited me out and I agreed. He introduced me to Miller's Lite beer, which I still prefer today. When he brought me home after our first date, we sat in his car and talked. No kissing. I said I had to go to the bathroom. I thought he would say "good night" and leave. But no, he said, "I'll wait in the car for you."

After I came back out, I kissed him good night so he would leave and I could go inside to bed.

That summer we all made a substantial amount from our tips. We opened saving accounts at a local bank and deposited our money every week. The average meal was three dollars, so parties of two spending six dollars for their dinners usually gave us a fifteen percent tip or one dollar. Sara made the most from a single tip, five dollars from one gentleman. We tried to avoid waiting on the French Canadians, because they only tipped ten cents per person. On average we earned fifteen dollars a day.

My favorite tip was not money, but a poem. A Philadelphia lawyer, along with the standard gratuity, gave me his business card with a limerick penned on the back of it:

There once was a lassie named Judy
Who lacked neither intellect nor beauty
Of one thing I'm certain
All the boys will be hurtin'
To wed this adorable cutie.

The four of us were Catholic and attended Mass every Sunday at St. Francis Xavier Church in Hyannis. During the summer, casual attire was permitted. We wore Bermuda shorts, instead of skirts or dresses. However, it was proper decorum to cover our heads, so we used a mantilla or handkerchief in place of a formal hat.

In August, Nancy and I needed to travel to Springfield, Massachusetts, to be bridesmaids in Marilyn's wedding. The Friday of that weekend, my boyfriend, Ben, agreed to drive us, because Nancy's house in Auburn, Massachusetts, was near his home, where he would spend the weekend. Then, Nancy's father drove us to Springfield for the weekend wedding and came back to pick us up. Late Sunday, Ben drove us back to the Cape.

Although we had agreed to waitress through Labor Day, by late August, I wanted to go home. My brother and a friend drove down to visit us. We let them stay in the hallway of the apartment building. The police found them there and accused them of trespassing. My brother said the girls in the next apartment suggested they could sleep there. So early Sunday morning, the police pounded on our door and demanded to know if Judy Heaney were there.

I opened the door. "I'm Judy Heaney."

"Is Don Heaney your brother?" one of the policemen asked.

"Yes," I said.

"Did you tell him that he and his friend could sleep in the hallway?" Again, I said, "Yes."

"Don't you know this is private property and that's against the law? We won't arrest you, if you leave Hyannis right now with your brother."

I gathered my things, said goodbye to my friends, and left for home.

***

On my return to campus for senior year, I encountered and wrestled with situations only applicable to seniors. We lived in the sorority house instead of a dorm. Courses were geared toward a declared major. English majors were required to write a thesis. We contemplated plans for the future after graduation: graduate school, employment, marriage—or all three possibilities.

On a personal front I had two immediate priorities: to lose my summer fat and to reconnect with Connie. Living in the Chi Omega house presented an obvious method for losing weight. The house was situated at least a mile distance from my classes. We prepared our own breakfast. I ate a piece of toast, coffee, and juice. I did not return to the house for lunch.

I skipped all lunches and lost the fat. Don't forget, I was only twenty years old. My second priority also proved easy. Connie wanted to date me again.

My courses for first semester:
English Novel, Defoe through the Victorians
Major American Writers
Journalism, Communications
Marketing, Advertising
Philosophy of Religion

My favorite course was Defoe through the Victorians taught by Doctor Allen, a professor whom I remembered and liked from freshmen year. For the time period 1600 -1800, the syllabus listed nine English authors: Daniel Defoe, Jonathan Swift, Henry Fielding, Jane Austen, William Thackeray, Charles Dickens, Anthony Trollope, George Eliot, and Thomas Hardy. We read one novel from each writer.

I was familiar with all of them except for Anthony Trollope. He became my favorite among the novelists. I remember the reason, vividly. Reading Trollope, I entered vicariously into the Victorian household. These people were not different, old-fashioned, or unapproachable to me. They seemed like my next door neighbors. I understood from Trollope that all humans, no matter the age in which they lived, were the same with universal emotions, desires, and motives.

My other salient memory from the class was the final exam, which I aced. This course was one of the few in which I earned an A in college. For the final, Dr. Allen presented nine paragraphs, from nine novels, from the nine different authors, but from books of theirs we had not read. After studying the one paragraph, we were to identify each author and to explain why we came to that conclusion. I loved puzzles and enjoyed the challenge. Also, maybe, I received an A because Anthony Trollope was also Dr. Allen's favorite Victorian author.

In a letter home, dated December 16, 1958, at mid-semester, my first correspondence to my parents after returning to school from Thanksgiving break, I wrote:

As I told you before I returned to school, I didn't know how I was going to live through the next three weeks. I had campus varieties rehearsal every night, 3 exams, and 2 term papers. Well, now, everything is over but 1 term paper. Campus varieties were a big hit and I had a ball doing it. I don't know how I made out on this last round of exams, but I didn't tell you the round before.

In my horrible Philosophy of Religion class I got a B-, in Advertising a B+, and in novel a B. So I'm still hoping that I'll make Dean's List....Guess what? I passed the Civil Service Entrance Exam. Three friends didn't pass. I don't understand how those kids didn't pass. Now I have to fill out about a million forms and return them.

Over Christmas vacation I'm going to write to advertising agencies and airlines to make appointments for interviews...I'm still going out with Connie, and he's gone home already to start work at the post office over Christmas...Oh, I almost forgot. Daddy don't you dare, dare go to Korea or anywhere. I want you to come to my graduation since you missed my high school graduation, and I hope eventually I'll be married in the next 2 or 3 years, and you have to give me away. So, don't you dare go.

By this time, I was dating Connie exclusively. Of all my boyfriends, Connie was a friend before he was a boyfriend. Once, he commandeered two bicycles from somewhere and threw pebbles at the Chi Omega house windows and yelled, "Can Judy come out to play?"

Another time he borrowed a friend's car and kidnapped me. I kept telling him I had to be back to waitress at the house. (We all took turns waitressing at meals.) I didn't want to get in trouble by being late. He brought me back late, but the kids covered for me. Connie and I played bridge and tennis, and went to fraternity parties and dances. We double dated with a QTV friend of his and a Chi Omega sister of mine, a sophomore. I brought him home to meet my parents.

My mother said, "I think you two like each other more than you will admit."

Playing bridge at Chi Omega, me in middle, Sara to my left

Besides dating Connie, I spent a lot of time with the paisans. Before dinner at the house, we gathered in the living room to play bridge.

When we returned to school after Christmas vacation, it was the big push studying for first semester finals. Unlike the other Chi O's, I never "pulled an all-nighter." When I couldn't concentrate any longer, I went to bed, and the kids woke me two hours later. I also pursued job interviews. A letter home:

I have written to 5 advertising agencies, 1 publishing house, 2 television studios, and 2 airlines asking for interviews. I have received 2 replys (sic) from 2 adv. agencies and I have appointments. We're looking around for rides now. We'll probably be able to get one...I'm all excited about working in New York next year.

Finals were over the second week in January. Nancy, Sara, Phyllis, Cleo, and I (the paisans) planned a getaway to New York City over the semester break. All five of us considered this trip the highlight of our college career. We left on Tuesday, January 20, at 3 p.m. for New York City. We had reservations for four nights at the Biltmore Hotel of "Meet me under the clock at the Biltmore" fame. The cost of the room was sixteen dollars a night for two double beds. We smuggled Phyllis in too, who had first gone home to her family's apartment in Yonkers, New York. Split five ways, the cost was less than four dollars a night.

Our goal was to see one Broadway show each night. We did. The most memorable one was Leonard Bernstein's *West Side Story*. We snagged stand-by tickets at the Winter Garden Theatre on Broadway.

Approaching the ticket booth, we asked if there were any tickets available for that evening's performance.

"You girls are in luck. I have five seats in the loge to the right of the stage for five dollars apiece. Do you want them?" he said.

So began a night we never forgot. Sitting in a private box, fifteen feet above the stage, we heard the operatic score for the first time. The songs remain classics today:

"Something's Coming"
"Maria"
"America"
"Somewhere"
"Tonight"

"Jet Song"
"I Feel Pretty"
"A Boy Like That"
"One Hand. One Heart"
"Gee, Officer Krupke"
"Cool"

The next morning our first stop was a record store to buy the album to relive the magic.

Back at school for the last semester of my college career, I changed my future plans and curriculum. I decided I wanted to go to medical school. Ever since I was a young girl, I wanted to be a

My West Side Story original album cover

doctor. My mother discouraged me saying, "You can't be a doctor, and a wife, and a mother too."

I believed her and did not pursue my dream, but this was my last chance. I realized I needed chemistry and physics credits for medical school. Both of those departments would not waive their requirements for their disciplines in the middle of the year. However, the Zoology Department let me enroll in Embryology. It was an eight-hour lab and lecture course. Officially, I continued as an English/ Journalism major and was responsible for writing a thesis.

My courses for second semester:
Embryology
Bible as Literature
Romantic Poetry
Africa, South of the Sahara
Speech and Diction

I chose to write my thesis for my Romantic Poetry class. We studied the three well-known romantic poets: John Keats, Percy Shelley, and Lord Byron. I was never a poetry aficionado. I preferred clear prose with words used in unusual ways to undecipherable poetic stanzas. But since one of America's foremost poets had lived in Amherst, I chose Emily Dickinson for my thesis. The UMass Library and Amherst College's Library offered easily assessable reference material.

Her home was at 280 Main Street, Amherst. It was privately owned and not open to the public until 2003, when Amherst College acquired it and it became a museum. When working on my thesis, I strolled by the property and looked through the black wrought iron fence. In my thesis I attempted to connect Dickinson's prolific output of about 1700 poems to the three romantic poets we were studying.

Emily Dickinson's home, Main Street, Amherst

I was unsuccessful. I earned a C on the paper.

By the end of senior year, Connie and I were unofficially engaged. We each claim the other one proposed. I recall the proposal in this way:

Standing on the edge of the dance floor at a QTV fraternity party, each sipping a drink, Connie said, "Who is going to get up to get the orange juice?"

I didn't understand his question. "What did you say?"

He repeated, "Who is going to get up to get the orange juice?"

The next day, he claimed that he was barraged by my friends congratulating him for being engaged to me. As a gentleman, he didn't deny it.

As explanation for my interpretation of this creative proposal, I reasoned that Connie was pretending we were married and we were lying in bed and he said, "Who is going to get up to get the orange juice?"

That constituted a proposal to me. How simple is that!

Graduation day arrived on June 7, 1959. That summer all the paisans went to New York City to pursue jobs. While we searched for work and an apartment, we lived at Phyllis' family's apartment in Yonkers, New York, as her parents ran a summer camp in the Berkshires. Connie also came to New York City. He accepted a job as a management trainee at a large insurance company. We were on our way to becoming Mr. and Mrs. Cash McCall. We planned an early fall wedding in September 1960. However, soon all our plans changed due to the threat of the draft.

Judith Heaney
UMass, 1959

Conrad Rousseau
UMass, 1959

Me on
Graduation Day,
June 7, 1959.
Yes, my father
was there.
He took the photo.

Photos from the yearbook

Copy of my transcript from UMass

Chapter Twelve

Sex in the City

The summer of 1959 we paisans followed our dreams to New York City. Living rent-free in Phyllis's family's apartment in Yonkers, Westchester County, we searched for our first meaningful jobs. Nancy, Phyllis, and I accepted positions as management trainees at MONY, Mutual of New York Insurance Company, for a salary of $72 a week, plus free lunch. Sara, holder of a science degree, worked as a lab assistant, and Cleo landed a dream job at the J. Walter Thomas Advertising Agency.

Connie secured a trainee appointment at another New York insurance company. Like a true-life Cash McCall, through the largess of his new boss, he acquired a sub-lease on East 67th Street, a posh address on the Upper East Side between Park and Lexington Avenues, but only for three months. Before the summer of 1959 ended, all our addresses would change.

Initially, Connie and I planned to marry in September 1960, return to New York City, and rent an apartment. However, compulsory military service interfered. The local draft board in Connie's hometown of Amesbury, Massachusetts listed him 1-A, which meant he was available for unrestricted military service—conscripted initially as a private—whenever needed. We could still get married but our income and living arrangements would be marginal. Since I had been an "army brat," I knew about the sub-standard housing accommodations allotted to the enlisted personnel. I refused to live as a private's wife. I promised Connie that I would wait for him during his three, long years of military duty. During that time, I planned to attend Hunter College in Manhattan, a part of City University of New York, to earn the chemistry and physics credits I needed in order to apply to a medical school.

Then, my father suggested an alternative path for Connie in order to fulfill his military obligation: apply to Officer's Candidate School and become a commissioned officer. The idea appealed to both of us, so Connie submitted an application. After taking physical, academic, and psychological exams, he was accepted into the November 1959 class at Naval Officer's Candidate School in Newport, Rhode Island. At the end of the four-month course, he would be commissioned as an Ensign in March 1960. We changed our prospective wedding date to June 1960, instead of September 1960.

Soon the summer would end. We paisans faced the challenge of finding an affordable apartment before Phyllis's mom and dad returned from their summer camp enterprise. Originally, we hoped to find a place in the Village, but that proved too expensive. On August 22, 1959, I wrote home:

> *We have located 2 apartments which we can have in Jackson Heights, which is in the Queens about a 15 minute subway ride to downtown Manhattern (sic). (I thing in this case my spelling is a result of my Boston accent.) One is $180.00 a month, very modern furniture, 2 bedrooms with twin beds in each, living room, and modern kitchen— gas and light included—an 8 month lease which is what we wanted— a modern brick duplex house with private homes all around. The other is about a 2 minute walk from the first—$150.00 a month but with one bedroom with 3 beds in it and a daybed in the living room, a 21 inch television, beautiful modern furniture but a 2 plate hot-plate and a rotisserie broiler instead of a stove.*

We sensibly chose the $180 accommodations that would cost each of us $45 a month. Phyllis would remain living at home with her parents in Yonkers. The eight-month lease would bring us to May and near to my wedding date.

Another major change occurred. I was offered a position to work at the Payment Center of the Social Security Office in New York City. In the August 22nd letter, I also wrote:

I have a new job-Civil Service- starting as a GS-7 or $4,980 a year, which is $95.77 a week. Isn't that the greatest thing that ever happened? I start Sept. 14, 1959. There is a 3 month classroom training period. The job is a claims examiner, no problem of mobility. The job is at 250 Hudson St., which is lower NY, but about a minute walk from the subway... There is no contact with people, but at least I know I won't be sent somewhere else. The hours aren't as good, of course, but not too bad: 8:15 to 4:45. Also, in a year, you are promoted to a GS-9 at $6,000 a year. Pretty good deal, huh? I'm going to give my resignation on Monday. I'm so excited.

Then, under the heading—The Real Corporate World—all my enthusiasm vanished as I faced a fiscal crisis. I thought I acted responsibility by giving a two-week notice, but the department boss terminated me, on the spot, saying I had not been employed long enough to train anyone, so I was dispensable. He blithely told me to apply for unemployment insurance. I was devastated. I had two weeks before I began my new job and the government withheld the first two weeks' pay, so it would be a month before another pay check. I needed money for my share of food and rent at our apartment. What could an enterprising woman do?

First, I called the Social Security Office and they agreed to let me start one week early. Next, I applied at a Temp Office and secured a job for the coming week. I did not apply for unemployment benefits. At the time I did not know the employer paid for the benefits with an unemployment tax. I thought it unethical to take money from the government for doing nothing. Then, I wrote home and borrowed money from my parents. Crisis averted.

Being single and twenty-one in New York City met all our expectations. One Saturday we spent all day and all night in the Village, went to 6:00 a.m. Mass, and slept all day on Sunday. We saw every Broadway play and musical. We shopped every Thursday night at Bonwit Teller and Saks on Fifth Avenue to the point we became bored with the stagnant merchandise. Every Friday on payday we dined on meatless meals, either at a Chinese restaurant (shrimp and fried rice) or an Italian restaurant (cheese manicotti). On New Year's Eve we joined the throng in Times Square. On Easter we attended Mass at St. Patrick's Cathedral and joined in the Easter parade strutting down the middle of Fifth Avenue.

After Connie went to OCS in November, on free weekends he hitchhiked back to New York City. Sara's boyfriend, Bill, preparing to enter Naval Flight School, also joined us. At that time, their wedding date was not finalized.

Since the five of us were virgins, we discussed the unknown details of sex, not covered in our college Marriage and Family Course—it was our version of *Sex in the City*. After the honeymoon, the first of us to marry promised to answer three questions with a "Yes" or "No" response. The three sexual mysteries were:

Question #1 Does it hurt?
Question #2 Does it bleed?
Question #3 Is it worth it?

In that hectic first year after college graduation, my plans changed again. I dropped my chemistry class at Hunter College because studying in the apartment with three roommates was impossible, and my eventual goal to attend medical school was unrealistic. In February, Bill completed his flight program and was ordered to Guam immediately. Sara and he

My engagement picture, spring 1960

planned a March wedding so she would be able to join him. She had a simple ceremony with her sister as maid of honor in her hometown of Pittsfield, Massachusetts. All the paisans attended. After a brief skiing honeymoon, Bill left for his assignment and Sara prepared to follow in a few weeks. We forgave her for not answering the "sex quiz."

However, now we had to split the rent three ways, instead of four. Plus, Cleo hoped to return home before the lease was up to pursue a Master's Degree in Education. (She eventually earned a PhD in psychology and became a school counselor.) Connie was commissioned in March on schedule, but was assigned additional study at Naval Justice School in Newport for two months. Then he would be assigned to a navy base or a ship. We prayed that I would be able to go with him. The timetable fit our plans for a June wedding. We became officially engaged in February and set the date for June 11, 1960. Nancy would be my one attendant as maid of honor.

Now Phyllis and Nancy needed to formulate a plan for the next year. Two Chi Omega sisters from the class of 1960 decided to join them in New York City. The four women rented an apartment in Manhattan. Thus, our first year of adult life ended successfully for all the paisans.

Connie graduated from Justice School and was assigned to the *USS Antietam*, an aircraft carrier stationed in Pensacola, Florida. We were married on June 11, 1960, and drove to the Pensacola Navy Base on our honeymoon. We spent the first three days at the Coonamessett Inn at Falmouth on Cape Cod. I honored our agreement and sent a postcard to my awaiting sisters with one brief sentence: "Yes, to all three questions."

My mom, Connie's mom, Connie, me, and Nancy in the receiving line

As a young married Catholic, I was cognizant of the Church's doctrines concerning the controversial subject of birth control. I knew its mandate was inviolable, as did my mother, a paragon for attacking burgeoning problems in their infancy.

A month before my wedding date, Mom handed me a calendar /chart with instructions on how to use the rhythm method to avoid pregnancy or increase the likelihood of pregnancy. By accurately recording your menstrual cycle, the system predicted your days of ovulation when you were most likely to become pregnant. To avoid pregnancy, abstain from relations during that time period, or conversely, engage in sex to enhance the possibility of conception. The method was most effective with a regular menstrual cycle. This was the only birth control behavior approved by the Catholic Church, as it was in reality a form of abstinence. Connie and I planned on using the rhythm method to avoid pregnancy for a few years, because we hoped to tour Europe after Connie's service commitment

Unaware of the prejudice against Catholics in the sixties in the South, I looked for a job when we reached Pensacola. One option was to teach elementary school. After reviewing my college transcript, the principal asked, "What is your religion?"

"I'm Catholic."

"Sorry, but we can't consider you for employment. We find young married Catholic girls become pregnant in their first year of marriage and don't finish the school year."

Catholics were not unique in their stance against contraceptives. Before 1930, all Protestant denominations banned the use of birth control in their religious teachings. That year, 1930, at the Lambeth conference, a decennial gathering of Anglican churchmen, begun in 1887 by the Archbishop of Canterbury, voted (193 for to 67 against) to allow contraception in some circumstances. Soon the Anglican Church approved all methods of contraception and the other Protestant churches followed its lead.

The Catholic Church continued to forbid artificial birth control. Almost forty years later, in 1968, Pope Paul VI issued his landmark encyclical letter, *Humanae Vitae* (Human Life), in which he reemphasized the Church's teachings that the use of contraception to prevent pregnancy was wrong and against God's design of "natural law."

Marriage is one of the seven sacraments of the Catholic Church. During a life span most practicing Catholics receive at least six of the seven sacraments: Baptism, Reconciliation (Penance), Eucharist (Holy

Communion), Confirmation, Marriage, or in its place Holy Orders (Ordination to Priesthood), and Anointing of the Sick (Last Rites of Extreme Unction).

The inclusion of marriage as a holy sacrament illustrates the divine importance God bestowed on the sanctity of marriage. The conjugal act is for the purpose of procreation. God's additional blessing of pleasure from sexual intercourse strengthens the bond of intimacy, respect, and love between husband and wife while it encourages the nurturing of children. In his 1968 pronouncement, Pope John IV extolled God's gift of the sex act, along with its accompanying pleasure and intimacy, but emphasized it must not be abused by deliberately frustrating its natural end—procreation.

Chapter Thirteen

Young Navy Bride

Futile job searches and loneliness plagued the summer of 1960. After arriving at Pensacola Naval Air Station in June, we rented a furnished apartment in town. No quarters were available on base. By the end of September, I still had not found employment. I knew no one and Connie was away overnight, or for days or weeks on the ship.

On September 29, 1960, in a letter to my parents, I bemoaned my situation:

> *Only 2 more nights and one more day and Connie will be home again. This has been a long, lonely week what with no job or anything. I still don't have a job. The Chemstrand Plant didn't have anything and the Fiesta people don't know yet. Honestly, this is the worst town in the world to find a job.*

Remember, I first applied for a teaching post, but that idea did not work out due to my religion. Finally, I landed a job as a caseworker for the Florida Welfare Office. Then, my efforts to transfer my credentials to the Pensacola District Social Security Office were successful. The branch director called and offered me a position as claims interviewer at the GS-7 level. The pay was twice Connie's salary. I rode the bus to work and Connie commuted to the base with our car. My government job was very lucrative because we often worked overtime at time and a half. I saved most of my wages for our future travel plans and down payment on a house.

In a letter home I raved about our dreams for the next three years:

Connie and I love New York and I don't think we would be happy anywhere else. Latest great plans...the Caribean (sic) this summer, Mexico next summer or fall, and Europe in the spring of 1963 when Connie gets out of the Navy. We will have the Navy fly us to Europe for free. They will send us anywhere we want to go when we get out. Of course, we'll have to pay our way back but we still save. Great idea, eh what? <u>We really are doing these things!</u>

And at that time, we believed we would do those things. We did none of them. While at Pensacola, we only took short vacation trips. We went to New Orleans where we joined Nancy and Phyllis for three days. Once Nancy visited us at Pensacola and twice my mother visited— one trip for the birth of our first child.

I remember three unpleasant facts of Florida life. First, the weather. During the winter months, in the mornings I donned wool outfits, suitable for the temperature, but at lunchtime when I stepped outside from the air-conditioning, I roasted.

Second: the cockroaches. I complained about them in a letter to my parents:

There are cockroaches here, but they only come out at night. If the lights are out in the kitchen and bathroom and we are in the living room when we go into the 2 mentioned rooms we usually find one. None have been in the drawers etc. yet. Our landlady insists on calling them water bugs. I guess she can't bear to think there are cockroaches in her house. Some of them are pretty big guys. If the situation doesn't get any worse, it is OK.

Third: the lonely life of a navy wife. Even though we were lucky that Connie wasn't assigned to a fleet at sea, he had the duty every third night and slept on the ship. We wives were ferried out for dinner and the ubiquitous movies, bridge, or acey ducey games afterwards, but then we drove home to empty beds. And often the ship was sent on maneuvers for one or two weeks at a stretch.

After I met other navy brides, we kept ourselves busy with bridge games, sewing get-togethers, or nights out at the movies. And every third night, when our husbands were on duty, we enjoyed dining on a four-course dinner on the ship, elegantly prepared and served by uniformed waiters.

During our second year in Pensacola, a one bedroom apartment became available on the base. We moved in and I was allowed to choose furniture from a huge warehouse and have the upholstered furniture recovered in the fabric and shade of my choice. I selected white. My father wrote, "What an inappropriate color for masking sticky little fingerprints covered with jam." He hoped for a grandbaby, sooner than later.

Since we now lived on the base, the commuting situation reversed—Connie walked to work and I drove our new acquisition, a green Volkswagen Beetle (christened Valerie), to work in Pensacola. We paid two thousand dollars on time for our new car.

One day Connie brought home a set of Patty Berg and Sam Snead golf clubs he had purchased for fifty dollars each on the ship. We began to play regularly.

Me, dressed for church, and Valerie Volkswagon in front of our quarters on base

We made many friends who remain friends today.

Friends with Connie and me at Officers' Club party

I remember two cooking incidents: one a disaster, one an impressive feast. Our first Christmas, the two of us celebrated the day together. I decided to begin the holiday fare with shrimp cocktail. I had never fixed shrimp before and I had never seen my mother prepare shrimp. I purchased a bag of frozen shrimp at the store. I defrosted them, arranged them atop crushed ice in stemmed glasses, and doused them in cocktail sauce. I thought it strange the shrimp were grey as I believed they were usually pink, but I didn't dwell on the color. Later I learned they needed to be cooked to turn pink. We suffered no known ill effects from my Christmas Day culinary calamity.

The other epicurean adventure occurred when I was seven months pregnant. Discovering the recital of this repast in one of my letters home, I was amazed at my chutzpah. I wouldn't attempt this menu today after fifty years of cooking.

I had Louise and her husband and this other couple to dinner last Thursday. We had cocktails and our'd'heures (sic) to begin. Then roast leg of lamb with spiced peaches, browned potatoes, stuffed mushrooms, peas and onions, celery and olives, hot French bread, and ambrosia for desert. (sic) It was yummy!

On July 19, 1962, I delivered our son at the Pensacola Naval Hospital. We only paid for his food, a cost of ten dollars. The navy's medical plan covered all other expenses. I felt this was a strange regulation. Since the navy obstetrician discouraged breast feeding, why wouldn't the government pay for the child's formula?

At the Navy Chapel we christened him, Conrad Ernest Rousseau, III with my mother and us in attendance. Absent were his godparents: Connie's brother Bobby and my friend Nancy.

At the beginning of my marriage I was a practicing Catholic and believed in God. Within three years, a traumatic incident left me questioning the existence of God

Christening of
Conrad Ernest Rousseau III,
July 1962

and his omnipotence. The birth of our first child, due to the unreliability of the rhythm method of birth control, and the resulting cancellation of our travel itinerary, did not weaken my faith. Yes, we gave up our idea of a grand European tour, but we formulated new plans and loved our little Terry (the name we chose to call him, derived from the Latin word *tertious* that means the third), with the fervent zeal of all new moms and dads.

I didn't always recall attending Mass at my various childhood locations. However, I believe because church attendance was routine, I didn't consciously remember every church or chapel in my history. I have enough memories to assure myself that I did attend church every Sunday and Holy Day of Obligation, and that I always followed the dicta of no meat on Fridays and no use of mechanical birth control. I admit I did not confess my sins and receive Holy Communion on a regular basis. I don't think Connie ever went to confession or communion.

Nevertheless I was steadfast in my belief in God and the teachings of the Catholic Church. I intended to raise our children Catholic. Connie did not question my decision in this matter, although in hindsight at this writing, I think he questioned the truth of the Church, but kept quiet about it. So, to this point in my life, nothing caused me to doubt the existence of God. I did doubt the power of prayer to bring about miraculous cures or grant wishes. As a young Catholic child, I studied the Catechism, not the Bible, so I gave little credence or thought to all the miracles claimed in the Bible. As an adult, due to biological facts, I dismissed the story of the Virgin Mary as a myth.

I based denial of miracles on personal empirical evidence. Two long-sought and fervent prayers went unanswered. In the fifth grade I discovered I could not read the blackboard from my seat. I hated the thought of wearing glasses. Every night and also during the day at school, I prayed to God to let me see the blackboard. No miracle occurred. I required glasses which gradually became thicker and uglier. Through the miracle of contact lenses I discarded my coke-bottle lens, and now through the miracle of medical science and cataract surgery, I see 20/20 ... with not one transcendental miracle involved.

My other unheeded prayer occurred during my freshmen year at college. I plotted my activities freshmen year in hopes of being elected to the Sophomore Honor Society, the Scrolls. I prayed every night for God to grant this one wish. I failed, and God failed me. Due to a misunderstanding, my dorm's housemother blackballed me. God ignored my request, even though I met all the qualifications for the honor.

In fairness, I remember one answered prayer. At age nine, I lost a sterling silver charm bracelet on the playground. While searching through the weeds, I prayed for God's help. I found it and attributed my success to God. Did God help me find the bracelet? What do you think?

Connie's three years of active duty ended in April 1963. We thought we would be in Pensacola until that date. Nothing is permanent or definite in the navy. The *USS Antietam* was ordered to the Philadelphia Naval Base for decommissioning in January. Connie went with the ship and I flew home with Terry to stay with my parents until Connie was discharged in April. Most weekends Connie drove to my parents' home in Marblehead, Massachusetts to be with us.

Again, I was a navy widow. My father reveled in his role of granddaddy. If I believed in God, I would thank Him for those months that He allotted to my father with his first grandson, as it was the only one he lived to cradle. This was my father's first look at Terry, because he did not visit with my mother at his birth. My father was an early riser, as was Terry. I savored many mornings of extra sleep as my father carried Terry on his shoulders through the house and around the yard while pointing out and naming every object in sight. The two of them were best buddies. But when Connie arrived for the weekend, my father disappeared from sight in order to let Connie engage with Terry.

Connie and me in front of my parent's house January 1963
Off to church

Connie was discharged from the navy in April 1963 with the rank of Lieutenant Junior Grade. He remained in the Navy Reserves. This commitment meant two weeks of active duty each year, but also meant credits towards retirement pay.

Our plans for the future included a job search and law school for Connie. Our nest egg from our savings account allowed us to buy a house. In the sixties, a 20 percent down payment was mandatory. Marblehead proved too expensive. We purchased a five-room ranch house in the rural suburb of Topsfield, Massachusetts in June 1963, for $15,500.

My father and Terry in the yard
Terry walked at seven months.

Chapter Fourteen

To Believe or Not To Believe?

Our small five-room house boarded the road connecting the town of Topsfield, Massachusetts to the town of Ipswich, Massachusetts. Deciduous trees surrounded the one-acre lot on the sides and in the back. Few neighbors. No sidewalks. No stores within walking distance. The rural setting was quite different from the established towns of Swampscott and Marblehead where I grew up.

A young couple, Maureen and Dick, with three young children ages newborn to three years old, lived on the lot next to us. We became instant friends and remain friends today. Our children played together almost every day.

Besides being stay-at-home moms, Maureen and I both played golf. That year, a new nine-hole golf course, New Meadows, opened in Topsfield, only five minutes away. We joined its Ladies League with the appropriate name, "Over Pars,"

Our first house in Topsfield, Massachusetts, Valerie in the driveway

where we golfed once a week, on Wednesday mornings. Dick, a dentist with Wednesdays off, babysat for Maureen while my mother drove the sixteen miles from Marblehead to babysit for me.

Connie worked in Boston at Hartford Life Insurance Company. As we only had the one car, Valerie, he drove to the subway station in Revere on Monday through Thursday for his commute to Boston. On Friday, with Terry strapped in his car seat, I drove him to the subway train and picked him up in the evening, in order to have the car for shopping and errands.

That summer we spent weekends at nearby Crane's Beach, famous for its dunes and white sand. Terry celebrated his first birthday with a few of the neighborhood children and his cousins. We attended church at St. Rose of Lima Parrish Church in Topsfield. The idyllic country life ended on November 22, 1963—the day of President John F. Kennedy's assassination.

Typically, I didn't listen to the radio or television during the day. Maureen rushed over to tell me the news. Connie called from work. Most stores and businesses closed for the weekend.

Besides the national tragedy that occurred that fateful November weekend, I experienced a wrenching personal tragedy, which changed my life forever and pulled me in two metaphysical directions.

On Sunday, November 24, my brother, a civil engineer, arrived at Boston's Logan Airport after working in New Guinea on a government assignment with NOAA, the National Oceanic and Atmospheric Administration. My parents met him at the airport. Connie, Terry, and I planned to drive to Marblehead later in the afternoon.

On that late autumnal morning, strings of diaphanous clouds trailed across the heavens. A distant sun attempted to warm the hardening earth. My sixteen-month old son, Terry, and I twirled and jumped in the fallen leaves. Inside, Connie read the newspaper. Through the half-opened kitchen window I heard the telephone ring. I thought it must be my mother calling to say they were back from the airport and to come after lunch and Terry's nap. I was unequivocally wrong.

As Connie ran out of the house towards me, I recognized a primal, universal look of fear etched on his face. No Messianic angels, seraphim, or cherubs appeared. Only the atavistic, biological, hormonal gene that foreshadowed danger flooded adrenalin through my veins and deep into my stomach. Connie grabbed me and enclosed me in his arms.

"Judy, sweetheart, that was Mr. Bevins on the phone."

Mr. Bevins was my mother's next door neighbor. My anxiety heightened. I wondered why he would be calling us on a Sunday morning.

Connie struggled to say, "Your father had a heart attack."

"He's OK, right?" I demanded.

"No, he died," Connie whispered to me through his tears. "It happened instantaneously."

"No. No. No! My father can't be dead. He would have let me know somehow. He would have communicated with me. I know he would have. I didn't *feel* anything. He can't be dead. He can't be dead..." I repeated over and over.

In my grief, I toppled to the ground. Thinking it was a new game, Terry jumped on me. I held him tight and sobbed.

After my father died, the legacy of his sudden, unexpected death lingered in my heart, mind, and soul. I could not shake the pain of not being immediately aware of his death. God had failed me. This realization produced the first chink in my faith in God. I was pulled in two polemic directions: *God exists; God does not exist.* If there were a God, He would have let me know that my father was in heaven with Him. There was no subliminal sign, no spiritual message, no transcendental vision, not even an intuitive feeling. Why were we expected to believe in an afterlife if there were no proof? I needed some metaphysical sign to supplement my faith. If my father were in heaven, his soul would have communicated with me.

Since I didn't sense anything, I began to question myself: Is there a God, or heaven, or any abstract dimension in our cosmos?

I flashbacked to a night when, at age eight, I saw a quintessential fairy queen, dressed in blue gauze, wearing a gold crown and waving a gold wand at the foot of my bed. I remembered to pinch myself, as directed by old wives' tales, to assure myself that I was not sleeping. The nip of the physical twinge startled me awake. The vision vanished. Nevertheless, I knew with the certainty of childhood innocence that things you see were real. The royal specter was real. In the morning, I shared the mystifying experience with my father.

He said, "If fairies inhabit this world with us, you, Judith, would be the first little girl they would visit." He didn't dismiss my genuine belief in the nighttime apparition "as just a dream." He validated my fantasy without violating the truth. I never forgot his genuine respect for me and my mystic visitor. My father had a soul. He was my Atticus Finch.

After that tangible and theological life-altering event of my father's death, I hoped to become pregnant again. I did. On October 24, 1964, our second child and second son was born, one day before what would have been my father's sixty-second birthday. We named him Donald Heaney Rousseau after his grandfather. Despite my wavering faith, we baptized him at St. Rose of Lima Catholic Church in Topsfied. Connie's brother's wife, Frankie, became Donnie's godmother and my brother, Don, became his godfather in absentia.

In 1965, we grappled with many decisions. Connie decided to matriculate at Suffolk Law School in its night sessions. Then, Hartford Life Insurance Company made plans to move its main office from Boston to Hartford, Connecticut. They offered Connie a tempting promotion to move with them. My mother joined in the discussion. Since she was a widow, she opted to sell her house and move with us.

Donnie's baptism with aunt Frankie and cousins, Jennifer, Suzanne, Robby, and brother Terry

In the planning stages, Connie and I made several house-scouting expeditions to Hartford suburbs. Soon, we put our house on the market, and my mother listed hers too. We expected her house in Marblehead to sell first. Instead, our house sold within a month for a thousand dollar profit. We moved in with my mother until our relocation to Hartford.

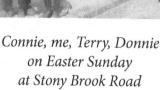

Connie, me, Terry, Donnie on Easter Sunday at Stony Brook Road

Then, plans changed again. Connie did not want to forgo law school. He declined Hartford's offer and took a job as an insurance claims adjuster until he finished law school. We lived with my mother for about a year and a half in Marblehead. In the spring of 1967, we bought a five-room, cape-style house at 10 Stony Brook Road, Marblehead for $22,500.

Three major events occurred in my life at Stony Brook Road, Marblehead. Two were secular and one spiritual.

One, Connie graduated from Suffolk Law School in May 1968. In June, he joined New England Life in Boston as an attorney.

Two, we welcomed our third child, third son, on December 13, 1969. I had hoped for a daughter, but Terry and Donnie were thrilled with their little brother. They jockeyed to be his favorite big brother. We named him Bryant, my mother's maiden name, William, after his paternal grandmother's father, Rousseau. Soon, nicknamed Bry, our determined, stubborn little imp charmed us all. We named him, but we did not baptize him, due to the third event, my religious apostasy.

Connie graduates from Suffolk Law School, May 1968

After we moved to Marblehead from Topsfield, our church attendance dwindled. My mother never went to church as she thought of God as Mother Nature. My father, who might have accompanied me, was dead. Connie spent Sunday mornings studying his law books. I hesitated to go to Mass by myself, or with two small children.

However, in the fall of 1969, a religious obligation confronted me. Terry was seven and entering second grade, the year for receiving the sacrament of First Holy Communion. My Catholic conscience and my father's memory compelled me to act. I realized I needed to take him to church and enroll him in Sunday school for First Holy Communion instruction. I called Our Lady Star of the Sea Church in Marblehead about Sunday school registration. I learned Sunday school was now

Bryant William Rousseau, age five months

Monday school and taught in the homes of lay teachers, usually the mothers of one of the children in the class.

Then, my informant asked, "Mrs. Rousseau, would you be willing to teach the catechism to the children in your son's class from the Gerry School? We can't find a volunteer in that area of Marblehead. Our records indicate there are three boys and three girls in that class who are Catholic and need instruction. To date, we don't have a volunteer."

Completely surprised, I stammered, "What qualifications do I need?"

"Just to be a Catholic in good standing and a willingness to teach the children. We give you a three-hour training session. Once a month we have a brief meeting with all the teachers to offer suggestions and answer questions. Of course, the second grade is one of the most important grades because of the preparation for communion," she answered.

I was five-months pregnant with a baby due in December. Did I have the energy, time, and personal commitment to undertake this task? I liked interacting with children and I wanted Terry to make his First Communion on time. I owed it to the memory of my father. He would have wanted and expected me to raise Terry as a Catholic.

After all these thoughts filtered through my mind, I said, "Yes, I'll do it."

So began a volunteer job that altered my theological position about God and the cosmos and compelled me, many years later, in my seventies, to write this book and share my internal conflict with family and others. Up to this point, my apostasy had been slowly evolving.

In one Monday school class, near to Christmas, Terry with an astute and relevant observation grasped the incredulity of religious belief with starling, innocent insight. Its clear truth converted me from a wavering Roman Catholic to a wavering, yet reluctant atheist.

Terry tended to simple and obvious deductions. At age two, he coined a word that linguistically, in my estimation, should be the proper adaptation. From the grammatical structure of *today* and *tonight,* he invented the word *tomorning.* For several months, he used the word in his speech: "*Tomorning,* Boy, play with blocks." Calling himself "Boy" was another one of his original speech patterns. I imagine the reason being since we always called him "a good boy," he thought his name was "Boy." Eventually, he unconsciously corrected "his mistakes" after hearing the constant repetition of adults saying "this morning" and "Terry."

In teaching the First Communion lessons from the catechism, I struggled to explain the concept of God's powers. The children were sitting in a circle on the floor of my living room. I was sitting in a comfortable chair due to my "baby bump." Each child read one answer in turn from the question that I asked from the lesson, entitled "God is Great." The question was "Does God know all things?" The answers listed in the text:

Yes, God knows all things.
God knows all things on earth.
God knows all things in heaven.
God knows what happened long ago.
God knows what we are doing now.
God knows what is going to happen.
God knows when we are good.
God knows when we are bad.
God knows all the things we do.
God knows even what we are thinking.
God watches us because he loves us.[1]

In an attempt to give meaning to the rote answers and God's unquestioned power, I intended to use the material in the teacher's guide. In the manual, even to adults, God's existence was called a mystery. Section I entitled, "Mystery of God" stated:

God is a mystery to people because God can never be totally known by people. We can only know God insofar as God reveals Himself to us. That is why we say that the mystery is at the center of Christian faith: the mystery of God the Father who continues to reveal Himself to people; the mystery of Jesus, risen, who shares his life with people in and through the church; the mystery of the Holy Spirit alive and active among us.[2]

My intent was to call God a mystery to adults as well as to children, and by our faith we knew of God's existence and of His powers. I planned to explain faith as unquestioning belief and trust in God. First, however, I wanted to hear the children's ideas before I presented the Church's view on the subject.

To begin, I asked the class, "Why does God know all things?"

Quizzical faces stared at me. Then, Terry waved his arm in the air and answered, "I know why! I know why! God is like Santa Claus. God's magic!"

I was stunned. It was near to Christmas, but I had not thought of this fairly obvious connection in the eyes of children. The class seemed to accept and understand this answer. Magic did not need any more explanation. Magic explained magic. The children knew the meaning of the word magic without further interpretation. The *Webster Unabridged Dictionary* defined the word as any mysteriously, seemingly inexplicable or extraordinary power. Originally from the Greek word *magiké* that in turn is from the Persian word *magūs* that means a priest skilled in sorcery.

What could I do now? How could I dispel Terry's proposal of magic as an explanation for the mystery of God without tarnishing the myth of Santa Claus? I acknowledged that Santa Claus was indeed magic, but God's power was not based on magic, but on faith. Faith was belief and trust in God without visible proof. A mystery even in the eyes of adults, but believed because of the Holy Spirit that God put in our souls and because of the teachings of Jesus Christ.

I knew this was a difficult concept for children to understand as they believed in what they saw. At this age, it was easy to believe in Santa Claus because they saw actual presents under the tree on Christmas morning. No one can witness faith. It is an abstraction, not easily explained by a theologian and certainly not explained by me, a lay person.

After the children went home, I thought about Terry's answer. He was right in the same way the little boy in Hans Christian Andersen's tale of "The Emperor's New Clothes," was right. Most of us are familiar with the story of the vain emperor who was swindled by weavers who claimed they spun the most marvelous cloth that possessed the quality of being invisible to anyone who was unfit for office, or stupid. Naturally, no one would admit they could not see the cloth. When the emperor marched in the grand procession wearing the new suit woven from the magical silk, all his subjects exclaimed, "What a magnificent new outfit," until a young lad said, "But he has nothing on at all." The fable ended with the father of the child saying, "Good Heavens! Listen to the voice of an innocent child." And one whispered to the other what the child had said, "But he has nothing on at all," until the whole crowd cried the refrain.

The young lad was right, as Terry was right. God is magic or a delusion. To date, the only way to "prove" the existence of God is by circular reasoning or by infinite regression that means the answer to a question raises another question. Simply stated, if God is all powerful and made everything, who made God? That would imply something more powerful than God and that would be a contradiction of terms. Someone or something more powerful than God cannot be. And round and round.

On that winter Monday afternoon in 1969, my questioning of religion and God's existence began again. I was evolving from a fledgling skeptic to a burgeoning agnostic. As Richard Dawkins elegantly said in his 2006 international best seller *The God Delusion,* "We are all atheists about most of the gods that humanity has ever believed in. Some of us just go one god further." I recommend this book to anyone who is serious about studying religion and its origins.

I completed my assignment as Monday school teacher for the class from Gerry School. In May 1970 all my pupils received their First Holy Communion, even Terry. In December, we did not baptize our third son, Bryant, born that December 1969. Donnie did not receive his First Communion. We did not attend church again, except maybe on an occasional Easter or Christmas. I really don't remember. I did not proclaim myself an atheist at the time, but I began to search for the truth. If, as I believed, God did not create us, then who or what created us? This was the beginning of many years of research to learn about the evolution of life on earth and whether science or religion was the answer.

1. *The New Saint Joseph First Communion Catechism* (New York; Catholic Book Publishing Co.,1963),12-13.
2. *Children's Catholic Catechism* (Dubuque, Iowa; BROWN-ROA,1989), 1.

Chapter Fifteen

My Life's Dash from 1969-2007

God ceased to exist for me at age thirty-two.

***

Even after this religious conversion, for almost forty years from age thirty-two to age seventy, with no apparent or outward signs of inner conflict or anguish and to borrow a phrase from Darwin's famous quote expressed at the end of his *On the Origin of Species*, I had gone cycling on through life according to the fixed law of expectancy for middle-class American women of the Silent Generation, those citizens born between 1925 and 1945. The pattern of my life unfolded to include all the promised expectations: a stable, loving marriage; the joy, work, and pride of motherhood; family and romantic vacations; rewarding part-time employment as substitute teacher in the public school system, associate English professor at a local community college, and English as a Second Language instructor for adult immigrants; numerous volunteer positions in the Parent Teacher Association, League of Women Voters, Marblehead Art Festival, local library, and as Cub Scout den mother for all three sons; personal endeavors such as, golf, skiing, tennis, jogging, sewing, knitting, needlepoint, bridge games, book clubs, studying Spanish, and writing—always attempting to pen the great American novel. Along with these tangible activities, I experienced most of the emotions allotted to *Homo sapiens*, such as happiness, sadness, shame, pride, doubt, anger, gratitude, boredom, confidence, stress, regret, grief, frustration, jealousy, surprise, and most of all the love of my husband, sons, daughters-in-laws, grandchildren, other family members, and friends.

I could have continued writing the details of my life in chronological order, chapter by chapter, from age thirty-two to seventy. But that is not the story I want to tell. I am reminded of the recent best-selling novel, *What Alice Forgot,* by Liane Moriarty, an Australian writer. The heroine hits her head, suffers amnesia, and forgets ten years of her life from age twenty-nine to age thirty-nine; the very formative and defining years of Alice's life.

My formative years were the first thirty-two years of my life. I think I could hit my head, forget my life from age thirty-two to seventy, and then read the biography of any American wife/mother to fill in the blanks of my lost years. Not that I would want to forget those years, but they are not the focus of this book.

When Connie and I retired to Florida in the early 1990s, we were in our late fifties. We built our house in a golf and tennis community on the West Coast of Florida. During the first twelve years, we played golf, tennis, bridge, made new friends, attended and hosted many parties and functions, and entertained friends and family from up North.

In due time, the universal claims of the recently retired afflicted us. Too busy. Not enough time. If the newspaper is thick, it must be Sunday. A retired husband is a wife's full-time job. Life is a game, but golf is serious. How did we ever have time to work in our earlier years?

At this point in my retirement, two unfulfilled dreams nagged at me. I had not written the great American novel, and I had not solved the mystery of how life began. Could I possibly combine the two? How many years did I have left? Although my mother lived to age ninety-six, she suffered from some form of dementia beginning in her late eighties. Would I fall subject to the same condition at the same age? How many years would it take to research and write a book about evolution and the origins of religion? I was neither a scientist nor a theologian. I needed to do a ton of research. I did not have a lot of time left. I knew I had to begin.

So, at age seventy, in 2007, I began by reading books on evolution. That was easy and fun. I loved to read. I fell in love with Charles Darwin, and his Victorian writing-style. I read his three major works in their entirety: *The Voyage of the Beagle, On the Origin of the Species,* and *The Descent of Man.* I read books by current authors and scientists who agreed with Darwin and offered additional proof to bolster his theory. I read books that argued against his theory. I admit I did not understand all the scientific terminology, but I understood enough to realize that his theory was considered a scientific reality or fact by almost all of the scientific community.

I studied books on religion. I attended religious services with friends, or by myself, in my hometown of Venice, Florida. I organized and saved reams of clippings and notes in manila folders on my desk. For three years I did not write one word. I only did research. I think, that is, I know, I was afraid to actually begin writing.

Then, in June 2010, we planned to celebrate our fiftieth wedding anniversary on an Avalon Waterways river cruise on the Rhône River from Nice to Paris, France. The riverboat scheduled stops at small French towns for daily tours. We walked through Arles, Avignon, Viviers, Tournon, Vienne, Lyon, Mâcon, Tournus, Châlon -sur- Saône, and Beaune with a group and guide, or on our own. We had planned our itinerary to leave and return from Boston, so we could also celebrate the occasion with our sons and family living in the Boston area.

While on the cruise we met and chatted with other passengers. Several times at dinner we joined a family of five, a matriarch with her two daughters and sons-in-law. She was a college professor and author.

Connie and me on our trip to France

I opened up to her and mentioned the book project I was contemplating. She asked, "How much have you written?'
"Nothing yet," I confessed. "I have been doing research."

"My dear," she said. "You are not a writer until you write. You must begin writing, even though you are still investigating your subjects. Put it down on paper. You can always rewrite, especially with the ease of computer technology these days. I am quite impressed with your topic and hope to read your book someday."

Buoyed by her encouragement and advice, I was ready to write on my return to Florida.

Over the July Fourth holiday, after our return from France to Boston and Marblehead, we hosted a family dinner in the Oak Room at the Copley Plaza in Boston with our three sons, daughter-in-law, and two older grandchildren.

Our family arriving at the Copley Plaza, Boston, via limo

That July 2010, on my return to my desk in Venice, Florida, I put pen to paper or actually fingers to keyboard and began to write. I joined a writers' group at the local library. With much apprehension, after two or three weeks observing the routine, I submitted a chapter to be critiqued at the meeting. As I left home for the library that evening, my concerned husband wished me luck. My fear was unfounded. Not that I was declared a wonderful writer, but the feedback was wonderful. Thoughtful readers read my material and praised it where warranted, and offered helpful corrections and suggestions where needed. Cliché or not: I was on my way.

Chapter Sixteen

Unexpected Chance to Visit the Holy Land

After the admonition from the matriarch on the river cruise in 2010, for three years I wrote, read, and researched, while also venturing out on investigative field trips to churches, temples, mosques, and religious cults. Then one day in September 2013, my college roommate emailed me about her plans to visit the Holy Land in the fall of 2014. The trip was sponsored by her church, St. Ignatius Catholic Church, in Baltimore.

Beginning in 2005, members of her church had taken a series of pilgrimages to holy sites in Spain, Turkey, Portugal, and the Baltic. Nancy and her husband, Ward, had gone on the Spain trip and enjoyed the group, and the combination of foreign exploration, coupled with religious history. Now Ward had Parkinson's disease, and would not be able to accompany her to the Holy Land. Nevertheless, she had always wanted to go to Jerusalem and felt the church group would be a perfect opportunity for her to realize that dream. Their son, Jim, would stay with Ward during the two-week period.

I wondered if this were also the perfect opportunity for me to travel to the Holy Land.

Since it was more expensive traveling as a single, I figured Nancy would be sharing a room with another church member. I decided to ask her if a non-member of the church could join the group. I emailed back and asked if it would be possible for me to accompany them and share a room with her.

A long week of apprehension followed. I wondered if Nancy was hesitant to include me because she knew my status as at least an agnostic, if not an avowed atheist. Since she was a practicing Catholic, maybe she feared I might embarrass her in front of the other parishioners.

A week later, Nancy answered my email.

"Judaline, I was so surprised when I received your email. I never imagined you would want to travel to the Holy Land, as I know your beliefs about religion. I would love for you to join me. It would be one last great adventure for the two of us. I checked with the church office and it would definitely be OK for you to join our group."

The trip was scheduled for September 2014, a year away. St. Ignatius Church had contracted Father Donald Senior to lead the pilgrimage. Father Senior had impeccable credentials as President Emeritus from the Catholic Theological Union, a graduate school of theology and ministry, located in Chicago. He was also a well-known biblical authority, author, lecturer, and tour guide. He agreed to include fifteen people from Baltimore as part of his planned September 2014 Holy Land Tour, along with fifteen pilgrims from the Chicago area.

Early in January 2014, after the date, price, and travel arrangements were set and announced, Nancy and I rushed to remit the requested deposit in order to secure our place among the fifteen from St. Ignatius. We were the first two to enroll from Baltimore.

Then, Nancy and I began emailing back and forth, comparing our preparations for the trip. Father Senior's assistant, Anne Marie, sent all the fellow pilgrims practical travel information with the most important considerations highlighted with yellow marker.

Besides sound, sensible advice familiar to all seasoned foreign travelers, the communique noted many considerations unique to our visit to Israel and Jordan. Due to the visits to Christian, Jewish, and Muslim holy sites, we needed to wear modest clothing. No shorts, sleeveless blouses, or tank tops for either men or women. Cropped pants, long pants, or long skirts were ideal for the ladies. Skirts could be an advantage at some hole-in-the-floor restroom facilities. Head coverings were required for both sexes at many religious shrines. At some Jewish sites (such as the Western Wall), a *kippah* (skullcap) would be provided free for the men. Bring water shoes for wading or swimming in the Sea of Galilee or the Dead Sea to protect our feet from the salty, calcified sea bottom. Also, bring toilet paper because some of the rural bathroom stops along the bus route did not provide paper.

The information included answers to our financial concerns. We would obtain the best exchange rate for the local currency in our hotels: shekels in Israel and dinars in Jordan. Both countries honored Visa and MasterCard. American dollars were also accepted. Anne Marie suggested that we bring a cache of twenty-five to fifty single denomination dollar bills for buying post cards, bottled water, and small trinkets from the local children. This stack of small bills proved to be a very valuable asset. Also, we were to make provisions with our own cell phone company for communications home.

My husband and friends in Venice, along with my family in Marblehead, worried about my decision to travel to Israel, considered a volatile area at any time. I dismissed their concerns and continued preparing for the September departure. I paid the air and tour expenses in full.

Then, on July 8, 2014, the Israel-Gaza conflict or Operation Protective Edge erupted. Father Senior sent several communications assuring us that we would be safe. We would not go anywhere that would be dangerous. We would obey all state department advisories. The trip was a "go." Nevertheless, in the same letter, we were asked if we would be available for a later date in the fall. The Ayala Travel and Tour Company would try to reschedule the trip for November, just in case. Most of our group agreed to the November date, if necessary.

During all these considerations and possible rescheduling, I was steadfast in my commitment to go to Israel. Connie, my sons, and my friends were vehement in opposition to the trip at any time. Nancy and I remained determined to make our pilgrimage.

Then, the decision was taken out of our hands. On Tuesday, July 22, 2014, all American and European flights to Israel were canceled after a rocket landed about a mile from Ben Gurion International Airport in Tel Aviv. The FAA canceled all flights until further notice. Now we had no choice. The Holy Land Tour Agency succeeded in rebooking our excursion for November 9 -21, 2014, with basically the same itinerary. Almost all the original participants, including, of course, Nancy and me, indicated our continued availability. We crossed our fingers and hoped for a cease-fire and removal of travel restrictions by November.

In retrospect, after reviewing the news reports from that summer, I realized the seriousness of the situation. I compiled a brief and objective summary of the Israel Gaza conflict in the summer of 2014. Both sides claimed they were in the right. Both sides claimed the other side was the aggressor.

The Israelis claimed the hostilities began because of the kidnapping of three Israeli teenage boys on June 12, 2014, at a bus/hitchhiking stop in the occupied West Bank. On a taped call, one of the boys whispered, "They kidnapped me," while Arabic and gunfire were heard in the background. Their bodies were found in late June. Two suspect Hamas members were identified, detained, and sentenced.

On the other side, the Palestinians cited the true cause of the 2014 conflict was the killing of two Palestinian youth on May 15, 2014, by sniper fire near the Ofer military prison in the West Bank city of Beitunia. The kidnapping of the Israelis was in retaliation to the deaths of the Palestinians.

Then, in response to repeated rockets fired from Gaza, the IAF (Israeli Air Force) launched a military operation of air strikes on the Hamas-ruled Gaza Strip on July 8, 2014, the official beginning date of the conflict. The Palestinians continued their rocket attacks. On July 17, Israeli ground troops invaded Gaza with the aim of destroying the Gaza tunnel system, built by Hamas for access to Israel. The back and forth fighting ended on August 26, 2014, with a cease-fire brokered by Egypt. More than 2,100 people had been killed, the majority of them Gazans. Both sides claimed victory.

According to Israel, Hamas was weakened and achieved none of its demands, while Hamas claimed Israel was repelled from Gaza. If one picture is worth a thousand words, maybe the two pictures, one from each combatant, will help you understand the concerns of both sides.

As it turned out, since the cease-fire was signed in late August, the September travel date to Israel would have been as safe as any, but in a way,

A tunnel leading to Israel in the Gaza Strip

we lucked out. November weather in the Middle East is much cooler and more pleasant than September weather. We were now advised to bring light jackets or sweaters for the evening, as the temperature cools quickly in the desert.

Our departure date was November 7, 2014, from Dulles International Airport, Washington, D.C. On Thursday, November 6, I flew to Baltimore and spent the night at Nancy's house. On Friday afternoon we joined the group of pilgrims at St. Ignatius Church for the bus trip to Dulles International, to catch our red eye Air France flight to Paris, and then on to Tel Aviv, also on Air France. Our original airline was Delta, so we thought we had lucked out again. We hoped the airline food on Air France would not be airline food, but true French cuisine.

Ruins of a residential area in the Gaza Strip

The flight of seven and one-half hours left Washington at 6:50 p.m. Friday evening and was scheduled to arrive in Paris at 8:25 a.m., which took into account the six hour time difference. The air bus was at full capacity with eleven seats across—three, five, and three in each row. Nancy and I were not assigned seats together. I was in a three-row section in an aisle seat, next to Michelle, a traveler with our group in the middle, and a young Israeli woman returning to her homeland in the window seat. When Michelle and I showed her our itinerary for the trip, she was impressed.

Nancy and me, waiting to board the bus at St. Ignatius Church to begin the Holy Land Trip

She said she had not visited all those sites and did not believe we could complete such an extensive tour in our allotted time. But we did.

As we had hoped, we did luck out with French cuisine, including an apéritif and red or white wine with dinner. Menu in French and English:

Repas	Meal Service
Salade de leves de soja fraîches et maïs	Fresh soybean salad with corn
Poulet à la moutade à l'ancienne	Chicken with grain mustard sauce
Riz pilaf et petite légumes ou Pâtes conchiglie au thon	Rice pilaf and baby vegetables or Conchiglie pasta shells with tuna sauce
Fromage, Compote de fruits	Cheese, Fruit compote
Gâteau croquant au chocolat	Chocolate croquant cake
Café et thé	Coffee and tea

The dinner was delicious. For breakfast we were served coffee/tea, croissant with butter/jam, and fruit. After arriving at De Gaulle Airport, we had two hours before our four-and-one-half hour Air France flight to Tel Aviv at 10:50 a.m. We arrived in Tel Aviv at 4:30 p.m. From there we went on a one hour chartered bus ride to Jerusalem.

We checked in to the Mount Zion Hotel. This eighty-year-old hotel is situated in the center of Jerusalem within walking distance of the Old City and the Temple Mount. The hotel is unique as the lobby is on the top floor. You take the elevator down to your room. After showering and changing from our travel clothes, we rode up to the dining area and outdoor patio to meet Father Senior, Anne Marie, and the pilgrims from Chicago for the first time. We were a diverse group: single women or women traveling without their husbands, like Nancy and me, two single men, and the rest couples. Mixed ages, just a few in their thirties, most in their fifties or older.

My first impression of Father Senior was very positive. I knew he was in his seventies, but he was very energetic, youthful-looking, and quite handsome. Dressed in casual attire, he greeted everyone personally. Anne Marie was a pretty, young woman in her early thirties. After cocktails and nibbles, we went into the dining room for an elaborate buffet dinner. Soon we learned all the dinners at the hotels were buffet-style. They included options of both traditional American food and Mid-Eastern fare of fish, lamb, or chicken, plus many salads, vegetables, and delicious desserts.

After dinner, Nancy and I returned to our rooms for an early night. We called and requested a six a.m. wake-up call, before resting our heads, bodies, and "souls" in the Holy Land.

Chapter Seventeen

First Day in Jerusalem

Although each day was unique because of the different sites and cities that we visited, each day also had a calming sameness to it. At 7 a.m. we ate a very ample breakfast, characteristic of the Middle-East, with salads, breads, fruit, and eggs. At 8 a.m. we boarded the bus. Shafik, a Christian Palestinian, drove our modern bus. He supplied us with cold bottled water for one American dollar and guarded any valuables left on the bus while we were touring. We switched our bus seats daily to allow everyone a chance for the front positions. We toured all day, lunched on the road, and did not return to our hotel until late afternoon. After we comfortably settled in our seats, the bus pulled away from the hotel and Father Senior led us in prayer. I liked the morning ritual. I felt safe.

Even though our travel packet contained a written itinerary for the thirteen-day trip, each morning Father Senior reviewed the sites and adventures planned for that day, always with an appropriate biblical reference. (Biblical references in the text are taken from The Authorized King James Version.) With charm and wit, he explained background and current relevance and answered our many questions. I wrote furiously in my soon-to-be-famous or soon-to-be-infamous small pocket notebook.

Sunday morning, November 9, the first stop on the first day of our pilgrimage was The Israel Museum. Our introduction to Jerusalem was an acre-sized 50:1 scale model of the city as it appeared in 66 CE, the year of the Great Revolt against Rome that led to the destruction of the Temple and the city in 70 CE. At that date depicted by the model, Jerusalem had an estimated 50,000 to 80,000 residents and covered 450 acres, more than twice the size of the Old City today. Truly the most spectacular scale model of a city that I have ever seen—an appropriate introduction to the wonders to come.

At this same site we visited The Shrine of the Book Museum, a building in the shape of a white dome that houses The Dead Sea Scrolls. They were discovered between 1947 and 1956 in eleven caves near the Wadi Qumran. We were scheduled to visit Qumran National Park, an archaeological site on the West Bank, about one mile from the Dead Sea, on Wednesday, November 12.

Model of the city of Jerusalem 66 CE (scale 50:1)

The next stop was Yad Vashem. Here, early on my first morning in Jerusalem, I cried many times. This memorial park is a research institute and a museum depicting the horrors of WWII, as well as an archive for the more than six million names of the victims of the Nazi Holocaust. To enter the site we strolled along the Avenue of the Righteous Among Nations, lined with plaques naming the Gentiles who put their lives at risk to help the Jewish people. I have an aversion to using the word "Jews" and whenever possible use "Jewish people" in its place. I guess from somewhere in my childhood I equated the word "Jew" with a pejorative meaning.

From the information in the visitor's guide pamphlet, I learned about the conception and history of Yad Vashem:

> The State of Israel made a commitment to remember and never to forget the crimes perpetrated against the Jewish people. Yad Vashem, the Holocaust Martyrs' and Heroes' Remembrance Authority, was established in 1953, by an act of the Israeli Knesset. It is entrusted with the task of commemorating the six million Jews murdered by the Nazis ... preserving the heritage of the thousands of Jewish communities destroyed ... and paying tribute to heroic fighters who risked their lives to save Jews.

The Yad Vashem Campus, free of charge but donations accepted, covers approximately fifty acres, and houses twenty-one buildings and exhibits. I loved learning about the significance of the name, Yad Vashem. In Hebrew "*yad*" means place and "*shem*" means name—so, a place and a name. The Hall of Names lists over three million names in English and Hebbrew and the entries continue to grow. These victims never received the dignity of a Jewish burial, or any burial in most cases. A quote from the Old Testament (Isaiah, 56:5) gives additional meaning to the epitaph: "And I shall give them in My house within My walls a memorial and a name (a 'Yad Vashem')...that shall not be cut off."

Father Senior, in middle, speaking to our group

Nancy and me along the Avenue of the Righteous Among the Nations

I snapped pictures of three of the many sculptures exhibited on the Yad Vashem campus. The first two are memorials to the victims in the camps. The third is to Janusz Korczak, a pseudonym for Dr. Henrik Goldschmidt, the Polish-Jewish educator, who tried to save the 200 children that he cared for in his orphanage. But all, including Janusz Korczak, were sent to death camps in 1942.

First death camp sculpture

Second death camp sculpture

After a short walk we reached The Hall of Remembrance. As I entered the dark interior, I did not know what to expect. It was like entering a tomb, and, in fact, I *was* entering a tomb. After my eyes adjusted to the darkness, I slowly walked down the incline that surrounded a fenced-off lower floor that listed the names of Nazi murder sites. A memorial flame burns continuously next to a crypt containing ashes of victims brought to Israel from the extermination camps. We filed in silence down, around, and back up again. All was silence and all were silent. When we exited out into the sunny morning, our silence continued. I did not think I could be so moved. I was so wrong. The next exhibit could and did touch me more—then, now, and I know, forever.

Memorial sculpture to
Janusz Korczak

The Children's Museum at Yad Vashem is a monument to the 1.5 million Jewish children killed during the Holocaust and hollowed out from an underground cave. Once again, we entered a chamber in semi-darkness. Over our heads a simulated night sky twinkled with what appeared to be millions of stars. The effect emanated from tiny lights representing memorial candles—a Jewish tradition to honor the dead. As we walked along the narrow path in the cavern, young voices murmured the names, ages, and countries of origin of the murdered children. No one could, or should, or would ever forget the meaning of those millions of stars dancing above us in the Holy Land of Israel.

Subdued, we boarded the bus for a ride around the Old City walls, on our way to the Mount of Olives overlook. We were all ready for a more cheery view of the Holy Land. For Christians studying the life of Jesus, no mountain has more meaning than Olivet or the Mount of Olives. On this hill, Jesus taught his disciples, prophesied the destruction of Israel, and wept over its fate (Luke 19:37-41). In earlier times, olive trees covered the slopes, but the Romans cut them down to build ramparts for their siege of the walls of the Old City in 70 CE, during the Jewish revolt against Rome.

Father Senior knew how to herd his flock. He knew we were ready for lunch. He had conducted so many tours of Israel that he knew where to go for quick, efficient, and reasonable lunches. Unless we had a special treat, our lunches were salads, some version of falafel, and soft drinks for the equivalent of ten American dollars. The restaurants all catered to the tourist trade, but Father Senior knew the best ones, and always seemed to know the owner.

View from Mount Olive overlooking the Old City and Temple Mount/
Dome of the Rock.

Falafel is traditional Mid-Eastern fast food. It is a fried chickpea patty, usually served in pita bread, with garnishes of tomatoes and lettuce. The ingredients are chickpeas, scallions, garlic, cumin, coriander, and egg that are blended in a mixer and fried in olive oil. Delicious … the first, second, and third time. Then, enough of the falafel! To be fair, we did have some variety in our lunches. I especially liked the Peter's fish lunch at the Sea of Galilee.

Refreshed, we returned to the bus and Shafik drove us to the Old City, but not into the city. The narrow streets would not accommodate the bus. Father Senior had planned an extensive walking tour of Jerusalem's old walled city. We entered through the Damascus Gate, the principal gate into the city that leads directly into the heart of the open-air Arab market or *souk*. The direction going out of this gate, built by the Sultan of the Ottoman Empire in 1537, leads directly to the road to Damascus, Syria, roughly150 miles northeast from Jerusalem.

The phrase "road to Damascus" has the idiomatic meaning of a sudden turning point in a person's life, derived from the sudden conversion of the apostle Paul on the road from Jerusalem to Damascus to arrest Christians (Acts 9: 1-27).

As we entered through the gate into the *souk,* we encountered a cacophony of sounds, a panorama of hues and movements, and an intoxicating aromatic mixture of cinnamon, cumin, and unknown smells. Father Senior had promised us numerous shopping opportunities

The Damascus Gate into the Old City of Jerusalem

over our thirteen- day trip, but this was not to be one of them. He suggested we come back on our last day in Jerusalem, when we had a free afternoon. Although most of us were eager to sample the spices and goods arrayed in bins lining the narrow allies, we hustled to keep up with the long-striding Father Senior. Along the way, very young and very old vendors jostled us offering postcards and religious relics for one American dollar.

Muslim women buying and selling in the souk

Jerusalem is considered holy to the three Abrahamic religions: Christianity, Islam, and Judaism. Both the Israelis and the Palestinians claim Jerusalem as their capital. It became a United Nations World Heritage site in 1981. The Old City consists of .35 square miles and is divided into four quarters: Armenian, Christian, Jewish, and Muslim. All the major religious sites inside the walls are within easy walking distance of each other. This afternoon, after entering into the Muslim quarter, we turned right toward the Christian quarter and our destination, The Church of the Holy Sepulcher.

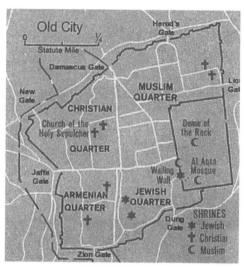

Map of the
Old Walled City of Jerusalem

After making our way to the courtyard of the basilica, we gathered around Father Don, while he told us the history of the sacred site. He reminded us that many of the locations that we visit are not historically accurate. In regards to the structure itself, history indicates that the first basilica was built by Roman emperor Constantine, between 326 and 335 CE, at the suggestion of his mother, St. Helena. That church was destroyed by an Egyptian sultan in 1009, rebuilt by a Byzantine emperor in the 1040s, and enlarged by the crusaders between 1114 and 1170. Repairs were needed in 1808 after a fire, and in 1927 after an earthquake.

Courtyard of the
Church of the Holy Sepulcher

Be it fact, myth, or legend, Christians believe the Church of the Holy Sepulcher is built on the site of Christ's crucifixion, burial, and resurrection—the most important church complex in Christendom. Here within the compound is the Hill of Calvary, the Holy Sepulcher where Jesus is buried, and the room where Mary anointed her Son after his crucifixion. The Stations of the Cross from ten through fourteen are said to have occurred here.

The tomb of Jesus, the holiest place in Christendom

Since a Sunday Mass was in progress inside the basilica, as well as there being throngs of other pilgrims jockeying to visit the shrine, we only had time to view Jesus' tomb. As we moved slowly forward, we observed the holy depictions on the walls and the beautiful mosaic tiles on the floor. When we reached His tomb, we knelt briefly and intoned a quick prayer.

The last destination for the first day of our Holy Land pilgrimage was right outside the Zion Gate and atop the hillside, known as Mount Zion. Here we visited the Church of the Dormition and the Cenacle, the site of the Last Supper. The Neo-Romanesque Church was built in the early 20th century and is said to be where Mary fell into an "eternal sleep." Tradition suggests an early church was built on this spot in 4 CE, then a larger basilica constructed in 6 CE, which later fell into ruins. When the Crusaders arrived in Jerusalem around 1100 CE, they built a Gothic church and chapels that they consecrated to the Dormition of the Virgin and The Last Supper. Only the first floor of one of these medieval buildings remains today.

Of course, before our trip, I knew the biblical story of the Last Supper. In fact, in 2010 I had attended a staged, but realistic Last Supper at the Holy Land Experience Theme Park in Orlando, Florida. Now I was anxious to visit the actual place of the Last Supper. Father Senior had made arrangements to serve Mass and the Eucharist to us in this very holy place, where Jesus sanctified his own Body and Blood for the first time. One of the men, a lector from the Baltimore contingent, would assist Father at Mass.

The Cenacle, derived from the Latin word *cenaculum*, meaning dining room and also known as the "upper room," is considered the site of the Last Supper. Christians believe the "upper room," is also where the Apostles stayed while in Jerusalem and is the site of the first Christian church (Acts1:13). The room is unadorned except for Gothic arches.

As I sat next to Nancy and anticipated the distribution of the Eucharist, in one of the most holy of all places in the Christian world, I faced a dilemma ... a Gordian knot that I needed to solve quickly, but in a manner tolerable to my conscience. I had not received Holy Communion since my apostasy at age thirty-two. When attending Catholic funerals, where I felt compelled to go to the communion rail in order to honor the deceased, I had learned the proper approach was to cross your arms over your chest and bow your head. Then, the priest knew to give you a blessing instead of a wafer.

Would I embarrass Nancy and myself if I asked for a blessing instead of taking communion? Would this action plant a disapproving seed in Father Don's mind? Would it be a mortal sin to accept communion, when in the eyes of God I was a heretic? Could I live with myself after I acted in such a hypocritical way?

Then, my rational mind jumped to the forefront. I was on an academic trip researching the origins of religions, as well as searching for any remaining flame of religion within myself. I was a guest of Nancy and her fellow church members. After every biblical and historical lecture, I gained more respect for Father Don's expertise as a guide. I did not believe the communion wafer really was the Body of Christ, but I did believe my fellow pilgrims believed this, and I respected their right to do so. As a guest on their trip, I wanted them to like and respect me.

So I decided the most logical path was "when in Rome..." or in this case, when in Jerusalem, do as the believers do. I took communion with them in deference to my fellow pilgrims, not in deference to the wafer,

Our group awaiting Father Senior to begin Mass in the Cenacle

which had no transcendental meaning for me. I thought Nancy was relieved by my decision.

Listening to Mass, singing hymns, and walking with folded hands in a line with congenial friends to receive the Eucharist at the alter of a church, built by the Crusaders on the prescribed spot, if not the actual spot, where Jesus held the Last Supper, was a spiritual experience, even for me.

After Mass, we followed Anne Marie and met Shafik at the bus. He drove the quiet, tired group back to the Mount Zion Hotel. Nancy and I decided to go to dinner promptly and return to our room for an early night. In our email correspondence, we had admitted to each other that we were poor sleepers, even snored, and often woke to switch on a light to read. That night, if Nancy woke, snored, or turned on a light I did not know it.

Chapter Eighteen

The Essence of Jerusalem

On the second day in Jerusalem, the Temple Mount/Dome of the Rock headed our itinerary. I wondered why this landmark situated half in the Muslim Quarter and half in the Jewish Quarter of the Old City bore two names. From pictures of Jerusalem, I knew the iconic golden dome symbolized the religious fervor which dominated and divided the city of Jerusalem. Its photograph adorned the cover of the travel guide that I had bought in preparation for the trip. With a quick flip through the pages, I realized how ignorant I was of the history and biblical references that seeped mystic mystery into the lands of Palestine, Israel, and neighboring areas.

In contrast, when Nancy first read our itinerary, she sent me a hurried email.

"Judaline, I cannot believe that we are actually going to see Petra. I have wanted to go there all my life," she typed.

I hastily googled "Petra" to understand her excitement. I had never heard of the place. After reading about the hidden, ancient city, I became as excited as she to visit Petra.

Since the purpose of my trip, besides enjoying the company of my former college roommate, was to study religion and its origins, and to convince myself that religion was not for me, I began reading non-fiction books on Israel's history and on the histories of religion. I also read historical fiction accounts such as *The Dovekeepers*, by Alice Hoffman, about the siege at Masada; *The Source*, by James A. Michener, the epic tale of the Holy Land; and *Ben-Hur, a Tale of the Christ,* written in 1880, by Lewis Wallace, about Rome and Jerusalem at the time of Christ.

The next few paragraphs contain many dates and many names of ancient tribes and peoples in both the BCE and CE time periods … perhaps too many. But this abbreviated history of their Holy Land is necessary to explain why all three major monotheistic religions consider these deserts and hills to be the Holy Land. Most of the cities and core places I visited on my pilgrimage are mentioned in stories that date back 12,000 years to the burgeoning of civilization and continue through centuries of wars and conquests, in pursuit of the Holy Land.

The prehistory of the Holy Land dates from 10,000 BCE at Jericho, where archaeologists unearthed evidence of settlements near the numerous springs in the area. Stone Age groups abandoned their nomadic lifestyle to pursue farming. By the third millennium, the Canaanites, a civilization of city states and worshipers of numerous Gods, including Baal, dominated the area. In 1468 BCE, an Egyptian army defeated the Canaanites, who then became subjects of Egypt.

In 1200 BCE, the Philistines invaded from the sea and named the land Palestine. Biblical scholars and historians offer many different versions for the etymology of the name Palestine, and for the origin of the people. At about the same time, the twelve Hebrew tribes arrived and united to form a sovereign kingdom under Saul. His successor, David, reigned from 1010-970 BCE. King Solomon followed from 970-930 BCE. According to the Old Testament, David captured Jerusalem and made the city the capital of the Israelis. Solomon built the first Jewish temple on the site of the Temple Mount. Inside the Inner Temple, the Ark of the Covenant resided in a chamber named the Holy of Holies. Several references in the Bible refer to the Mount of the Lord, where Abraham was asked by the Lord to sacrifice his son, Issac—this site is now believed to be the location of the Temple Mount (Genesis 22:14; Chronicles 3:1; Isiah 2;3 and 30:29; Psalm 24:3; and Zechariah 8:3).

New nations entered the struggle for the Holy Land. After Solomon died, the Jewish nation split into two parts: the Kingdom of Israel to the north and the Kingdom of Judea to the south. In 722 BCE, Assyrians conquered the Kingdom of Israel and deported its people. In 587 BCE, the Babylonians defeated the Assyrians and destroyed Solomon's temple and the Holy Chamber inside it. Soon afterward, in 538 BCE, the Persians defeated the Babylonians and allowed the Jews to return to Israel.

After returning in 515 BCE, the Jewish people built a Second Temple on the same site as the first. Then, in 332 BCE, Alexander the Great of Macedonia, the area north of Greece, defeated the Persians and won the land called Palestine. After Alexander's death, fights ensued over the spoils of the large empire. Syria claimed Palestine. In 164 BCE, King Antichus, a Seleucid from Syria, intended to rededicate the Jewish temple in Jerusalem to Zeus, and make observance of Jewish law punishable by death. Led by Judas Maccabeus, a Hasmonean priest, the Jews rebelled, defeated the Seleucids, took control of Jerusalem again, and reconsecrated their Temple.

Almost immediately, the Jewish high powers began fighting among themselves. The Pharisees, a high religious sect, demanded the Hasmonean kings relinquish the priesthood. Both factions asked Rome, the new military and political power of the period, for help. Rome did not miss this proffered opportunity and sent their legions to storm Jerusalem. They appointed a Jew, Herod the Great, as procurator or client king of Palestine. He reigned from 37-4 BCE. Herod constructed massive architectural projects such as Masada, the port city of Caesarea on the Mediterranean Sea, and the reconstruction and enlargement of the Jews' Second Temple in Jerusalem.

After Herod's death in 4 BCE (this date disputed by some researchers), his three sons reigned for a short period. The burdensome conditions imposed on the Jewish people such as heavy taxes and the implementation of Roman culture, culminated in the revolt against the Romans in 66 CE, without success. By 70 CE, the Romans had captured Jerusalem, destroyed the city, demolished the Temple, and, three years later, routed the Jews at Masada.

Soon the Jews rebounded and rose up again. After a Second Jewish War from 132-5 CE, the Romans attempted to thwart any further Jewish rebellion. They rebuilt the city of Jerusalem, forbade the Jews to enter the city, and sold them into slavery. Some managed to flee and escape. This scattering of the Jews is known as the Diaspora. Nevertheless, during this period in the second and third centuries, some Jews remained in Palestine and began to record their oral law in a text now known as the Talmud.

By the fourth century, the Christians, who had also been persecuted by the Romans, were granted freedom of worship by the Byzantine Emperor Constantine. As the son of Roman Emperor Flavius Constantine and his consort Helena, Constantine rose in the ranks to become emperor of the Eastern Empire. He built his imperial residence at Byzantium

The Byzantine Empire 565 CE

and renamed the city Constantinople, after himself. Currently known as Istanbul, as well as New Rome during Constantine's time, the city was the capital of the Eastern Roman Empire, or the Byzantine Empire, for over one thousand years.

As a Christian convert himself, Emperor Constantine reopened the Holy land to the Christians. Christian churches and monasteries were built on the sites where Jesus and his disciples had lived and preached, including the first Holy Sepulcher Church that we visited on Sunday.

Relative calm reigned in the Holy Land during the Byzantine Era until 614, when the Persians arrived, massacred the Christians, and desecrated their holy sites. Then, ironically, in 628, the same year that the Byzantine Empire defeated the Persians and recaptured Palestine, the Prophet Muhammad conquered Mecca in Arabia.

Six years after Muhammad's death, in 638, Omar, Muhammad's *caliph* (the word means leader of Islamic policy and successor to Muhammad), defeated the Byzantines at the Yarmuck River in what is now modern-day Syria. A new era began as the Muslims became the rulers of Palestine.

The Muslims, as one of three monotheistic religions that traced their origin to the patriarch, Abraham, regarded Jerusalem as a Holy Land. The Muslims believed that the Prophet Muhammad ascended to Heaven on his Night Journey from the same rock on which Abraham was asked to sacrifice his son. Thus, they cleared the Temple Mount area and there they constructed two mosques: one, the Dome of the Rock in 691, and the other, El-Aqsa, in 705. Jews and Christians were denied excess to the site, but could live and worship in Jerusalem if they paid an "infidel" tax.

For several centuries the situation remained static, until 1009. In that year, caliph El-Hakim destroyed the Church of the Holy Sepulcher. For

Taking of Jerusalem by the Crusaders, 15th July 1099,
painted by Émile Signol in 1847 and displayed in the Palace of Versailes

several decades, the tension between Muslims and Christians continued to escalate. In 1071, the Seluk Turks seized Jerusalem and forbade Christians entrance into the Holy City. Due to the hostile action of the Turks, in 1095, the European Christians came to the aid of their brethren, the Eastern Christians or the Byzantines, and launched a series of Crusades to free the Holy Land.

Pope Urban II ordered the First Crusade with the cry, "God wills it!" The knights passed through Constantinople, engaged the Muslims in Anatolia, Turkey, captured the city of Antioch, and marched through Syria and into Palestine.

On June 7, 1099, the Crusaders reached Jerusalem. For five weeks, the Muslims defended the city. On July 15, the Crusaders breached the walls and slaughtered the Muslims in the streets.

In the struggle to keep Jerusalem in Christian control, history recorded several Crusades over approximately two hundred years. The Second Crusade ended in a defeat at Damascus, in 1148. In 1190, Richard I of England, the Lionheart, set out on the Third Crusade. He failed to retake the Holy City, but his negotiations won the right of Christian pilgrims to enter the Holy City and visit sacred sites. Louis IX of France led the last major Crusade in 1270. The Mamluks defeated the last of the

Crusaders at Akko, a city on the coast of what is now northern Israel in 1291.

Two important monastic orders arose during the time of the Crusades. One, the Hospitallers, built a hospital, large enough to care for as many as 2,000 people at one time. The other, the Templars, were a skilled fighting unit which used the Temple Mount as their headquarters, thus earning them the name of Knight Templars. At the time of the Crusades, the Muslim mosque, the Dome of the Rock, became a Catholic Church, renamed the Templum Domini or Temple of the Lord. The Templars actually lodged in the smaller mosque, the Aqsa Mosque. Information and the history about these two religious orders, whether myth, conjecture, or fact, is available online, and in numerous books.

Artist depiction of a Knight Templar

Depiction of a Mamluk nobleman

In the succeeding centuries, warring empires continued to fight over and rule Palestine. The Mamluks, a military caste of former slaves, who ruled Syria and Egypt from 1250 – 1517, also ruled the Holy Land. They were somewhat tolerant in their treatment of the religious factions. The Franciscan Friars maintained a presence at the Cenacle (site of The Last Supper) and many Jews returned from Spain after the Inquisition in 1492. The Ottoman Turks defeated the Mamluks in 1516. The Ottoman dynasty, led by the great Turkish sultan, Suleyman the Magnificent, accounted for many architectural projects in Jerusalem, including rebuilding the walls and gates of the city.

By the eighteenth-century, the Ottoman Empire was in decline due to a series of weak sultans. Europe began eyeing the region. In 1798, Napoleon landed in Egypt, but was repelled by the Ottomans. The Jews continued to come and settle in communities in Galilee, where they joined the Sephardic Jews from Spain.

"The British are coming. The British are coming." Those famous words ascribed to Paul Revere could be applied to Palestine. In 1831, when the Egyptian ruler, Muhammad Ali, seized Palestine from the Ottoman Empire, the British military helped the Turks regain the territory. Soon after, in 1838, a British consul arrived in Palestine, and soon after that, diplomats from France and Prussia arrived. In fact, one cause of the Crimean War (1854) was a dispute between France and Russia over guardianship of the Holy City.

With the decline of the Ottoman Empire and the rise of European colonial powers in the nineteenth century, a growing Jewish movement called for the creation of a Jewish state. In 1896, Theodor Herzl, an Austro-Hungarian Jewish journalist, published the pamphlet, *The Jewish State.* Jews worldwide joined in the cry for a creation of a Jewish state. The next year, Herzl and his followers formed the World Zionist Organization with its aim "to create for the Jewish people a home in Palestine."

Zion comes from the Latin *sion,* which means hill. To the Jewish people it is the hill in Jerusalem, the site of the temple and royal residence of David and his successors,that is the symbol of the center of Jewish national life. Zionism, coined in 1898, means the national movement of the Jewish people to return to their homeland, and to resume Jewish sovereignty of the Land of Israel.

Predictably, the Zionist movement incensed the large indigenous Palestinian Arab population, as well as the other Arab nations, and incited resistance.

As the history of Palestine and Israel moves into the twentieth and twenty-first centuries, the hostilities between the two peoples continues. My aim is to tell their story with facts, with a skeletal timeline of major events, and without judgment.

Again, here come the British and T. E. Lawrence, now famous as the exotic hero, Lawrence of Arabia. While attending Oxford, Lawrence spent a year in the Middle East, compiling his thesis on the medieval castles of the Crusaders. During World War I, the British asked Lawrence, who knew Arabic and the region, to persuade Faisal and the Arabs to join them in ousting the Turks from the Middle East, in return for autonomous control of the Arabian Peninsula and Palestine. Lawrence and the Arabs succeeded in capturing the oil-rich regions from the Turks, but the British reneged on their agreement.

For a detailed account of the life of Lawrence of Arabia and the actions of the British, I watched the documentary, *Lawrence of Arabia: The Battle for the Arab World,* available from Netflix. I also rewatched the epic 1962 Oscar-winning, not quite four-hour drama, *Lawrence of Arabia*, starring Peter O'Toole and Alec Guinness. When I first saw the film in 1962, I was a new mom and I remember the luxury of sleeping through most of the film in the darkened theater.

Lieutenant Colonel Thomas Edward Lawrence in 1919

The Arabs expected control of Palestine, as they had been promised for their help in defeating the Turks, but the British, urged on by the Zionist Movement, favored the creation of a national Jewish state in Palestine. In 1919, The Paris Peace talks awarded control of the area to Britain and the arrangement was ratified by the League of Nations in 1922. To appease the Arabs, the British allowed Emir Abdullah, eldest brother of Faisal, to rule Trans-Jordan, but under the supervision of the British. In 1946, the territory became independent with Abdullah named king.

At the end of World War I, 500,000 Palestinian Arabs lived in the Holy Land and about 85,000 Jews. In 1929, the Arabs, concerned about the Jews praying at the Western Wall and possibly restoring their claim to the Temple Mount, attacked the Jews in Jerusalem, Hebron, and Safed. The Western Wall Uprising resulted in 133 Arab fatalities and 110 Jewish fatalities. In spite of these skirmishes and with tensions rising in Europe, over 250,000 Jews immigrated to Palestine. In 1936, an Arab revolt induced a six-month general strike. In 1937, the Peel Commission, headed by Lord Peel, searched for an amicable solution to the hostilities in Palestine and proposed partitioning the country. The Jews accepted, but the Arabs refused, stating that the most fertile zones were in the Jewish section. The proposal was rejected by the League of Nations. Subsequent plans were drafted, but all proved impracticable. On the eve of the forthcoming war, Britain published a "White Paper" that limited the number of Jews allowed to immigrate to Palestine. This was unenforceable, as the Jewish people, fleeing Nazism, continued their flight to Palestine.

At the end of World War II, the British presented the "Palestine question" to the newly-formed United Nations. On November 29, 1947, the UN voted to partition the Holy Land into an Arab state and a Jewish state with Jerusalem under international administration.

Britain announced it would leave Palestine on May 15, 1948. Before that date, both Jewish and Palestinians extremists raided and attacked one anothers' villages and

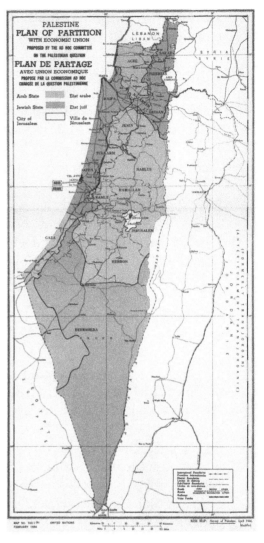

UN General Assembly Resolution for Palestine Partition

settlements in attempts to gain territory. On May 14, 1948, on the eve of Britain's departure, David Ben Gurion declared the birth of the State of Israel.

Since that date of statehood for the Israelis in 1948, and at this writing, the Palestinians and Jews have endured years of major wars, minor confrontations, numerous cease-fires amid peace talks, assassinations of leaders, and a few periods of tenuous peace.

The following dates and events include the most salient events in the interactions between the two adversaries:

The 1948 War: Immediately on May 15, 1948, the Arab states of Lebanon, Syria, Iraq, Jordan, and Egypt launched an attack on Israel with "the aim of casting the new state into the sea." Result, Israeli victory, Arab, defeat.

March 10, 1949: war ended.

July 20, 1949: Final armistice signed. Israel now occupied eighty percent of Palestine as compared to seven percent in 1948. Seven hundred thousand Jews immigrated to Palestine. Seven hundred thousand Palestinians were displaced. The city of Jerusalem was divided between the two factions.

1951: King Abdullah of Jordan assassinated by Palestinian extremists.

1956 Suez Crisis: Israeli army moved into Sinai under auspices of Britain and France to confront Egypt's attempt to nationalize the Suez Canal. Pressure from UN forced their retreat.

Six Day War: On June 5-11, 1967, Israel, alarmed by Egyptian build up on the border, attacked pre-eminently. In six days Israel's army captured Golan Heights from Syria, the Gaza Strip and Sinai from Egypt, and the West Bank from Jordan and retook the city of Jerusalem.

Yom Kippur War: In a surprise attack on October 6, 1973, Egypt and Syria attacked Israel on its holiday. There were initial losses for Israel, but it soon regained its territory. However, the hostilities paved the way for first peace talks between Egypt and Israel.

Camp David Talks: In 1979, formal peace treaty signed between the two nations. In 1982, Sinai returned to Egypt.

<u>Palestine Liberation Organization (PLO):</u> In the eighties, unhappy with the peace treaty, the PLO's guerrilla attacks against Israel garnered no international sympathy until the *intifada (shaking off)*. In late 1987, there was a grass-roots Palestinian revolt against Israeli occupation in the Gaza Strip and West Bank. Images of young Arabs throwing rocks at well-armed Israeli soldiers earned world attention.

<u>Oslo Accords:</u> Secret talks in Oslo resulted in the creation of the Palestinian Authority that held limited self-governance over parts of the West Bank and Gaza Strip, and resulted in a handshake between Arrafat, PLO president, and Rabin, Israeli PM, in 1993.

<u>Notable Deaths:</u> 1995, Rabin assassinated by Jewish extremist: 1999, King Hussein of Jordan died: 2004, Yasser Arafat died.

<u>Notable Date:</u> 2005, Jewish settlements withdraw from the Gaza Strip.

<u>Summer 2014:</u> The recent Israeli-Gaza conflict covered in preceding chapter.

The above chronological log is a brief list of the more important events in the past seventy-year history of Israel and Palestine and their struggle to coexist on the same land. The biblical and academic history explains the relevance of the region to the sacred heritage of the three religions, Christianity Islam, and Judaism.

However, I needed the guidebook to fully unravel the mystery of the double appellation: Temple Mount or Dome of the Rock. The Islamic architectural centerpiece, the golden Dome of the Rock sits within the rectangular esplanade, the Haram esh-Sharif, or Temple Mount. The area is technically not a mountain, but a man-made platform erected by Herod 2,000 years ago. For the past several years, non-Muslims have not been allowed to enter the shrine of the Dome of the Rock.

The Temple Mount/Dome of the Rock headed our agenda for Monday. Father Don cautioned us on our dress: no sleeveless blouses or short pants, and no visible religious jewelry (such as a cross). What I remember the most from our visit were the many Muslim monitors roaming the grounds to prevent any observable demonstrative actions. They prevented men and women from touching, holding hands, or putting arms around the shoulders of each other even for a picture. This Islamic shrine is the third in religious importance after Mecca and Medina to Muslims. Our group agreed to a professional group photo with the Dome of the Rock in the background.

Father Senior's Tour at Temple Mount with the Dome of the Rock in the background; Father Senior, top right with Sister Luna, a Catholic nun, visiting our group from Iraq; Anne Marie first row right; Nancy, top row fourth from left; me, third row, second from right.

Our next stop was the Western Wall, or Wailing Wall, an outer wall of the Temple Mount plaza. It is the only ancient wall that remains from the time when King Herod enlarged the temple grounds. In Jewish tradition, there is a men's side and a women's side. In reality, the plaza is an outdoor synagogue. Boys and girls celebrate their *bar* or *bat mitzvahs* there. We saw several ceremonies in progress. Some worshipers visit daily to sit and recite entire books from the Old Testament. A popular tradition is to write a prayer on a scrap of paper, fold it, and insert it into a crevice in the wall. Monday morning at breakfast, Nancy and I wrote our prayers, to be ready to partake in the tradition. Mine read: "Let us return safely to the United States."

Women praying at the Wailing Wall

Next, we boarded the bus for a trip to Jericho on the West Bank, a driving distance of about seventeen miles. From the bus window, I noticed the highway was modern and in good repair. As we traveled through the Rift Valley, I was surprised by the look of the desert. I always thought a desert consisted of fine, white sand, such as on the shore. No, this desert was red rock. Nothing but rock, no sand. Also, not far from the side of the highway, we viewed several Bedouin encampments.

Judean Desert on route from Jerusalem to Jericho

Archaeologists believe Jericho is one of the oldest inhabited cities in the world, dating back 11,000 years. The original attraction was the copious springs that pumped 8,000 gallons of water a minute in prehistory eras, and now produce at least 1,000 gallons per minute. Due to numerous palm trees around the oasis, Jericho was called the City of Palms. The Bible mentions Jericho in both the Old Testament and the New Testament. The biblical passage (Luke 19:1-5) tells the story of Zacchaeus who climbed a sycamore fig tree to view Jesus riding into town. The tree, said to be over 2,000 years old, is the main tourist attraction in the town. After viewing the tree we went to lunch.

Sycamore fig tree climbed by Zacchaeus in the Bible story

Driving back to Jerusalem, we stopped to view The Monastery of the Temptation on Mount Qarantal. The Greek Orthodox Monastery built into the mountain can be reached by cable car. It is said to be on the site where Jesus went into the mountains after his baptism, to fast for forty days, and was tempted by the Devil (Matthew 4:1-11).

On returning to Jerusalem, Shafik let us off by the Dung Gate which led into the Jewish quarter. Father Don knew it was time for a bathroom and snack break. Anne Marie led us into Hurva Square, a pleasant spot for a cup of coffee or an ice cream, where we chatted and watched children play.

After our brief respite, we walked to St. Anne's church, a Byzantine Church built in the 1100s that is believed to stand on the spot where Anne and Joachim, parents of the Virgin Mary lived. Next to the church are the Pools of Bethesda, where Jesus was said to cure a paralyzed man (John 5: 1-15).

At 4:30, Shafik delivered his exhausted group to the Mount Zion Hotel. Nancy and I showered and then joined the others for cocktails and a buffet dinner. We retired early, because Father Don had scheduled Mass the next morning in the Shepherds' Field in Bethlehem, at 10:00 a.m. He also promised a shopping spree at an authentic Palestinian Co-op that allocated its proceeds to the contributing native artisans.

The Monastery of Temptation

Chapter Nineteen

Exploring Bethlehem

Today's activities provided my most enduring spiritual memories and my most meaningful, tactile mementos from my trip to the Holy Land. Before traveling to Bethlehem and our scheduled Eucharist al fresco in the Shepherds' Field at 10:00 a.m., Father Don paraded us once again to the Mount of Olives overlook. Below us lay a grid of above ground crypts in the Jewish graveyard. Many Jews wish to be buried in the 3,000 year old cemetery, because from there, close to the Valley of Jehoshaphat, they believe mankind will be resurrected on the Day of Judgment (Joel 3:1-2 and Joel 3:9-12).

As we stopped to listen to Father Don's lecture along the iconic overlook, I snapped this photo that I used for my 2014 Christmas card, deceptively claiming it was taken in Bethlehem.

We strolled down the narrow, cobbled path and gathered in the courtyard of the Basilica of the Agony or the Church of All Nations, so named because it was built in 1924 with donations from many countries. The current, modern church sits on the foundation of a Crusader chapel built

Jerusalem from the Mount of Olives overlook

in the twelfth century. The site enshrines the spot where Jesus prayed prior to his arrest (Mark 14:32-42).

Shafik and our bus awaited us at the foot of the overlook on the Jericho Road. Although today our destination was not Jericho, but south to Bethlehem, a distance of approximately six miles. Once aboard, Father Don extolled the privilege of celebrating Mass at the Franciscan Missionary church in the fields, where the angels appeared and told the shepherds to travel to Bethlehem to adore the new born Christ child (Luke 2:8-15). Months in advance, he made reservations for use of the site.

Unfortunately, we encountered an unaccustomed snag in Father's planning. Due, I guess, to the rescheduling of our pilgrimage, another group was occupying the outdoor church. We had to settle for one of the many sheds provided for religious services, near, but not actually in, the fields. Since the Greek Orthodox claim another field as the exact site of the angel's appearance to the shepherds, I figure we were near enough. After celebrating Mass, complete with hymns, robes, and communion wafers, Father Don took us shopping, as he had promised.

The Holy Land Handicraft Co-op, an authentic Palestinian craft store, sold vibrantly painted ceramics, genuine olive-wood sculptures, and mother-of-pearl jewelry, among other artifacts. We were allowed one hour to shop.

All the members of our group, including the men, spent the hour examining and buying many of the hand-made items displayed in the store and workshop. I found perfect souvenir gifts to bring home to my friends: hand-painted refrigerator magnets of Bethlehem and the Christmas star for two American dollars each. I purchased ten of them. For myself, I bought an olive-wood, hand-carved angel to display at Christmas time with my crèche. The artisans hinted that any of the olive-wood items may have been carved from trees growing in Bethlehem at the time of Christ's birth. For my husband, I began a search to find a gift pertaining to pomegranates, a common and popular fruit grown in Israel, and his favorite juice. I did not succeed in the pomegranate quest until the very last day, in a shop in Jerusalem.

Our busy morning ended with lunch at Ruth's Fields, a well-reviewed restaurant located near the Shepherds' Fields. We enjoyed a pita sandwich, French fries, and iced tea. Ruth, herself, greeted each member of our tour group. Father Don hurried us back to the bus, because we had an appointment at Bethlehem University at 1:30 p.m.

Father Senior prides himself in showing his pilgrimages both sides of the Israeli/Palestinian conflict. With a population of thirty thousand (seventy percent Muslim and thirty percent Palestinian Christian), Bethlehem is a city on the West Bank, administered by the Palestinian National Authority.

Israeli citizens are barred from entering Bethlehem. Palestinian travel into Jerusalem is regulated by a permit system. As American tourists, our mobility was not restricted, as Bethlehem's economy relies on tourism.

Bethlehem University, the first university established in the West Bank, is a Catholic co-educational institution, founded in 1973, by the La Salle Christian Brothers, who trace their educational involvement in Palestine and Egypt to 1893. In 2014, student enrollment totaled 3,293 with seventy-seven percent female, twenty-three percent male; seventy-four percent Muslim, twenty-six percent Christian; and forty-nine percent from Bethlehem, forty-one percent from Jerusalem, and ten percent from other locations.

After wandering through the small campus and chatting with the English-speaking students, we settled into an auditorium for the presentation by a panel of Palestinian students, five girls. After a short movie, the students introduced themselves and shared their majors and plans for the future. Few men attend the University, because most Palestinian male students

Bethlehem University campus

matriculate outside of Palestine, for the better opportunities offered in disciplines of engineering or law. The popular departments at Bethlehem University are nursing, education, and hotel management/tourism.

The students were eager to answer questions about the Palestinian situation. They discussed the 1948 War and the Six-Day War in 1967. All of them were resentful of the restrictions applied to them. They required permits in order to travel, and envied our freedom to move unhindered throughout the Holy Land, their homeland. However, all felt safe on the university campus.

Although some of us nodded off in the comfy seats, we admired the young people and their determination to acquire a college education, and navigate the difficulties of living in a barricaded and war-conflicted land. Our group thanked them and Father Don for supplying us with this true and intimate look into the lives of young Palestinians.

Panel of students at Bethlehem University

Our next stop in Bethlehem was the Herodium, built and eponymously named by Herod the Great, the Roman client king of Judea, who reigned from 37-4 BCE. Although considered the greatest builder in Judeas's ancient history, as the designer of the expansion of the Second Temple in Jerusalem, of the port city of Caesarea Maritima, of the fortress at Masada, and of the circular fortress, Herodium, he was also a madman. He ordered the killing of many of his own family members, numerous rabbis, and the purported massacre of innocent Jewish baby boys (Matthew 2:16-23).

The Jewish historian, Flavius Josephus, documented the Herodium as the site of the entombment of Herod after his death in Jericho. In 2007, an archaeologist from Hebrew University claimed to have discovered Herod's tomb at the exact location described by Josephus. But in October 2013, other professors reasoned the tomb was too small and challenged the discovery. At this writing, I cannot find evidence that the dispute has been resolved.

To me, one of the more surprising aspects of this ancient land was how much history has still to be unearthed or discovered. Almost like in Europe, where all cathedrals begin to look alike, in Israel almost all tourist attractions look alike, due to a dig in progress. I think there are more Roman ruins in the Holy Land than in Italy.

After a long day touring Bethlehem's religious and secular sights, our last stop imprinted a lasting memory into my heart and consciousness. If I believed I had a soul, the sensation would be lodged there as well, for it was a spiritual happening.

In November, evening darkness curtains the Middle East by late afternoon. Shafik let us off at Manger Square at 5:00 p.m. Dusk surrounded us. Street and shop lights were turning on. At the top of the hill, our destination was the Church of the Nativity, the church built over the cave that Christians venerated as Christ's birthplace. We began our climb. Pealing church bells calling Christians to daily Mass intermingled in the night air with the mournful Muslim call to prayer, emanating from the muezzin's chant atop the minaret of the nearby Mosque of Omar.

At that moment in Bethlehem, hearing the adham summons from the tower and approaching Baby Jesus' birthplace, I hoped for a divine, metaphysical sign from God. If He were there, this would be the perfect time to poke me. I experienced chills and goose bumps in my physical self, but no awakening in my spiritual self. Once again, my prayer went unanswered, but the memory of that powerful moment lives within me.

After we had all arrived in the courtyard, we gathered around Father Don to listen to the history of the church. In 160 CE, St Justin Martyn first promoted this location as the birthplace of Christ. In 326, Emperor Constantine ordered the construction of a church at the site. Damaged by the Samaritans in 529, the church was rebuilt by Byzentine Emperor Justinian a century later. The Crusaders redecorated it in the 1100s; but in the 1500s, the Ottomans looted much of the valuable marble during their control of the Holy Land. Refurbished in1852, custody is now shared by the Roman Catholic, Greek Orthodox, and Armenian churches.

We stooped to enter the main door into the nave, known as the Door of Humility. The Crusaders reduced the door to its tiny size to prevent the Ottomans from pillaging, by driving their carts and horses through the original entrance. The opening is four feet high and two feet wide.

The Door of Humility at
the Church of the Nativity
Look closely and you can see the
original lintel over the opening.

We all bowed in humility as we entered through the door, still intact since the time of Justinian.

The wide nave dates to Justinian's era. Thirty of the forty-four pink limestone columns depict Crusader scenes of saints and the Virgin and Child. Most of the columns have been recycled from the original basilica. This magnificent ancient church is listed as a World Heritage Site, and is also listed on the UNESCO'S List of Heritage Sites in Danger ... I assume due to its location in Palestine's West Bank.

Nave of the Church of Nativity

Along with many other pilgrims in the basilica, we inched to the front of the church where we descended the narrow, curved staircase to the Grotto, the focal point of our visit. A silver star on the floor marked the spot where Mary had lain Christ at his birth. I enjoyed the pretense, but I did not believe I was actually standing at Christ's manger. I was not touched in the way that I had been walking up the hill, while listening to the chimes and chants, calling believers to devotion.

Silver star marking Christ's birthplace

Before returning to the bus in Manger Square, I made one last purchase at the Church of Nativity's shop, to remember my day in Bethlehem. I am not sure it is a genuine relic, but it is certified as soil from the Holy Land; perfect to use as a bookmark in my Holy Bible.

Certified package of soil from the Holy Land
(A small plastic bag containing the soil was attached by the staple.)

After returning to Hotel Zion, Nancy and I and our group met for cocktails and dinner … then an early evening, because we were leaving this hotel in the morning. We had instructions to place our bags outside our doors by 7:00 a.m. and to be on the bus at 8:00 a.m. Our itinerary for Wednesday included driving southeast to visit Qumran, Masada, and the Dead Sea. Then, after lunch, we faced a three and one-half hour bus ride to the Arava border crossing into Jordan.

Chapter Twenty

Miracle at the Jordan Border

On Wednesday, our visits to the Qumran National Park and the Masada National Park would highlight the morning's adventures. Then, a promise of lunch and a mud bath awaited us at Ein Bokek, a waterside resort on the Dead Sea. After the respite at the Dead Sea resort, Shafik would drive us about 130 miles to the Jordan border crossing at Arava. We would arrive after dark. At the border, both Nancy and I encountered serious, but unrelated problems ... both resolved by miracle or karma.

As a small and tourist-fueled economy, Israel regulates tourism through the Israeli Nature and Parks Authority, part of the Ministry of the Environment. Visitors may purchase a Green Pass 'For Tourists Only' for a fee of 150 NIS (New Israeli Shekel), approximately forty American dollars. This ticket entitles them admission to sixty-one Nature Reserves and National Parks, valid for fourteen days from the date of the first park visit. The symbol for the Authority is an ibex named Artsy. I purchased one of the stuffed mascots for my young granddaughter.

On the northwestern shore of the Dead Sea, our first stop of the morning was Qumran National Park, managed by the Israeli Park Authority. Here in 1947, while looking for a lost goat, a local Bedouin shepherd boy discovered the Dead Sea Scrolls hidden in a cave. After the initial discovery, Father R. de Vaux and his team of French archaeologists eventually excavated 190 linen-wrapped scrolls, preserved in jars (due to the arid climate) for over 2,000 years. Academics and rabbinical scholars continue to debate over the authors and meanings of the historical find.

Most agree that the Essenes, a Jewish sect, lived and studied at Qumran from 4 BCE to 6 CE. Two ancient scholars and authors, Flavius Josephus, and the Roman writer, Pliny the Younger, mentioned the Essenes in their writings. They lived an ascetic, reclusive, messianic and possibly celibate lifestyle. Although most historians attribute the scrolls to the Essenes, some skeptic scholars believe orthodox Jewish sects living in Jerusalem were responsible for the scrolls and hid them in the caves to protect the sacred writings from the Romans.

Artsy, ibex mascot of the Israeli Nature and Parks Authority

In my research, I read many facts about the Essenes. Two fascinated me: one profound and one scatological. Either could be true or false, but both are eminently notable. Similar to scientific "facts" that are updated through further discoveries, anthropologists change their interpretations when new historical evidence becomes known.

E. Planta Nesbit (1895) in his book, *Jesus, An Essene,* wrote that at the time of Jesus there were three Jewish sects, the Sadducees, the Pharisees, and the Essenes. Jesus often rebuked the Sadducees and the Pharisees, but never mentioned the Essenes by name. Flavius Josephus wrote that, during the time of Jesus, about 4,000 Essenes lived in Palestine. After reading this, I concluded that Jesus probably was an Essene, as his teachings and lifestyle fit with what I have read about the sect.

Accurate or not, the second revelation evokes an unforgettable image. Due to the Essenes' obsessive preoccupation with cleanliness, members refrained from defecation on the Sabbath.

At the Qumran Park archaeological site, we walked through the actual excavated rooms and workshops where the Essenes lived in a communal society. A map, given to us at the entrance, led us through the various areas, such as the scriptorium, the kitchen, the assembly hall, the pottery workshop, kiln, and cattle pen. The scrolls were found in the caves surrounding the settlement.

Remains of living quarters at Qumran

Caves at Qumran

Back on the bus, we drove south on Route 90 through the Jordan Rift Valley, with the Dead Sea and Jordan to the left, and date palms and Israel to the right. The Dead Sea is the lowest point on Earth at 1,300 feet below sea level. It drops one meter per year. The sea is mined for potash and magnesium.

During our thirty mile drive to our next destination at Masada, which means "fortress" in modern Hebrew, Father Don entertained and informed us about the history of the imposing mesa. It is such a popular tourist attraction, that a small airfield is located near the site. Masada was one of the few attractions on our pilgrimage familiar to me. In our book club we had read *The Dovekeepers*, a fictional novel based on the few women and children who escaped the slaughter by the Romans to report the massacre. One member of our book club had recently returned from a visit to Israel and reported about the spectacular site to us. It did not disappoint, except for the searing heat atop the plateau.

The cliffs at Masada rise 1300 feet above the Dead Sea to a plateau twenty acres in size. The Hasmoneans, a ruling dynasty of Judea between 240 BCE and 116 BCE, constructed the first fort at Masada to protect from invasion from the east. During his reign from 37 BCE to 4 BCE, Herod rebuilt and fortified the bastion for a winter palace, by adding bath houses, a swimming pool, store houses, an elaborate cistern system, and small guest palaces. The only entrance was via the narrow Snake Path that could be defended easily.

After the fall of Jerusalem in 70 CE, a group of 960 Jewish men, women, and children escaped to the fortress and defended it from the Romans for three years. The aforementioned novel, *The Dovekeepers* by Alice Hoffman, is an excellent fictional account of the historic episode. Her believable tale of three years of isolation and rebellion are substantiated by the historical record written by Josephus. After the Jews realized they could not defend the fortress any longer from the Romans, their leader, Eleazar Ben Yair, convinced his followers to end their own lives, as well as those of their families, rather than live as Roman slaves. According to Josephus, two women and five children hid in the cisterns and lived to tell the Romans what had happened on that first day of Passover, 73 or 74 CE.

Masada is maintained by the Park Authority with every amenity: guest house, sound and light show, two overnight campgrounds, restaurants, toilets, walking paths to the top, wheelchair access, and a cable car to the summit ... and quite possibly ibex sightings. We chose the three-minute cable car ride, as opposed to the forty-five minute climb up the Snake path, or the fifteen-minute walk up the Roman siege ramp.

First view of Masada from the bus window

Cable car at Masada

Niches for funerary urns of the ashes of non-Jewish members of Herod's court

Ruins at Masada

Exhausted and hungry after the hot morning tour atop the Masada plateau, we climbed aboard the bus for the short eight miles to the Dead Sea hotel and resort district at Ein Bokek. The Dead Sea is actually a hypersaline lake. Although toxic to fish, the lake has been valuable since the time of hunters and gatherers. Its Hebrew name, *Yam Hamelach,* means the Sea of Salt. In the Bible, it is the site where the Lord condemned the cities of Sodom and Gomorrah, and turned Lot's wife into a pillar of salt (Genesis 19:24-26). During the Roman occupation, they controlled the salt deposits at Mount Sodom just south of Ein Bokek, and Herod the Great built a resort spa in the area.

Dermatological professionals consider the rejuvenating minerals, revered for thousands of years, effective today. AHAVA and PREMIER are two retail brand names for the Dead Sea Natural Skin Care Products.

The famous Dead Sea black mud is a mixture of salts and minerals rich in magnesium, natural tar, and silicates. The mud bath softens and cleanses the skin, which produces a wonderful glow, while also stimulating blood circulation. Some of the more adventurous and younger among us were anxious to try a mud bath swim or float in the sea.

At the resort, Nancy and I ate our lunch on the seaside terrace and watched some of our fellow pilgrims coat themselves in the black mud before rinsing it off in the therapeutic waters. I did venture to the shore and waded in the warm waters. I was amazed by the sugar-cube-size blocks of salt that lined the shoreline, like shells along our seacoasts.

Me wading in the Dead Sea, note cubes of salt along the shoreline

Sharon and Kevin coated in Dead Sea mud

After lunch and a toe dip in the Dead Sea, Nancy and I settled into our seats for a long two-to-three-hour bus ride, to the border crossing at Arava. Father Don and some of the other seasoned travelers prepared the group for what to expect at the border.

First, the Israeli bus could not cross the border. So we were each responsible for transporting our own luggage through the check point. We were warned that there may or may not be luggage carts available at the crossing.

Second, have your passport in your hand and open to your photo at all times.

Third, be ready for possible baggage inspection.

Fourth, have a buddy watch your belongings while taking the bathroom break that we would all need at that point.

Fifth, stand by your luggage to identify it until it is loaded onto the Jordanian bus, before boarding the bus yourself.

Sixth, it will be dark, so try to be vigilant at all times.

Seventh, Father Don assured us he had never encountered any problems ... yet.

At Avara, Nancy and I were apprehensive, but not worried. We said "goodbye" to Shafik. We would not see him again until we boarded his bus at the northern crossing, at the Husseini Bridge Crossing on Saturday morning.

Hooray! There were luggage carts. Nancy and I became separated getting in line for the checkpoint crossing. Nancy was ahead of me.

When I placed my luggage on the conveyor belt and watched it glide forward toward inspection, I saw that up ahead Nancy was pulled aside and was being questioned by the authorities. Another woman from our group was with her and apparently helping her and calming her down. Also, Father Don and Anne Marie were by her side. So I was not too concerned. After my bags made it through the inspection with no problem, I restacked my luggage trolley and stood in a line again to push the cart across the actual border. I dutifully had my passport open in my hand. I kept looking down at the cart and counting my bags.

Suddenly, from behind me, two twenty-something Jordanian men tapped my shoulder and showed me a wallet open to a photo.

"Is this you?" said one in accented English.

I was immediately suspicious. Who were these guys? Why were they asking me if this were a photo of me? It was dark with very few lights in the area. I really couldn't see the picture.

"No, that isn't me," I said.

They seemed to stare at me for a few seconds, and then ran ahead to the next person in line. I looked down at my pile of luggage. I thought I had balanced my wallet atop my handbag, when I had pulled my passport from my wallet to have it ready for inspection. No wallet. At that second, I realized my mistake. It was my wallet that the young men had found.

I deserted my cart and chased after them yelling, "Yes, that's my wallet."

They ran back and gave it to me. They flipped it open to prove all the contents were still there. Before I had time to thank them and give them a reward, they took off running.

After I reached the safety of our group waiting by the new bus and started telling my miraculous story of the honesty of the two young Arabs,

Nancy arrived with her story. She thought she had lost her passport. She and the others had helped her search through all her belongings. Finally, one of them suggested she look in her jacket pocket. Voila! The passport!

By the time we had boarded the new bus and gone the five or six miles to our hotel in Aqaba, Jordan at the northern tip of the Red Sea, we were back to equilibrium, either by miracle or karma. And to our delight, an Arabian night spectacular awaited us at our Five Star accommodations, the Mövenpick Resort and Residences Hotel, on King Hussein Street.

After showering and donning fresh clothes, we joined the others for cocktails and a dinner show. Mature and young belly dancers, in traditional Arabian attire, swirled and gyrated among the tables, as we dined on lamb, fish, and exotic fruits.

Nancy and I rued one decision from that magical night. We had not ventured out of the hotel to view the Red Sea. The next morning at breakfast, Kevin and Sharon, or was her name Scheherazade, shared their tale of an Arabian Night swim in the Red Sea.

Chapter Twenty-One

Petra...Here We Come

Wednesday evening, belly dancers entertained us at our five-star hotel. Thursday morning, the breakfast fare surprised us. Along with eggs, bread, salads, and fruits, we dined on pork, ham, and bacon ... items definitely not on the menu at the Orthodox Jewish Hotel Zion in Jerusalem. We soon learned Jordan was its own country, with its own laws and traditions.

Father Don was no longer our only official guide. Jordanian law required all tours to hire a local guide. This practical regulation provided much needed jobs for their country's population. Also, the law mandated all tours with more than fifteen tourists in the group to hire an armed policeman to accompany them on the bus. For the next three days, Haitham, our Jordanian guide, and a policeman escorted us on our visits to Petra, Madabah, Mt. Nebo, Amman, and other sites in their native Jordan.

Before leaving the dining room, Father Don advised us to pack a lunch to bring with us to Petra. Our breakfast buffet offered many choices: cheese, meat, breads, fruits, and sweets. From experience, Father knew the lunch options inside the confines of ancient Petra were expensive and limited. With goody bags stashed in our backpacks, we boarded the new bus for the two-hour drive north to Petra. After Father led us in our morning prayer, Haitham manned the microphone.

He shared a few facts about himself and encouraged us to ask questions at any time. His ancestry was Bedouin. Unlike in Israel, where the Bedouins continued their nomad lifestyle, King Abdullah II built permanent housing for them. From the bus window, we viewed some of these communities. The reason for the flat roofs on most of the houses was practical. Land was expensive and families tended to live together. When a son or daughter married, the new generation built a house on top of the parents' house, who had built on top of their parents' house. So most structures looked unfinished, but in reality, they were houses-in-waiting.

As we rolled along the modern divided highway, Haitham corrected some of the previous misconceptions I held about the culture and history

A typical town in Jordan

of Jordan. I had thought the British created Jordan as an Arab country after WWI and the Lawrence of Arabia era. Actually, the Nabataeans, an Arabic people living in northern Arabia, built the city of Petra as the capital of their ancient Arab kingdom between 400 BCE and 160 CE. They controlled the trading from Syria to the Red Sea, but no exact boundaries defined their kingdom in the desert regions. Like the other nations in the area, the Nabataeans were conquered and ruled sequentially by the Romans, then the Ottomans, and eventually yes, the British.

Post WWI, Britain and France divided the Arab kingdoms. In 1922, the League of Nations recognized Transjordan as a state under a British Mandate. Abdullah I, who had collaborated with Lawrence of Arabia, was appointed Emir of Transjordan. In 1946, Jordan became an independent state, and Abdullah I ruled as king until his assassination in 1951 by a Palestinian. He was succeeded by his son, Talal, who soon abdicated, due to mental illness, to his son, King Hussein, who then ruled from 1952 until his death in 1999. Hussein was succeeded by his son, King Abdullah

II, the ruler of Jordan at the time of my visit. His Majesty is a forty-third generation descendent of the Prophet Muhammad.

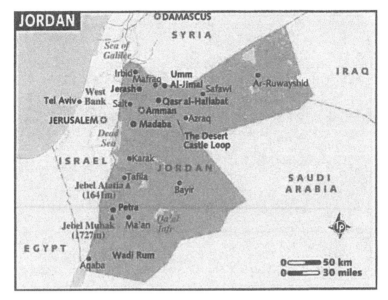

Map of Jordan, 2015

Besides telling us about the history of Jordan, Haitham discussed the geography, demographics, and culture of his country. Although the weather is normally hot and dry, Haitham loved telling us that it snowed in each of the last three years...global change, but not global warming! Jordan is about the same size as our state of Indiana, and has approximately 6.72 million residents with a literacy rate of over ninety percent. Jordan's capital city is Amman, with a population of over one million; its ethnicity is ninety-eight percent Arab; and its religion is ninety-two percent Sunni Islam and six percent Christian. Internationally, Jordan receives high marks for its willingness to accept both Christian and Islamic refugees fleeing persecution.

Concerning cultural observances, I asked Haitham, "Do the different colored scarfs worn by the Arab men have any clan or status significance?"

"No," he said. "The colors don't designate anything. The scarves are called *ghutras* and the rope tied around the head is called an *agal*. They're usually white, red and white, or black and white and are worn for protection from the sun and the sand."

From the bus window, the landscape was majestic, mountainous, and monotonous. I did not see one plant or tree for miles. Haitham told us that in the 1920s, the British destroyed five million trees for fuel to feed the steam engines of the trains they had brought with them.

The Jordanian desert on the road to Petra

We arrived at Petra at about 10:00 a.m. and left our luggage in the foyer of the Möevenpick Resort Petra, a five-star hotel situated near the entrance. My excitement was mounting. In 1985, Petra's world-wide acclaim earned it recognition as a UNESCO World Heritage Site. In 2007, in an online vote to choose the New Seven Wonders of the World, Petra placed second behind the Great Wall of China. Also, the *Smithsonian Magazine* listed Petra as "one of the twenty-eight places to see before you die."

After the ancient city was annexed by Rome in 106 CE, Petra's trade declined because the Romans used sea routes for trade, instead of land routes that normally passed through Petra. Then, an earthquake in 363 CE destroyed many buildings and the water system, and after another one in 551 CE, the Nabataeans abandoned the city. During the Middle Ages, the Byzantines used it for a provincial capital, and the Crusaders built fortresses in the area. But its existence and its ruins were ignored by the West, until its rediscovery by Swiss explorer John Ludwig Burckhardt in 1812.

Born Jean Louis Burckhardt in 1784, in Lausanne, Switzerland, he used the aliases John Lewis, Johann Ludwig, and even Sheikh Ibrahim Ibn Abdallah as a cover when searching for the lost city of Petra. An ardent adventurer, in 1809 he accepted a commission to discover the source of the Niger River in Africa, its third longest river. He spent three years preparing himself for the African expedition by studying Islam and Arabic, and also assuming the name and guise of a Muslim scholar, Ibraham Ibn

Abdallah. In 1812, on his way to Egypt, he passed through Jordan and heard rumors of a lost city in the mountains, hidden from Westerners.

With cunning and careful subterfuge, he persuaded a local guide to lead him to the city on the pretense of offering a sacrifice to the Prophet Aaron. He was the first to visit Petra from the West in almost a millennium. After news of his discovery was published in Europe, more adventurers trekked to the hidden city. Since daguerreotype photography was not invented until 1839, many explorers were also artists, and sketched their impressions of the buildings, ruins, and landscape seen in their travels. One of the more famous was a Scottish painter, David Roberts. His representations are so detailed and accurate, they appear the same as the photographs taken today.

El Deir (The Monastery) at Petra by David Roberts

Although I bought a guide book at a bookstore in Petra, the most complete information about Petra and Jordan can be found online in the book, *Jordan Jublilee*, which can be accessed at this internet address: www.jordanjubilee.com.

After gathering outside the hotel, Haithan told us that it was about a mile walk through the Siq to the Al-Khazneh el-Faroun or the Treasury of the Pharaoh, the most photographed of the temples at Petra. Its name, the Treasury, comes from Bedouin folklore. The locals believed gold or treasure was deposited inside the rock walls. However, the inner chamber is only fourteen square yards deep and houses an ablutions basin used in religious ceremonies. No treasure was found.

The Arabic word *siq* literally means "shaft." In some guide books it is defined as "passage." The Siq is the deep valley entrance through the rock facade into the ancient city of Petra. Haitham pointed to the many modes of transportation lined up at the entrance to transport tourists wishing to ride instead of walk. While Anne Marie paid our entrance fee, we eyed all the available transportation options:

Horse cart option

donkey rides, camel rides, horseback, horse cart, or motorized dune buggy. But, if we chose to ride, we would miss Haitham's and Father Don's informative talks along the way, so most of us chose to walk, including Nancy and me. If desired or necessary, we knew the rides would be available for our return trip.

Djinn blocks near the entrance to the Siq

So began our unforgettable visit to the ancient city of Petra. Even before we reached the Siq, we saw our first monument, the Blocks of Jinn or Djinn. These square blocks of stone are believed to be the earliest tombs in Petra. Prior to Islam, in Arabian folklore, jinns or djinns, were supernatural beings or genies. Early Nabataeans worshiped the god, Dushara, Arabic for "Lord of the Mountain," commonly represented by a block of stone. Twenty-six djinn blocks are found in and about Petra.

As we strolled down the slight decline through the Siq, we looked right, left, and skyward to view the height and structure of the rocks, which peaked at over 1,000 yards. The colors in the sandstone rock blended and changed into hues of red, black. blue, yellow, and white, depending on the light, or time of day. My words cannot convey the beauty of the topographical formations created or carved either by wind, water, or man, from the mountains in the desert city of Petra. Only by pictures can I share the wonder of these sights.

Walking through the Siq

Haitham would stop and wait for stragglers to point out the monuments and water channels along the edge of the lower rock formations. Due to the natural slope of the Siq, the Nabataeans devised an aqueduct system. We marveled at the ingenuity of the water troughs as we walked along.

Water troughs along the edges of the Siq

After more than a mile's trudge, scrunching through the red sand of the Siq, Father Don took the mike from Haithan and said, "Stop. Turn around, gather close to me, and close your eyes. When I tell you, turn and open your eyes."

"Turn! Open!"

Pictured below is the awesome sight!

The first view of the Treasury though the narrow entrance from the Siq

Our group in front of the Treasury: Nancy, third from left, second row, me in black hat, back row, Haitham, second from left, front row

In front of the Treasury, our walking group reunited with our other members, who had taken buggies or camels through the passage into the square. An Arab hustler gathered us together for the traditional photo in front of the Treasury. Other Arab hawkers persuaded Nancy to ride a camel. I had ridden one in Morocco years ago and never again would I sit atop one of those nasty beasts.

Nancy atop one of the nasty beasts

Lower town of Petra

The Monastery at Petra

After our group picture, we were on our own to explore and return to the hotel on our own time. Father Don pointed us in the direction of the lower town, another one-half mile further into the basin. This area was where the town of Petra once prospered. Today there were souvenir shops, rest rooms, and a small restaurant, where we ate our bag lunch and bought drinks. I ordered a delicious, cold pomegranate juice drink.

Some of the younger members of our group elected to climb the 800 steps to visit the Monastery. This structure was built in the same architectural style as the Treasury. It was built in 1 CE for King Obodas I, who had achieved many military victories. The Byzantines used it during their reign, thus its name. It is one of the largest facades in Petra, at fifty-three yards in height and fifty-two yards in width. To me, from pictures, the Treasury and the Monastery look to be the same building.

It was 3 p.m. Nancy and I were tired, hot, covered with red dust, and ready for a bath. We began the long uphill trek back to our hotel. After conferring with friends who took the buggy ride, we decided walking was the safest method of transportation. One older couple who had ridden by buggy had clung on in terror. No seat belts, of course, and the quicker the driver could deliver you, the sooner he could barter for another fare.

With water bottle in hand, we trudged homeward. We discovered that even walking through the Siq was dangerous. At some sections of the passage, it was only three yards in width ... impossible for walker and buggy to pass at the same time. We learned to climb up on the water channel and let the driver and horse cart pass ... the only way to stay alive!

That evening, at cocktail hour and dinner, our group of awestruck, tired pilgrims agreed to a universal consensus of the day—Petra epitomized the Grand Canyon, the Rocky Mountains, and Disney World in one.

Buggy racing through the narrow Siq

Chapter Twenty-Two

Tour of Jordan

Our twelve-day tour of the Holy Land was half over. We had visited Petra on the sixth day of our pilgrimage. Today, Friday November 14, the seventh day, our schedule included three religious stops along the Desert Highway on our way to Jordan's capital, Amman, a distance of approximately 175 miles. The sites were Shobak Castle, Madaba, and Mount Nebo, where Father Don would celebrate the Eucharist. In Madaba, Father Don promised a stop at the Madaba Arts & Handicraft Center. This factory store trains the locals in the intricate, ancient art of mosaic design. The items produced range from table coasters to patio tables. I was sure I would find some type of souvenir inlaid with colorful mosaic tiles depicting pomegranates to bring home to Connie.

Leaving Petra, Haitham arranged for our policeman guard to meet the bus on the highway near his hometown of Wadi Musa. As we waited for him, Father Don led us in our morning prayer and then handed the mike over to Haitham. After our guard arrived and hopped on the bus, we were underway again. Haitham spent the thirty mile ride to Shobak Castle telling us about Jordanian daily life and its traditions, old and new.

Contrary to what many Westerners believe, marriages are not arranged. That custom ended more than thirty years ago. Women marry between twenty-eight and thirty years old, and men between thirty-eight and forty years old. Most couples have two to three children, not the ten to fifteen children common as recently as thirty years ago. Muslims may divorce, but Christians don't divorce. There are no civil marriages, only religious marriages. Islam allows men to have more than one wife, but few do. Most Jordanian women work, but do not serve in the military.

I tried to write down all the facts Haitham was telling us, but I could not write fast enough. This was information I could not read in a guide book. My notes were jotted down in poor handwriting in abbreviated phrases, cascading down the page, one isolated comment after another. I have no orderly way to organize his remarks, but they are worth repeating as a mélange of truths and myths from a genuine Bedouin. Pretend you are sitting on the bus with me and listening to the words of Haitham.

Jordan is a poor but stable country. We use nuclear power for electricity and buy some from other countries. Phosphate mining and cement production are major industries. Tourism is dying. Relatives from outside Jordan send money home. We like American movies. Jordan has very good hospitals and health insurance is free. The relations between Israel and Jordan are still not good, although peace was negotiated in 1995. We have peace in our hearts.

We eat camel meat and milk, but not goat meat. Camels can drink fifteen liters of water at one time, which sustains them for four to five days. We race horses and camels. Only the one hump species, the dromedary, is used for racing. Camels live an average of eighteen years.

As we approached Shobak castle, Father Don took over the microphone to give us some historical background. Also called, Krak de Montréal, the castle outpost was built in 1115 by the Crusader King Baldwin I of Jerusalem to guard the road from Egypt to Damascus. Although a magnificent fortress, it fell into ruins in only seventy-five years to the armies of Saladin in 1189.

Shobak Castle seen as a photo-op from the highway

Back on the road again to drive to Madaba, a distance of eighty-five miles, Father Don had time to give us the biblical and historical story of the Madaba Mosaic Map visited by up to a thousand tourists a day.

The Old Testament refers to the city of Madaba as a Moabite city conquered by the tribes of Israel (Numbers 21:30; Joshua 13:90). Like many other areas in the Middle-East, the Romans ruled the district in the first centuries of the Common Era, but by 4CE, Madaba had become a Christian city with its own bishop. Then, in turn, Persians, Muslims, and Mamelukes invaded and conquered the town. Eventually, by the 1600s the beleaguered inhabitants abandoned Madaba. In 1880 a group of Christians moved from Karak, a mountain city located about twenty-five miles south along the Desert Highway, to the deserted town to acquire more religious freedom. At that time, Muslim rulers allowed Christians to build new churches, but only on top of the locations of former ones. While clearing debris in preparation for constructing a new holy structure, the Christians uncovered the mosaic map. The workmen saved and incorporated it into the floor of the new St. George's Church. Ten years later archaeologists recognized its value as a mosaic designed during the reign of Justinian (527-65 CE).

Madaba is sometimes called the "white city" because its buildings are made from white stone. An Archaeological Park in the center of the city encompasses St. George's Church and several other sixth century churches, which also house archaic mosaic scenes.

Upon arrival at St. George's Church, Father Don ushered us into the outer chamber of the church where there was a reproduction of the map on the wall. Historians agree the map is accurate for its time and corresponds to modern cartography. The depiction of Jerusalem is enlarged in a separate illustration at the lower left of the display. In this enlarged square map of Jerusalem, the Zion Gate, the Damascus Gate,

Copy of the Madaba Mosaic Map with Father Don and Jerusalem map at left

the Church of the Holy Sepulchre, and the Basilica on Mount Zion are clearly recognizable. The map itself portrays the Jordan River, the Dead

Sea, Jericho, Bethlehem, Gaza, Mount Sinai, and the city of Karak. A total of over two million tesserae comprise the mosaic.

After marveling at the geographical knowledge and workmanship required to make such a map from tiny colored stones, we were eager to visit the Madaba Arts & Handicraft Center to learn more about the artistic and painstaking work involved in the craft of mosaics.

The well-run workshop impressed us all, even though I did not see one mosaic pomegranate in the entire shop. Father Don told me to have patience. He knew of a shop in Jerusalem that specialized in pomegranate artifacts and would take me there on our last day in the Holy City.

Before viewing the walls lined with mosaic plaques and other mosaic items for sale, we entered the working area of the establishment where the stones used in the productions were stored and where the students and artists worked. We learned Mosaic Design 101.

All mosaics have been made in the same way by hand for centuries. The tesserae, the small blocks of stone, tile, or glass are chipped from a larger piece with a tile nipper and placed onto a design or drawing. Once the composition is completed the tiles are glued down leaving small gaps between each individual piece. The pattern from the gaps is part of the design. After the adhesive is dry, the gaps are filled with grout. To do this, smear the

Woman making mosaics in the Madaba factory

grout over the entire picture using a rubber squeegee to fill in the cracks. Then, clean the grout off the tiles with a damp sponge. When dry, wipe off any grout residue. Voilà, your mosaic is finished after five months of intense but satisfying labor.

Next, we walked into the sales area where the walls were covered with thousands of intricate mosaic designs, but not one pomegranate among them. The most popular motif seemed to be the representation of the Arabic Tree of Life. The Tree of Life is a world-wide and historic symbol which is portrayed by different themes and images depending on the country. The Arabian design symbolized the tree of life as giving life to deer who in turn gave life to lions. Could it be a pomegranate tree?

Traditional design of the Arabian Tree of Life

Nancy and I did not buy any mosaics, as the handmade items were very expensive and alas there were no pomegranate designs. But one shopper in our group purchased a large patio table for about $4,000 that included shipment to his home in the States. Then lunch, before the short six-mile jaunt to Mount Nebo.

According to the Old Testament, at the summit of Mount Nebo, Moses viewed the Promised Land as described to him by God, but died before reaching it (Deuteronomy 34: 1-12). We viewed the Jordan River and the Dead Sea far below us from atop the outlook which rose 3,500 feet above the valley. A directional map posted on the outlook railing indicated the locations of the Dead Sea, Bethlehem, the Mount of Olives at Jerusalem, and Jericho among some other places that we could see in the distance.

Before entering the Mount Nebo Church to observe Mass, we admired the Brazen Serpent Monument, a serpentine cross sculptured by Italian artist, Giovanni Fantoni. The piece symbolized the bronze serpent created by Moses in the Wilderness (Numbers 21:4-9), and also the cross upon which Christ was crucified (John 3:14).

Directional map posted at Mount Nebo

After Father Don celebrated Mass and the Eucharist we boarded the bus for the last leg of the trip to Amman, the modern capital city of Jordan. Haitham seemed to know we wanted to rest and close our eyes so he ended his lectures for the day with a bit of Jordanian wisdom and wit.

"We Jordanians," he said, "know to be prepared, to be cautious, and to count to ten before acting. So when jumping out of a plane, we always have a parachute, and we always remember to count to ten before pulling the cord. But...we hit the ground in seven seconds. That is the Jordanian way."

Mulling over the meaning of this metaphorical maxim, I nodded off, not to wake until we pulled into the entrance to our accommodations for the night, the five-star Hotel Le Meridien on Queen Noor Street, Amman, Jordan, where a genuine Turkish steam bath awaited adventurous, weary pilgrims. I did not indulge.

Brazen Serpent Monument atop Mount Nebo

Chapter Twenty-Three

Good-bye Jordan, Hello Miracle in Israel

On Saturday morning, November 15, after enjoying another sumptuous breakfast spread, including bacon and ham, we boarded the bus for Haitham's Tour of Amman. Father Don suggested we eat hearty because we would not stop for lunch until we arrived back in Israel. He warned us that sometimes the border crossing could last two hours or more, depending on the number of buses at the checkpoint.

I snapped this photo of Hotel Le Meridien as we pulled away.

Hotel Le Meridien, Amman, Jordan

In contrast to our lively farewell toasts to Jordan the previous evening, Father Don added a reflective recital of Psalm 139 to our morning prayers. The only psalm I knew was the Twenty-third Psalm, very familiar to most Christians, which begins "The Lord is my shepherd; I shall not want."

All of the 150 psalms in the Old Testament praise the Lord or seek help from Him, as did this chosen selection. The main subject of Psalm 139 is God's constant presence wherever you may be, which made it appropriate for us traveling pilgrims. However, one of the places where God followed us surprised me and seemed to contradict traditional scripture. I would have liked Father Don to explain it to me, but I was too shy and too ignorant of liturgy to ask him. Here it is for you to ponder too. In the passage "thou" refers to God: "If I ascend up into heaven, thou art there; if I make my bed in hell, behold, thou art there." I wanted to know why would God be in hell?

After prayers, Haitham manned the mike again. As we traveled through the modern city of Amman, Haitham delivered historical facts and his own personal commentaries on life in Amman. Amman is a liberal, westernized modern Arab city with an estimated population of four million residents.

Haitham told us that a cup of coffee, depending on whether you bought it in a poor section or a rich section of the city, could cost either one dollar or four dollars. We were traveling in the high-rent district with potted topiary trees displayed on the sidewalks.

City street in Amman, Jordan

The city of Amman dates back to 7250 BCE which makes it one of the oldest continually inhabited cities in the world. Originally built on seven hills, it now encompasses nineteen hills consisting of twenty-seven districts. East Amman contains most of the historical sites, while West Amman is the economic center of the city. The Romans conquered the area in 68 BCE and many ruins remain. One of their large amphitheaters could seat 6,000 spectators and is still in use today.

Poster of King Abdullah II attached to an electric pole in Amman

As we drove out of Amman on our way to the highway, we noticed huge poster photographs of King Abdullah II attached to the electric poles.

Once on the highway, on our way to the border check point at the Hussein Bridge crossing, we traveled for about fifty miles through the Jordan Valley, an extension of the Great Riff Valley of Africa. We viewed many groves of orange, lemon, and grapefruit trees on the fertile land along the Jordan River. Haitham bragged that Jordanian strawberries were the best in the world. Vegetables are also grown in the valley. From the bus windows we saw tents of sheer fabric stretched over the growing produce to protect it from the heat.

Seemingly out of place in the middle of the fields was a large mosque. No towns or settlements were near the modern holy building.

We were all wondering whether our crossing would be hassle free. It was noontime and we were looking forward to lunch and a restroom break. When we arrived at the border procedures and necessities took over.

First, we unloaded our bags from the bus, dragged them to the X-ray machines, and then dragged them back to the bus to be reloaded. Next, we headed to the bathroom facilities to find toilets. Alas with no seats and no toilet paper. Then, we entered the police station to have our passports checked and confiscated. They would be returned to us on the Israeli side.

Modern mosque along the highway in the Jordan Valley

One more ride on the Jordanian bus to the Israeli border. We exited that bus for the last time, thanked Haitham, and said goodbye.

On the Israeli side, after retrieving our passports, we repeated the luggage drill. We identified our bags and placed them on the conveyor belt for an X-ray check. We too passed through an X-ray machine, similar to those at our airports. Then, our passports were checked by the Israeli border patrol. Next, we were questioned about any books we had in our possession. I later learned that contraband was often smuggled across borders in hollowed-out books. Security was thorough because we were entering into Israel near Palestinian Territories in the West Bank—territories occupied by Israel since the Six-Day War of 1967.

We had begun the check point inspections at noon. It was now 1:15 p.m. as we boarded our familiar bus with Shafik at the wheel. Not quite a quick crossing, but Father Don assured us we had been lucky in our timing. Not knowing how long the border questioning would take, Father Don had called ahead to Shafik and instructed him to purchase pizzas and soft drinks for our lunch. Shafik drove us to a public park with tables, benches, and modern restrooms. We shared the shady spot with young, Jewish families enjoying a Sabbath afternoon outing.

The next adventure on our agenda was a visit to nearby Bet Shean, often billed as the best-preserved Roman-Byzantine town in Israel. For me and my notebook, the site proved miracles still happen in twenty-first century Israel.

The town, first inhabited more than 5,000 years ago, prospered as a trading stop along the route between the Mediterranean Sea and Mesopotamia, the region now known as Iraq, Syria, and Kuwait. Like most of the cities in the Middle-East, Bet Shean passed through many occupations, including Egyptians, Canaanites, Greeks, Romans, Byzantines, Arabs, Crusaders, Mamluks, Ottomans, and yes the British. After fights between Jewish and Bedouin forces during the 1948 Arab-Israel War, the city of 17,000 citizens became an established municipality within the Israeli state of Galilee.

Half a mile north of town, the Bet Shean National Park administers a large archaeological tell and two significant Roman-Byzantine sites. A short distance from the entrance, Father Don led us to the almost perfectly preserved Roman theater capable of seating 7,000 spectators. We filed into the rows and settled down on the stone seats. Father Don stood and faced us to lecture on the ruins we would see in the complex. Behind him, we could see columns lining the Roman cardo or main commercial thoroughfare, a shopping mecca in ancient times. In the distance was the flat- topped conical archaeological tell, or mound. I pulled my notebook from my backpack and began writing.

Soon, Father Don was on the move again. He planned to lead us along the cardo and to the tell. Anne Marie suggested that those who did not want to walk the mile or so to the other sites could stay at the theater and the group would meet them on the way back. I was the only one of our group who decided to stay seated in the theater in order to catch up on my journal writing. Several other groups and individuals sat near me.

Roman theater with Roman cardo and archaeological tell in the distance

After about ten minutes of writing, I could see our group walking up the cardo. I decided I could catch them. So I jumped up and hurried after them. It was a longer walk than I had anticipated. I did not catch up with them, but met them as they were coming back. Nancy said all I missed was more Roman ruins.

Back on the bus, Father Don announced the next stop was Bet Alpha, only seven miles west. This was the site of a sixth century synagogue discovered in 1928 when a local kibbutz was plowing its fields for planting. It is amazing to me how many religious sites, towns, and antiquities are still being discovered in the twenty-first century in Israel.

Father Don began talking about the magnificent mosaic tile patterns found largely intact on the floors of the ruined building. The upper floor section depicted the Ark of the Covenant. The middle section was a Jewish adaption of the Greco-Roman zodiac wheel. Historians surmised that Judaism combined pagan symbols of the seasons with Hebrew labels. The lower floor told the story of Abraham being asked to sacrifice his son Isaac.

While Father Don was talking, I reached into my backpack to retrieve my notebook. No notebook. I became frantic. I pulled everything out, looked on the floor and behind me in my seat. I could not find the notebook. Eventually, I realized I must have left the journal on the seat of the Roman theater when I jumped up to race after the group. I had to have that notebook. How could I remember everything? I needed the information to write this book.

I climbed over Nancy who was sitting in the aisle seat and rushed to the front of the bus where Father Don was sitting next to Anne Marie and talking on the microphone. I'm sure Father Don realized I was in some kind of distress and interrupted his lecture to listen to me.

"Father Don, I hope you can help me. I can't find my notebook in my backpack. I think I left it on the seats at the theater at Bet Shean. Since we just left there, could we please go back so I could look for it? I have to have that notebook."

I knew Father Don had seen me constantly writing in its pages. His kind eyes conveyed a message of empathy. I felt he and Anne Marie wanted to help me. Everyone on the bus was wondering what the problem was. I was wondering if we would turn back.

Father Don retook the mike, "Judy has a problem that I think we can help her with. She thinks she left her notebook back on the seats at Bet Shean. This is what we can do. We'll continue on to Bet Alpha. We'll only be there for about half an hour. Then we'll have Shafik drive back to Bet Shean and we can ask at the ticket counter if anyone turned in a small, black and white-polka-dotted notebook. We have plenty of time.

In fact, we have time to kill because we can't arrive at the kibbutz before sunset on the Sabbath. Is that agreeable to everyone?"

Everyone agreed.

On the way back to my seat most of the group encouraged me saying: "Someone will have turned it in."

"No one would steal a notebook."

"You'll find it."

Soon, we arrived at Bet Alpha, run by the Israel Nature and Parks Authority. We saw more ruins and more archaeological areas cordoned off due to work in progress. All of Israel seemed to be one big dig. More ruins or not, the ancient mosaics were worth seeing. The panels reminded me of Egyptian artwork or of Grandma Moses primitives as the

The binding of Isaac

figures were one-dimensional. The comprehensive brochure handed to us at the entrance helped me interpret the mosaic painting at my feet.

The mosaic panel above depicts the "Binding of Isaac" (Genesis 22:1-18), the biblical story where God asks Abraham to sacrifice his son as a burnt offering to Him. At the right in the drawing is Abraham dangling Isaac over the fire as he raises his hand to perform the sacrifice. In the center, God symbolized by the hand, instructs Abraham to sacrifice the ram (pictured in the middle of the drawing) instead of Isaac. On the left are the two servants who accompanied Abraham and Isaac. I learned from reading the pamphlet that the "Binding of Isaac" was also a popular theme in early Christian art as a pre-figuration for the crucifixion. I learned from the internet that the Binding of Isaac was a popular 2011 video game. It resurfaced in 2015 as the Binding of Isaac: Rebirth.

After the visit, Shafik retraced the bus route back to Bet Shean—either to be a miracle mission or a waste of time. I was hopeful, but not optimistic. If I had actually left the notebook on the seats, we had been gone for more than an hour.

Father Don, Anne Marie, and Nancy hurried to the admission counter with me.

"No, sorry, no notebook of any kind has been turned in. However, if you would like, we will let you back in, and you can look on the seats where you were sitting."

Uttering apologies, the four of us scurried pass the people standing in line for admittance.

As we entered the stadium and descended the steps, we saw something lying on the stones where we had been sitting.

A miracle! It was my small, polka-dotted pocket notebook!

When we climbed aboard the bus, all the group cheered as I waved the journal in the air.

Even after backtracking to retrieve my lost notebook, Father Don had time to reschedule our itinerary. As it was the Sabbath, we could not check into our lodgings at the orthodox Kibbutz Lavi Hotel at Tiberias until after sundown. No work was allowed on the Sabbath, which began at nightfall on Fridays and ran until after sundown on Saturdays. So instead of visiting Nazareth on Monday, as originally planned, we drove there today.

The well-known Biblical city of Nazareth is often called the Arab capital of Israel. The population is sixty-nine percent Arab Muslims and thirty percent Arab Christians. In 1957 Jewish colonists founded a district just to the north of the city, called Nazareth Illit. Although never mentioned in the Old Testament, Nazareth is the town where Jesus lived as a young boy with his parents, Joseph and Mary (Matthew 2:21-23).

The focal point of the city is the Church of the Annunciation, built in 1969. This imposing modern church is the fifth church built over the site considered to be the place where the Angel Gabriel appeared to Mary to announce the birth of Christ. The lower level preserves the Holy Grotto, while the upper level serves as the major Catholic church of Nazareth.

Very near the basilica is the Church of St. Joseph, rebuilt in 1914, and purported to be the site of Joseph's house and carpentry workshop.

After visiting the traditional Christian holy sites, we boarded the bus for the twenty mile drive to Tiberias and the Kibbutz Lavi Hotel, our accommodations for the next three nights. Father Don wanted us to enjoy the flavor of luxury hotels as well as experience a stay at a kibbutz. I was curious to see the difference and to experience life in a kibbutz.

Tiberias is the largest town on the Sea of Galilee or Lake Tiberias. The body of water is the chief source of water for Israel and is fed and drained by the Jordan River. The area is a popular resort destination for Israeli citizens with many hotels and outdoor activities.

As we drove into the kibbutz complex along a well-maintained road, my first impression was very favorable. The hotel was a large, four-story, white concrete building similar to many hotels in Mid-Eastern cities. The Sabbath restrictions were over and the Jewish guests were checking out. Many of the men sported curled locks or peyos, and beards. The Torah forbids the use of a razor. The women were modestly dressed and most wore head coverings.

Once inside, my initial impression of the hotel radically changed. The lobby was sparsely furnished with no cocktail lounge. Moving very slowly through the reception area, a very old, very humpbacked cleaning woman pushed a very large trash container on wheels. Due to the many departures occurring at sundown, we waited a considerable time for our turn at the registration counter.

Upon entering our room, Nancy and I changed our impression again. The bedroom and bathroom were modern and clean with all the amenities offered in five-star hotels. We attempted to turn on the flat screen TV with no luck. We called room service. Soon a young man appeared at the door. Father Don had warned us that most of the staff did not speak English. The maintenance employee showed us how to operate the clicker with hand gestures, no words. The channel he selected for us was CNN with the announcer reading the news in English.

Then he said, "I'm sorry but we have no English-speaking channels here."

Nancy and I stared at each other in amusement.

The next surprise was the dining room. We were required to check in with the hostess who directed us to the tables reserved for Father Don's group. The room looked like a typical college dining commons with long rows of tables and chairs. Our group's table assignment was in the back. The service was buffet-style as it had been in all the hotels, but no table service at all. We had to go to the wine station to purchase white or red Israeli wine and charge it to our room. The food itself was good and similar to the fare served on the rest of our trip.

The Kibbutz Lavi Hotel in Tiberias

After dinner, Nancy and I relaxed in our room. I decided to write in my "miracle" journal. I flipped through the pages to review our day and found an entry not in my handwriting. A mysterious cryptic message appeared on the page where I had stopped writing and subsequently left the journal on the stone seats at Bet Shean.

> *You people of the book*
> *are wrong*
> *church bells & mineret*
> *at same time for 5 pm*

I showed it to Nancy and we tried to figure out who had written it, when it was written, and why it was written. We knew Muslims referred to "people of the book" as either Christians or Jews. So we surmised the answer to the "who" was a Muslim. The "when" must have been after I had left the book on the seats at Bet Shean. But the "why" stumped us. Had the author read in my journal where I had written about the sounds of the church bells and minaret chants mingling in Bethlehem at 5:00 p.m.? If so, then why did the writer claim "the people of the book" were wrong, since we agreed to the same 5:00 p.m. time for the sonorous calls to prayer? Nancy and I never did solve the question of "why."

Some might say only God knows the reason for the improbable miracle recovery of my notebook, and the reason for the curious, mysterious notation in that same notebook on that Sabbath Saturday, November 15, 2014, in the Holy Land of Israel.

Chapter Twenty-Four

Jesus' Ministries on the Sea of Galilee

On Sunday, November sixteenth, the ninth day of our tour, Father Don planned visits to locations near the Sea of Galilee, some of them familiar to Nancy and me through Bible stories. Later, when we recalled our trip, Nancy declared this was her favorite day, instead of her much anticipated visit to Petra. My favorite memory was the evening stroll climbing up the hill to the Basilica of the Nativity in the West Bank city of Bethlehem with the church bells tolling and the muezzin chanting from atop the minaret.

The Galilee is the true home of Jesus' ministries. Jesus was born in Bethlehem, lived his early years in Nazareth, but preached his sermons and performed his miracles around the shores of the Sea of Galilee, also known as Lake Tiberias or Lake Kinneret. Kinneret is an ancient word for "lyre." The shape of the lake reminded the Israelis of King David's musical instrument.

Once on the bus, Father Don outlined our itinerary for the day. We would circle the Sea of Galilee. The sea is actually the largest fresh-water lake in Israel. It is thirteen miles long, seven and a half miles wide, and fifty meters deep. Today and since biblical times, the lake has been famous for its abundance of fish.

The morning began at the Mount of the Beatitudes and ended in the Golan Heights at the Peace Outlook, overlooking Syria. Sunday Mass would be at 11:00 a.m. at Capernaum, an important shoreline town where a distinctive, modern church rests atop the historically documented ruins of the house of Jesus' disciple Simon Peter. For lunch we would stop at Ali's restaurant for St. Peter's fish, a traditional tourist treat.

Map of the Sea of Galilee [1]

Early on that beautiful Sunday morning the bus rolled out the gates of the kibbutz and headed north for about seven miles to Tabgha, derived from the Greek name Haptapegon, which means Seven Springs. In ancient times all seven water sources flowed into the Sea of Galilee. Today there are but five springs.

Our first stop was at the Church of the Beatitudes, built on the hill purported to be where Christ gave his Sermon on the Mount. The beatitudes are the eight blessings which Christ taught to his disciples and the multitudes as they gathered around Him (Matthew 5:3-11). Almost one year later, in remembering our trip Nancy wrote, "The most moving moment for me that I will never forget was when we were standing at the wall looking down over the hill and the lake and Father Senior read the Sermon on the Mount."

View of Lake Galilee from the hill as we listened to the Sermon on the Mount

Some, if not all of the Beatitudes, are familiar blessings known by Christians and non-Christians alike, either from the Bible or Western literature. Whether a believer in God and his teachings or not, I think the beauty of the Books of the Old and New Testaments appeals to all lovers of the language of poetry.

Blessed are the poor in spirit: for theirs is the kingdom of heaven.
Blessed are they that mourn: for they shall be comforted.
Blessed are the meek: for they shall inherit the earth.
Blessed are they which do hunger and thirst after righteousness: for they shall be filled.
Blessed are the merciful: for they shall obtain mercy.
Blessed are the pure in heart: for they shall see God.
Blessed are the peacemakers: for they shall be called the children of God.
Blessed are they which are persecuted for righteousness' sake: for theirs is the kingdom of heaven.
And Blessed are ye, when men shall revile you, and persecute you, and shall say all manner of evil against you false, for my sake.

Although biblical historians cannot prove this site is the exact spot of the Sermon on the Mount, pilgrims have been gathering here since the fourth century. The current church was built near the remains of a small church dating from 4 CE. The modern Church of the Beatitudes was constructed in 1938 by the Franciscan Sisters with support from the Italian ruler Mussolini. It was built as an octagon to represent the eight beatitudes.

Church of the Beatitudes

Nearby, we also visited the Church of the Multiplications of the Loaves and Fishes built in 1980. This is considered to be the site where Jesus performed the miracle of feeding five thousand people with five loaves of bread and two fish (Luke 9:13).

In the same vicinity was the Church of the Primacy of Peter. A black basalt Franciscan church built in 1943 on the spot where Jesus is said to have appeared to his apostles for the third time after his resurrection (John 21:1). Father Don chose this sacred site to expand on the story of the apostle Simon Peter. The Roman Catholic Church considers Peter to be the first Pope. In (Matthew 16:18), Jesus ordained Peter as the rock on which his Church would be built. Catholics claim the Primacy of the Pope dates from this anointment of Peter as head

The Church of the Primacy of Peter along the shores of the Sea of Galilee

of the new Church. Protestants believe the Primacy of Peter existed only during his lifetime.

The chart below lists the five popes of the first century in chronological order, beginning with Peter. The complete list of popes is published every year in the *Annuario Pontificio* by the Roman Curia, the administrative office of the Holy See, or the Vatican.

Pontiff number	Pontificate	Portrait	Name: English · Latin	Personal name	Place of birth	Age at start/ end of papacy	Notes
1	1 April 33 – 29 June 67 (34 years, 89 days)		St Peter PETRUS	Šim'ōn Kêpâ (Simon Peter)	Bethsaida, Galilea, Roman Empire	32 / 66	Greek Jew. Apostle of Jesus from whom he received the keys of the Kingdom of Heaven, according to Matthew 16.18–19⑨. Executed by crucifixion upside-down; feast day (Feast of Saints Peter and Paul) 29 June, (Chair of Saint Peter) 22 February. He is recognized by the Catholic Church as the first Bishop of Rome appointed by Christ. Also revered as saint in Eastern Christianity, with a feast day of 29 June.[4] The St. Peter's Basilica in Vatican City is named after him.
2	29 June 67 – 23 September 76 (9 years, 86 days)		St Linus Papa LINUS	Linus	Volterra, Italia, Roman Empire	57 / 66	First Roman pope. Feast day 23 September. Also revered as a saint in Eastern Christianity, with a feast day of 7 June.
3	23 September 76 – 26 April 88 (11 years, 216 days)		St Anacletus (Cletus) Papa ANACLETUS (Cletus)	Anáklitos (Klítos)	Athens, Greece, Roman Empire	51 / 63	First Greek pope. Martyred; feast day 26 April. Once erroneously split into Cletus and Anacletus.[6]
4	26 April 88 – 23 November 99 (11 years, 211 days)		St Clement I Papa CLEMENS	Clemens	Rome, Roman Empire	53 / 64	Roman. Feast day 23 November. Issued 1 Clement which is said to be the basis of apostolic authority for the clergy. Also revered as a saint in Eastern Christianity, with a feast day of 25 November.
5	23 November 99 – 27 October 107 (7 years, 338 days)		St Evaristus Papa EVARISTUS	Eváristos	Bethlehem, Judea, Roman Empire	49 / 55	Greek Jew. Said to have divided Rome into parishes, assigning a priest to each. Feast day of 26 October.

Chart of first century popes beginning with Peter [2]

Before joining Shafik on the bus, for the ride to Capharnaum where Father Don would celebrate the Sunday Eucharist, we dipped our toes or fingers into the warm water of the Sea of Galilee.

Two miles north of Tabgha we reached the town of Capharnaum, proudly declaring itself as the town of Jesus. Here Jesus gathered his first disciples—Peter, Andrew, James, John, and Matthew. Here he performed many miracles—healing Peter's wife's mother of a fever, bringing a child

Our group on the rocky shores of Galilee

back to life, curing a leper, casting out the spirits with his word, and healing all that were sick (Matthew 8:16).

Father Don hurried us along to our destination. Sunday Mass was scheduled at the modern Church of St. Peter built in 1990 over the remains of Peter's house, one of the few biblical locations believed to be the authentic site by most historians. From the first floor of the church we looked down

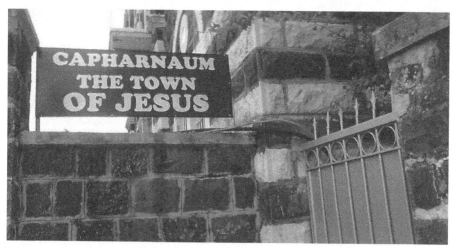

Gate to the town of Capharnaum

into the excavation site of Peter's home, the house where Jesus often resided during his visits to Capharnaum.

After Mass we explored the ruins of the White Synagogue, a two-story structure of white limestone built in the third century over the synagogue where biblical scholars believe Jesus preached in the first century. The ancient town often mentioned in the Bible was an impressive sight (Matthew 11:23).

Back on the bus, Shafik drove a few miles south to the town of Migdal. During the first centuries, the town's name was Magdala and recognized as the hometown of Mary Magdalene, the enigmatic woman revered as a saint or condemned as a prostitute depending on different interpretations of the Bible. According to the New Testament, Jesus visited the town by ship (Matthew 15:39). The Jewish historian Josephus described Magdala as a town with a population of 40,000 people and a fleet of 230 fishing vessels during the time of Jesus' preaching. Currently, the town's population totals under 2,000 residents, but boasts at least three tourist attractions—the Magdala Center, The Magdala Archaeological Park, and Ali's restaurant, renowned for its lake view and its excellent "St. Peter's fish."

Seated *al fresco* under a tent at Ali's restaurant with a view of the Sea of Galilee, I enjoyed two dining experiences that previously I never dared to undertake. First, the traditional tourist treat, "St. Peter's fish," is a species of fish that back in Florida I had sworn never to sample—tilapia—the common name for about one hundred species in the cichlid fish family, whose members frequent ponds and streams with water temperature of at least seventy degrees Fahrenheit. Tilapia populates the ponds on our golf course that are prone to run off from fertilizer and pesticides. To Floridians, tilapia is food fit only for the alligators that also populate our ponds. We always joke that we ship tilapia off to the unsuspecting New Yorkers as a tropical delicacy,

Second, I had to choose whether to have a whole fish cooked with its skin and head, or my default choice of a filet. With no indecision Nancy ordered the whole fish. One of our fellow travelers dared me to order the whole fish. He guaranteed that I would love it, plus he argued that I would never again be afraid to try a new culinary experience. He promised to show me how to lift the fish flesh right off its bones. I believed him and opted for the whole fish. I decided when in the Galilee; eat as Jesus and

My plate of "St. Peter's fish" before I devoured it.

his disciples would. Result: the most delicious fish I have ever eaten. Nevertheless, I will never eat tilapia in Florida and never, never in New York City.

Before boarding the bus again, I used the restroom at Ali's restaurant. Another new experience. In the stall over a small metal basket a sign read: DO NOT THROW TOILET PAPER IN THE TOILET. One of the more experienced travelers among us told me, "This is a common sign in undeveloped countries. Their waste systems cannot handle too much paper." Well, at least they supplied the toilet paper!

After lunch, Father Don brought us to the Magdala Center to see the new, modern church just recently dedicated on May 28, 2014 — so new as not to be listed in most of the guide books. The Duc in Altum Church is Latin for "Put out into the deep," and also the words of Christ (Luke 5:4). Its altar is in the shape of a first century fishing boat, often called a Jesus boat. The altar stands in front of an infinity pool that directs the eye to the sea beyond, and gives the illusion the altar boat is floating on the Sea of Galilee.

This church with its unusual and imaginative concept is part of the much larger complex, the Magdala Center, much of which is still under construction. When completed, the compound will include a hotel or retreat for pilgrims visiting the Holy Land and a teaching center highlighting the biblical significance of the area, while also promoting vocation for women.

Father Don shared the checkered history of the Magdala Center's director with us. In Mexico in 1941, Marcial Maciel founded the Legionaries of Christ, a Catholic congregation of priests and seminaries studying for the priesthood. Although Father Don characterized the organization as almost a cult, the movement grew to include members in twenty-two countries, with three bishops, 994 priests, and 1,515 seminarians. Maciel served as general director until January 2005, when the Holy See began investigations of alleged sexual abuse, which were later confirmed to be true. In 2006, Pope Benedict XVI removed Maciel from office. Since then, the order underwent extensive reform and rewrote its constitution. On November 4, 2014, just prior to the date of our visit, the Vatican approved the Legionaries of Christ's amended constitution.

Near the Magdala Center is the Magdala Archaeological Park. In the early 1960s, Franciscan archaeologists discovered the ancient port city. As recently as 2009, when the Legionaries were digging the foundation for their center, they uncovered a first-century synagogue. Most biblical scholars believe Jesus taught in the synagogue.

Our schedule indicated that the next stop of the afternoon was yet another archaeological site at Jordan River Park at Bethsaida on the northeast corner of the lake. I have no recollection, pictures, or notes from our visit there. One archaeological dig too many, I guess. I do remember the last destination of the day as the light was fading.

Altar shaped like a boat in the Duc in Altum Church, Migdal

Shafik drove the bus up a steep, narrow road to the Peace Overlook in the Golan Heights, a rocky plateau on the border of Israel and Syria. We all scrambled off the bus to peer over the cliff for our first actual view of Syria. Since the 1967 Six-Day War, both countries continue to claim the disputed territory. We looked down on an abandoned United Nations encampment that once served as a buffer zone between the two adversaries. Now the area is considered No Man's Land. At this writing, 20,000 Jewish settlers live in Golan Heights and 20,000 Syrians, most of them members of the Druze sect. Talks continue on and off in an attempt to resolve the conflict.

That evening, after dinner, I attended a lecture given by a long time member of the Kibbutz Lavi. His topic was the birth of kibbutzim in general, and the particulars of our host kibbutz, Kibbutz Lavi. The word kibbutz means group in Hebrew, but its definition connotes much more than that simple meaning. More formally, a kibbutz is a communal settlement in Israel of a voluntary democratic community where people live and work together on a non-competitive basis with an aim to be economically and socially independent while employing the principles of communal ownership of property, social justice, and equality. Many other such utopian communes in other times and other countries have come and gone, but the kibbutzim continue to thrive in Israel.

Our lecturer, Samuel, graduated from high school in 1961 and joined the Kibbutz Lavi in 1968. He has remained as a member for life. He began his talk with a brief history of the kibbutz movement. The first kibbutz, Debania, was established in 1909 by only twelve immigrants to Palestine, who wanted to be farmers. Economically, the only way to make a profit from farming was to band together.

Soon, the kibbutz phenomenon flourished. Seven hundred people lived on kibbutzim in Palestine in 1922. By 1927, there were 2,000 kibbuzim. At the beginning of WWII, 24,105 members lived on 79 kibbutzim or five percent of the Jewish population in Palestine. By 1950, the number had risen to 65,000 or almost eight percent of the population. In 1989 the kibbuzim population peaked at 129,000. Then, came a decline. In 2010 about 100,000 people lived in 270 kibbutzim.

The Lavi Kibbutz began in 1948 as a farm. Today its income is derived one third from farming, one third from furniture manufacturing, and one third from the profits from the hotel. One hundred twenty-seven families and two hundred fifty people live in the kibbutz.

It is a classical kibbutz, which means no one has any personal income. All salaries, even from members who may work outside the commune as teachers, lawyers, or accountants for example, are deposited in one account. All the work in the kibbutz is done communally. However, many of the hotel staff are hired from the outside.

All the meals are prepared in the communal kitchen. Instead of eating in the common dining hall, many residents bring the meal home to eat privately in their own dining rooms. Each family receives a home in accordance with the number of family members. The majority of the residents are in their mid-thirties with two to three children. A school on the ground teaches children in grades kindergarten through grade eight. The students attend high school outside the community. Grants are awarded to students who qualify to continue on to college.

Everyone contributes in some way. Residents ages sixty-five to seventy work twenty hours a week. At age seventy-six you may retire or continue to work if you wish. I remembered the elderly woman I saw pushing a trash trolley on the night we arrived. Women and men have the same opportunities. Forty percent of the kibbutzim children remain in the commune after completing their education, but most of them work in outside jobs.

At the end of the talk, I said good night to our group and returned to our room. I reported on the lecture to Nancy. She had chosen an early night and a chance to call her son and talk to him and her husband, Ward.

1. https://search.yahoo.com/yhs/search?p=map+of+sea+galilee&ei=UT (Accessed July 17, 2017)

2. https://en.wikpedia.org/wki/List_of_popes (Accessed July 17, 2017)

Chapter Twenty-Five

The Muse of Zippori

Monday, November 17, the tenth day on our Holy Pilgrimage, was our last day in the Galilee. On the bus, as we headed southeast from the Kibbutz Lavi Hotel, Father Don led us in prayer and then listed the stops for the day. Our first visit would be Cana, the small town where Jesus turned water into wine at a wedding celebration. For me, an improbable but fanciful feat—however, highly satisfying to miracle believers. Next, Zippori National Park, another among the many Israeli archaeological sites. The third stop was to be at the top of Mount Arbel with an acclaimed overlook of the Galilee. Here, Father Don would celebrate Mass. After lunch, we would tour the Ancient Galilean Boat Museum. Late in the afternoon, our last activity would be a boat ride on the Sea of Galilee, aboard a replica of an ancient Jesus boat.

I was both exhilarated and apprehensive by the thought of this last excursion. I definitely wanted to experience a boat ride on the Sea of Galilee, but I worried about becoming seasick, as I was prone to motion sickness. I had brought Bonine with me in preparation for this scheduled boating event. Anne Marie tried to convince me that my fears were unfounded because the sea was calm and the boat was seaworthy. Nevertheless, that morning, I put the tablets in my backpack.

Soon, we arrived at Kafr Kanna, which in English translates to the Village of Cana, a town catering to the Christian tourist trade. According to the biblical story (John 2:1-11), in this small town Jesus changed water to wine at a wedding ceremony. Although not mentioned in the three Synoptic Gospels of Matthew, Mark, and Luke, the Gospel of John devotes eleven verses to the water-to-wine miracle, considered by Christian tradition to be the first public miracle performed by Jesus. After all the available wine had been drunk, Jesus told the servants to fill six water pots with water and offer it to the governor, a guest at the feast. He tasted the water that Jesus had made into wine. Then, he said to the bridegroom: "Every man at the beginning doth set forth good wine; and when men have well drunk, then that which is worse, but thou have kept the good wine until now" (John 2:10).

Theologians continue to discuss whether the story is to be considered an actual transformation of water to wine or as a spiritual allegory. One interpretation suggests that John is referring to the appearance of Jesus himself as the good wine that all the multitudes have been awaiting.

Many Christians travel to Cana to renew their wedding vows at the Franciscan Wedding Church, built in 1879 over a sixth-century synagogue. They also purchase Cana Wedding Wine from the many shops along the narrow lanes. A nearby Greek Orthodox Church displays ancient water pots that the priests claim to be the original jars used by Jesus at the wedding feast. One archaeologist believes they are most likely baptismal fonts.

Back on the bus, Shafek drove a few miles east to Zippori National Park, the site of a former wealthy Jewish city that archaeologists believe

Franciscan Wedding church in Cana, Israel

One of the many Cana Wedding Wine shops lining the streets of Cana

dates back to the Iron Age. In Hebrew, Zippori or Tzipori means "bird." The city was thought to perch atop a mountain like a bird, also known as Seppkoris from the ancient Greek spelling.

Father Don prepped us for our visit with the long history of the city's legacy that included: Hellenistic, Jewish, Roman, Byzantine, Islamic, Crusader, Arabic, and Ottoman rulers and influences. Zippori was first mentioned in written records in 103 BCE during the reign of Alexander Janaeus, high priest of Judea. In 63 BCE, the Roman army conquered the region; in 55 BCE, after the murder of his father, Herod the Great retook Zippori. After Herod's death in 4 BCE, the Jewish people revolted and recaptured Zippori. However, the Roman army quelled the revolt, burned the city, and sold the Jews into slavery. Herod's son, Antipas, rebuilt the city. During these early years of the pre-Christian era, Zippori was the largest city in the Galilee and thought by scholars to be the birthplace of Mary, mother of Jesus, and hometown of Mary's parents, Anne and Jochim.

During the first major revolt of the Jews against the Romans in 66 CE, the citizens of Zippori procured a treaty with the Romans that protected their city from destruction. In the early second century, the city's name was changed to Diocaesarea—the city of the God Zeus and of Caesar—as pagan rulers replaced the Jewish rabbis.

At this time of renewed persecution and exile of the Jews from Israel in the late second century, 190 CE, Rabbi Judah Hanasi felt a need to write down the Oral Torah before it was lost. It was here in Zippori, after the leadership of the town was restored to the Jewish people, that Rabbi Judah Hanasi, a descendant from the royal line of King David and head of the Sanhedrin, the highest council of the ancient Jews, worked on editing and perfecting the Mishnah. He became so well-known and famous he was simply called "Rabbi."

At this point in the narration, Father Don briefly defined the meanings of Torah, Talmud, and Mishnah for those of us not versed in Judaism 101. The Torah (the Hebrew word for instruction or law) consists of two parts: The Written Torah and the Oral Torah, commonly called the Talmud. The Written Torah is the First Five Books of Moses—Genesis, Exodus, Leviticus, Numbers, and Deuteronomy—written down by Moses in 1273 BCE and includes all 613 commandants or mitzvah. The Oral Torah or Talmud was not allowed to be written down, but had to be explained orally by the rabbis. One could not be understood without the other.

With input from other Rabbis, Rabbi Hanasi compiled the information from the Talmud into the Mishnah, Hebrew for teaching. Because of the prohibition against writing down the Oral Torah, he wrote the work in code, so a rabbi was needed to decode it.

Using the example of one commandment, Father Don compared the Jewish law as commanded in the Written Torah to the detailed explanation for implementation of the law from the Oral Torah, as written in code in the Mishnah.

The Written Torah says: "When thou hast eaten and art full, then thou shalt bless the Lord thy God for the good land which he hath given thee" (Deuteronomy 8:10).

The Mishnah extends the meaning of the commandment. It specifies the blessing to be recited before and after each kind of food, and what to do if the wrong blessing is given by mistake.

At the height of the Jewish influence, eighteen synagogues and study houses flourished in the city. Then, in the early fourth century, 324 CE, Emperor Constantine declared Christianity the religion of the Roman Empire and Zippori became a bishopric under the Byzantine. Many churches were built, although the majority of the population remained Jewish.

As the bus was approaching our destination, Father Don condensed our history lesson to a few, quick, salient facts about Zippori. After an earthquake in 363 CE, the city was rebuilt. During the Crusader period from CE 1095 to CE 1291, Zippori became known as Le Saphorie, a fortified principality in the Galilee. By the eighteenth century Zippori was the small Arab village of Saffuriyyeh, which eventually was captured and its residents dispersed during the 1948 War of Independence. Excavations and archaeological research began at the site in 1931 and continue to date.

I tried to digest all three thousand years of Zippori history. Would this be another Israel archaeological dig with rock formations and cordoned-off trenches that I wouldn't remember?

As we had done at the many other ancient sites we had visited, we walked along the Roman cardo, or main thoroughfare of the city, while sidestepping the visible ruts left by the wagon wheels. We viewed another ubiquitous Roman theater with seats for five thousand spectators. We strolled by the fortress or citadel from the Crusader period. At this point, Father Don urged us on as he knew we were approaching the signature attraction at Ziporri, the Dionysus House or House of the Wine God. This house built in the third century CE was destroyed by the earthquake of 363 CE, but archaeologists have uncovered a spectacular mosaic design of a beautiful woman, almost intact on its floor.

Now, I knew I would not forget Zippori. I had found my distinctive icon, unique to this ancient city. I called her the Muse of Zippori. Many learned historians who had discovered her before me named her, the Mona Lisa of Zippori. Other researchers thought she was meant to be Venus. Oh well, each to his own *umwelt*, (pronounced OOM-velt) a word which means environment in the original German, but commonly translated to "each to his own self-centered world" in English. I planned to call upon my muse to help me write of my adventures in the Holy Land.

From Zippori, Shafek drove us northeast for about twelve miles to Mount Arbel where Father Don would celebrate the Eucharist atop the famed overlook. Although Father Don promised us a spectacular view

The Mona Lisa of Zippori or my own Muse of Zippori

Remains of the Roman theater at Zippori

from the top of the mountain looking out over the Sea of Galilee, the ascent meant 700 steps up and 700 steps back down. Four of us, including Nancy and me, decided not to attempt the climb. We sat in a covered rest area and drank cool drinks. Instead of celebrating Mass, we shared views on religion and Catholicism. I did not betray Nancy and admit my true beliefs, but listened to the others. It became apparent that many of the pilgrims in our group were "cafeteria Catholics," a term I had not heard before. It means a Catholic who picks and chooses which doctrines of the Church to follow. I agreed that that was a sensible idea.

The group returned in about an hour and reported the climb up the cliff was worth the effort. Nancy, Thea, another woman named Judy, and I promised not to miss the next mountain top. Then, we all boarded the bus for the drive to our lunch stop. After lunch, as a prelude to our boat ride on the Sea of Galilee, we visited the Ancient Galilean Boat Museum at the Yigal Alton Center at Kibbutz Ginosar.

Once again, Father Don gave us the background to this unexpected archaeological discovery— this time not a Roman ruin and this time not unearthed by eminent scientists, but a 2,000 year old wooden boat stumbled upon after the severe drought of 1986 at the Sea of Galilee by two brothers from Kibbutz Ginosar, who imagined themselves amateur archaeologists.

The excavation of the remarkable find was overseen by the Israel Antiquities Authority with the help of many volunteers. Its age was dated to 40 BCE (plus or minus eighty years) based on radiocarbon dating, and/or from 50 BCE to 50 CE based on pottery and nails found in the boat.

To preserve the hull, it was submerged in a specially-built pool filled with synthetic wax that replaced the water in the wood cells. After fourteen years, in CE 2000 it was placed on exhibit at the center.

Upon our arrival, before seeing the actual boat, we viewed a film detailing the historical importance of the find both to the Jews and to the Christians. For the Jewish people, the discovery revealed facts about the life of their ancestors as fishermen in the first century. For the Christians, the finding corresponded with the passages in the Bible depicting Jesus and his disciples as common fishermen in that area of Galilee. There is no direct evidence that Jesus used this exact boat in his ministries but its prototype is mentioned fifty times in the New Testament.

Commonly called the Jesus boat, it exemplified a typical fishing boat from the first century with a length of twenty-six feet, a width of almost eight feet, and a height approaching four feet. This boat on exhibit had originally been repaired many times, as twelve different woods were evident in the hull.

After inspecting the boat, we had time to shop at the museum store. It was here that I bought Artzy, the ibex mascot, symbol of the Israeli Park Authority, for my young step-granddaughter. A picture of Artzy appears in Chapter Twenty. The ten-inch stuffed animal was well made with

The ancient Galilee boat on display
at the Yigal Alon Center in Ginosar, Iseael

removable clothes for only ten American dollars. Of course, I also looked for anything "pomegranate," but I had no luck. I was becoming overtly anxious as our tour ended in two days. Again, Father Don assured me that on our last day in Jerusalem he would bring me to the pomegranate shop.

We settled back in the bus and were ready to pull away on our way to the pier at Tiberias for the boat ride. I reached into my backpack to pull out my polka-dotted notebook. I remembered writing down the exact spelling of Artzy so I wouldn't forget it. No note book. I panicked. Nancy and I searched the back of the seat, the floor, and under all our packages. I took everything out of my backpack. No notebook. I knew I had had the notebook in the museum shop since I definitely remembered writing down the name, Artzy. I thought perhaps I had dropped it at the counter.

I jumped up, ran to the front of the bus, and asked Anne Marie and Father Don to let me run back in the shop to search for my notebook. They both looked irritated but told Shafik to hold up for a few minutes. Anne Marie and I hopped off the bus.

This time we didn't have extra time. We were on schedule for our appointment at the dock in Tiberias. This time, Nancy didn't come with me. I think she was too embarrassed. Anne Marie and I looked all around the shop, and asked the clerks if anyone had turned in a small notebook. No notebook. This time I returned to the bus without my quarry. This time my fellow passengers did not cheer. This time they were annoyed at my carelessness. I was almost in tears.

Where was my Muse of Zippori? She was not looking out for me.

I slumped into my seat. Nancy whispered, "I'll help you remember."

"Thanks," I said, "but my project is lost. I'll never recapture all our adventures. I'll never remember all Father Don's historical and biblical information. Ten days gone forever."

To comfort myself, I decided to show Nancy the cute little ibex I had bought for Trinity, my granddaughter. When I opened the plastic bag, there nestled next to Artzy was my notebook. Maybe Artzy and not the Muse of Zippori would be my inspiration.

"Don't tell anyone," Nancy pleaded. "They are mad enough as it is. They'll think you were crazy and an irresponsible old lady not to look thoroughly before you stopped the bus."

"Okay," I said, as I began to worry about a new problem—seasickness.

Later, I did "confess" to Father Don and Anne Marie.

The bus headed southeast, back to Tiberias, where we had three o'clock reservations with Francis Jordan Sailing, Ltd. for a private excursion.

This company reenacts the biblical experience with the crew dressed in robes from the time of Jesus. They stayed in character and fished with nets similar to those used by the disciples. We circled the Sea of Galilee as Father Don pointed out biblical landmarks and recited biblical references to events which occurred on the Sea of Galilee. Jesus walked on water (John 6:19-21). Jesus calmed a storm (Matthew 8:23- 26). Jesus multiplied fish (Luke 3:1-8).

The sea was calm; the boat was steady; I had no hint of queasiness.

The sun was setting as we returned to the dock at the port of Tiberias. A weary group of pilgrims climbed aboard the bus for our return to the Kibbutz Lavi Hotel. After dinner, most of our group attended a scheduled lecture on the conflict between the Jews and Palestinians. Nancy and I skipped it for an early bedtime. A decision I knew I would regret, and I still do.

And that reminds me of a maxim to live by that I believe to be true. In simplest terms: We regret more the things that we didn't do than the things that we did do.

A crew member dressed as a disciple
preparing to cast a fishing net

Group picture on the Sea of Galilee Jesus boat
Nancy and me front row left

Tourist boats returning to dock at Tiberias at sunset

Chapter Twenty-Six

Caesarea on the Mediterranean Sea

I faced Tuesday, November 18, with sadness—our final full day and night in Israel. Tomorrow we flew home on a a red-eye flight. I rued the fact that the trip was almost over. As travelers do, I vowed to live this last day to the fullest. No more lamenting about Roman ruins. In fact, today's agenda listed another one, Caesarea. Until today, I was unaware of this "Granddaddy" of all Roman ruins, more spectacular than the Colosseum and the Forum in Rome, or the volcanic remains at Pompeii. At Caesarea, the splendor and scope and the bygone glory of ancient Rome awaited by the edge of the sea.

As we left the grounds of the Kibbutz Lavi Hotel, I also lamented that we had not had time or daylight hours to explore the campus of the kibbutz. Kibbutz Lavi sustained itself with a working farm and furniture factory, as well as the hotel. The guide map listed thirty-six points of interest on the grounds. Farm operations included a milking parlor with a peep-through window from which to observe the milking of 300 dairy cows; numerous chicken coops and gardens; and a stable. For the guests, the hotel provided a swimming pool, tennis courts, a children's playground, outdoor fitness center, and beauty spa. Also available was a guided tour of the Lavi Furniture Factory, the largest designer and manufacturer of synagogue furniture in the world. For the residents, the kibbutz maintained a school, infirmary and dentist facility, clothing store, garage, and gas station.

Listings unique to Kibbutz Lavi were the "All Senses Garden" for the visually impaired, an archaeological garden with artifacts from the

Second Temple era, and two separate mikvehs, one for men and one for women. Mikvehs are pools of water used for obtaining spiritual purity.

This morning the bus headed southwest for the twenty-five mile trip to our first stop, Megiddo National Park. As the bus rolled along, from the window I viewed fields which reminded me of my native New England, rocky but productive. At about eleven miles out, in the distance we saw Mount Tabor with the Basilica of the Transfiguration on its summit, and the peaceful town of Nain nestled at its foot. We stopped for a picture-taking opportunity, while Father Don recounted Bible stories.

Here in the town of Nain, Jesus brought the only son of a widow back to life (Luke 7:11-15). More importantly, for Christians, the miracle of the Transfiguration of Christ, celebrated on August 6, occurred on Mount Tabor. According to Catholic theology, the Transfiguration is the culminating point of Jesus' public life, as His Baptism is its starting point, and His Ascension is its end. Jesus brought Peter, James, and John to the mountain top. As the four were praying, a bright light illuminated Jesus. The prophets Moses and Elijah appeared and talked with him. A voice from out of the sky called him "Son" (Matthew 17:1-6; Mark 9:1-8; Luke 9:28-36; John 1:14). Besides all the biblical lore associated with Mount Tabor, in the twenty-first century, the mountain top is the hang-gliding capital of Israel.

*Mount Tabor with the basilica atop the mountain
and the town of Nain at its foot*

We reached Megiddo about mid-morning. Megiddo became a national park in 1966, and in 2005 a UNESCO World Heritage Site. Excavation work at the Megiddo is a continuous operation. Signs warned of open pits and restricted areas. To date, archaeologists have unearthed twenty-six layers of ruins dating from 7,000 BCE. The Old Testament mentions the city under many different names and as the site of many battles. In the New Testament Megiddo is predicted to be the site of the final battle, Armageddon (Revelation 16:16). Here, John the Baptist envisions the apocalyptic battle between the forces of good and evil.

Our time at Megiddo was limited, as this morning Father Don had us on a tight schedule. We were booked to celebrate the Eucharist at 11:00 a.m. at Murakah on the slopes of Mount Carmel, traditional site of Elijah's contest with the prophets of Baal. The site overlooks the modern harbor of Haifa, the country's third largest city, located on the map at the thumb of Israel. Like most of the areas in Israel, Haifa's history of continuous settlement dates back 3,000 years and includes rule by Phoenicians, Persians, Romans, Byzantines, Arabs, Crusaders, Ottomans, British, and Israelis. In the twenty-first century it is considered a non-religious city. The only one where buses run on Saturdays.

On my trip through the Holy Land and in my research for this book, I added to my biblical knowledge and to my insight on religious beliefs from unexpected sources. Such was the story of Elijah. I knew his name from the Bible, but I knew nothing about him. He is esteemed by all three Abrahamic faiths as a prophet during the ninth century BCE. In Christianity he is called St. Elias. In Islam he is called Ilyas. In Judaism he is known as Elijah.

Upon reaching Mount Carmel, we climbed up the mountain on our way to celebrate Mass at the Carmelite church at Murakah. We visited Elijah's cave where he lived and meditated before defeating Ahab, the King of Israel, and the false prophets. Ahab had married Jezebel, a Phoenician. She persuaded Ahab and the Israelis to worship her idols and the false god Baal, instead of the One True Invisible God, called Yahweh by the Jewish people. During a time of a severe drought throughout the land, Elijah proposed a competition to establish the supremacy of either Yahweh or Baal. The prophets representing Baal and the prophet Elijah gathered on Mount Carmel. Each side built an altar on which to sacrifice a bullock. Baal or Yahweh was to supply the fire. First, the prophets of Baal ranted, danced, and immolated themselves to no avail. No fire occurred. Then, on Elijah's request, the One and Only God sent a great fire that consumed

Elijah's altar, the sacrificial animal, and the surrounding earth. When the Jewish people saw this they cried out, "The Lord alone is God." And Yahweh sent a downpour which ended the drought (I Kings: 18:21-40).

Throughout his life Elijah continued to counsel the people of Israel in the belief of the One God. At the end of his life, after naming Elisha as his successor, Elijah was swept up to heaven by a fiery chariot and horse in the midst of a whirlwind.

In Jewish belief, Elijah never died and returns to earth during the Seder meal at Passover, at the circumcision of a baby boy, and every Saturday evening to bless the work for the next week.

While researching Elijah, I read many books. My favorite was a children's book entitled, *Journeys with Elijah* by Barbara Goldin with stunning and detailed watercolor paintings by Jerry Pinkney—a book to treasure, whether child, parent, or grandparent. But besides the artwork, the stories gleaned from Jewish folklore were entertaining and thought-provoking. One answered two enigmatic questions that have plagued all believers whether Jewish, Christian, or Muslim through the ages: Why do some people suffer even though they have done good deeds? And why are wicked people sometimes rewarded? I think these two questions are at the heart of the mystery as to how a just and loving God can allow misery and evil to persist in our world.

Elijah answers the questions with a parable. A rabbi accompanies Elijah on his travels about the countryside. At one poor farmhouse, a farmer feeds and houses them for the night. When they leave, Elijah prays to God to kill the man's cow and the cow drops dead. The rabbi doesn't understand but he had promised not to ask questions. The next day at a luxurious dwelling, a rich man gives them no food and only allows them to sleep in the yard. When they leave Elijah asks God to fix the rich man's crumbling wall.

Even though the rabbi had agreed not to question Elijah, he cannot stop himself. He asks Elijah to explain why he rewarded the selfish, rich man but punished the poor, generous farmer. Elijah agrees to tell him, but then they must part.

"As to the poor couple, I knew his wife was to die so I implored God to kill the cow instead. As to the rich man, I knew if workmen repaired the wall they would find treasure hidden in the walls that the rich man would claim as his. God works in mysterious ways. Everything is not as it seems. You must learn to trust and believe in God."

If you have faith and belief, I think Elijah's parables were as good as any I have heard to explain the unexplainable whys and ways of reward or punishment for the acts of good or evil. But to play devil's advocate, why does God need to exact a reward for His good deeds? Why not save both the wife and cow? Why not let the workmen profit from the hidden treasure? I was not convinced this parable was proof of a "just and loving" God.

Monument to Elijah at Mount Carmel

The Carmelite church was built in the late 1800s over earlier churches, all on the location presumed to be Elijah's cave. As this was our last Mass in Israel, Father Don treated us to a surprise. He presided over the sacramental rituals, but Charlie, our spiritual layman, gave the sermon. Charlie, one of the pilgrims from St. Ignatius Church in Baltimore, had served as proctor at all our previous Masses. For fun, his wife, Joyce, had calculated our many thousands of steps with her Fitbit.

Charlie's sermon tied our morning visits together by using transfiguration as an analogous theme. He suggested that the transfiguration of Jesus atop of Mount Tabor where he was transformed into a noble and transcendental figure with the prophets Moses and Elijah by his side was similar to when Elijah transfigured or transformed the Israelis away from their worship of the false god, Baal, to once again adore the One True God. In

Father Don celebrating our last Eucharist at the Carmelite Church in Murakah

the same manner, Charlie suggested our tour group had been transfigured into knowledgeable pilgrims of the Holy Land by our extensive trip covering so many biblical places. I congratulated Charlie for delivering a perceptive and relevant sermon. Was I becoming a believer again?

After Mass and our return to the bus, Shafik drove us to Daliyat Karmiel, a town of 13,000 inhabitants, almost all members of the Druze sect. Father Don directed Shafik to the restaurant, Temer Halabi, for lunch. The owners, a Druze family known to Father Don, served us salads, humus, falafel, and their specialty, a tiny cup of strong Druze coffee flavored with ground cardamon seeds. Their next door shop sold hand-made items such as woven bags, scarfs, and carpets. I bought a colorful scarf as a gift for my daughter-in-law, but I had no luck in finding a pomegranate-themed gift for my husband. I must learn to be patient.

Father Don told us a few facts about the Druze community in Israel. The Druze are a religious minority whose population in Israel continues to increase: 102,000 in 2004, 125,000 in 2010, and 140,000 at the end of 2014. They are Arabic-speaking Israeli citizens who serve in the Israeli Defense Force and some sit as members of parliament.

The Druze religion is secretive and closed to outsiders. Those born with a Druze mother and a Druze father are not allowed to leave the religion, and those not born as Druze are not allowed to join. One defining tenet is a belief in reincarnation. If you live a good life, you return as a good person, while the converse is true for those living a bad life. Al-Hakin, an Egyptian ruler, founded the religion in the early eleventh century by blending Islam's belief in one God with Greek philosophy and Hindu influences. Similar to the story of Jesus, the Druze believe Al-Hakin was God and ascended into heaven in CE 1021 and will return to make the world a wonderful place. They respect the writings of the Bible and Quran, but believe the Jews, Muslims, and Christians have turned from the "pure faith" due to their dependence on ceremonies and rituals.

Instead of the Ten Commandments, the Druze religion offers seven guidelines for living.

1. Veracity in speech and the truthfulness of the tongue.— Speak the truth.

2. Protection and mutual aid to the brethren in faith.—Take care of one another.

3. Renunciation of all forms of former worship and false beliefs.— Do not believe in any other religions.

4. Repudiation of the devil and all forces of evil.—Stay away from the demon and people who do bad things.

5. Confession of God's unity.—Live in harmony with each other.

6. Acquiescence in God's acts no matter what they be.— Accept all of al-Hakim's acts.

7. Absolute submission and resignation to God's divine will in both secret and public.—Act the way that al-Hakim would want you to.

From this smattering of information, I became fascinated with the Druze religion, maybe perversely because I could not become a convert. When I returned home, I searched four comprehensive books that purported to discuss most or all of the world religions. Not one mentioned the Druze sect. However, there is information available. Two books became my main source of information, as well as sites on the internet.

Wikipedia lists the regions of the world with significant populations of Druze. Up to eight hundred thousand in Syria, two hundred thousand in Lebanon, one hundred forty thousand in Israel, thirty-two thousand in Jordan. Outside of the Middle East: one hundred twenty-five thousand in Venezuela, forty-three thousand in the United States, twenty-three thousand in Canada, and nineteen thousand in Australia. In the United States the majority live in California.

One of the books, *The Druze* by Robert Brenton Bates, published in 1988, divided the data into three parts: Origin and Beliefs; Social Structure, Customs, and Demography; and Modern History. The text supplemented Father Don's information. The book stressed that the Druze religion combined all the ideas of religion and philosophy known at the time of its inception. Besides elements from the New and Old Testament and the Quran, the founder al-Hakim relied on concepts from Gnosticism, Neo-Platonism, Hinduism, and the teachings of Pythagoras.

Socially, the Druze do not drink alcohol or smoke. Sometimes the women wear veils and the men turbans. Marriage is often arranged and always to another Druze, often a first cousin. Some of the Druze, both men and women, may go to universities. In 1983, the Israeli census for Daliyat Karmiel listed 8,227 Druze, 229 Muslim, 3 Jewish, and 1 Christian.

The other more recent book, *Heirs to Forgotten Kingdoms: Journeys into the Disappearing Religions of the Middle East* by Gerard Russell, published in 2014, speculated that the Druze may actually be the modern-day successors to the Pythagorean Brotherhood, the secret society composed of the pupils and followers of Pythagoras. None of his teachings could be revealed to non-members, with any betrayal punishable by death. Russell explored many of the beliefs of the Druze and connected them to the beliefs of the Pythagoreans. He concluded his study with this observation:

> Pythagoras had thought that by recalling his past incarnations he could accumulate more than a lifetime's worth of wisdom. Similarly the Druze believe that since they are reincarnated in the community of the enlightenment, only they can ever hope to attain real wisdom. It is truly a Pythagorean notion.

To me, the logical reason no new converts are allowed into the sect can be simply explained, due to their belief in reincarnation. The Druze can only be reincarnated among themselves, a Druze to a Druze. Their souls belong to the ages. Their former selves walked with Abraham, Moses, Jesus, Mohammed, or al-Harkim.

The concept of reincarnation interests me, although I don't call it reincarnation. I have my own notion. I believe we do not die but continue to live on as a part of the cosmos. We revert to "stardust." Matter cannot be destroyed. It lives on in another form. We are made from the elements of the universe that are found in the stars or gases in space. Only six elements comprise ninety-nine percent of the human body: oxygen, hydrogen, nitrogen, calcium, carbon, and phosphorus. I don't believe souls rise to Heaven or enter another body. I believe when we die that our bodies or our matter return to the cosmos, the ether, the universe. In this way, we are still living, only in another form or dimension. In my will, I have requested that my obituary read, "She has returned to stardust whence she came."

After lunch, it was less than fifteen miles south to Caesarea. In 20 BCE, Herod built this magnificent city at the edge of the Mediterranean Sea and named it for Augustus Caesar. The historian Josephus writes of edifices of white stone, sumptuous palaces, theaters and amphitheaters, and a large hippodrome. Aqueducts carried water from the Carmel Range to the city, a distance of eleven miles. Historians estimated the population at 125,000 citizens and an urban area of 1.4 square miles. For 600 years Caesarea was the capital of the Roman province in Judea.

Until the 1950s and 1960s when archaeologists began extensive excavations at the site, historians thought Josephus' descriptions of the city were exaggerated. Now the ingenuity and splendor at Caesarea impresses both visitors and anthropologists. Sculptures discovered at Caesarea were

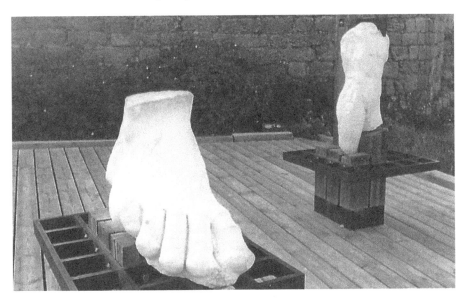

Giant white marble foot at Caesarea

on display on an outside raised platform. The giant white marble foot at least seven feet long suggested the enormous size of the original sculpture.

The excavation work continues. In December 2015, the Israel Antiquities Authority announced the discovery of a ram. The release stated the statue might have been from a Byzantine church dating to the sixth or seventh century, or possibly from an earlier Roman period.

Nancy and I were not disappointed by our final Roman ruin. We marveled at the size and location of this former jewel of the Roman Empire. Below are pictures taken as we strolled along the more than a mile-long cardo of ancient Caesarea.

By the end of the exploration at Caesarea Maritima, we had walked a distance of two or three miles. Most of our tired group slept on the return trip to the Mount Zion Hotel in Jerusalem, a distance of seventy-five miles. After a farewell cocktail party and dinner, Father Don handed

Our group walking along the shore at Caesarea

The Roman theater at Caesarea

Ruins at the edge of the sea at Caesarea

out the times of our bus departures to the airport in Tel Aviv. Most of us would leave for the airport in the late afternoon on Wednesday. For the morning Father Don had scheduled a few more group visits, but our afternoon would be free to explore Jerusalem on our own. Father Don again promised to direct me to a shop where he assured me I would find gifts decorated with pomegranate motifs.

After readying our bags for tomorrow's departure, Nancy and I went to bed.

At 4:00 a.m., a loud blast woke Nancy and me. We sat up in bed and stared at each other, each with our own thoughts. *What was that boom? Was it a bomb? Would there be another one? Were the Palestinians attacking Israel?*

We looked at each other for reinsurance.

"What was that?" we said in unison.

We hopped out of bed and rushed to the window. All was dark and peaceful. We didn't see anything. We heard no more booms. We climbed back in bed and whispered to each other to calm our fears. Finally, we fell back to sleep.

Chapter Twenty-Seven

Farewell to Israel

Nancy and I awoke with a purpose on Wednesday morning, November 17. our last day in Jerusalem. At breakfast we hoped to learn the source and reason for the loud boom in the middle of the night. All of our group, except for Father Don, had been awakened by the explosion. One woman looked out her window and witnessed a fire burst in the night sky.

The hotel staff confirmed the explosion and supplied the explanation. The Israeli government had revived a controversial policy, suspended a decade ago, of demolishing the homes of terrorists involved in attacks against Israeli citizens. In this case, the family home of the Palestinian man who plowed his car into pedestrians killing a baby and young woman was demolished as punishment. The border police evacuated about fifty people from his apartment building and nearby structures at 1:00 a.m., before detonating the bomb at 4:00 a.m.

The *International New York Times* quoted Prime Minister Benjamin Netanyahu, "We will restore security in Jerusalem...This morning we demolished the home of a terrorist."

The B'Tselem, an Israeli human rights group, opposed the demolition. In the *Times* Ms. Michaeli of B'Tselem said, "Our position is it's illegal and it's also immoral. It's a deliberate policy for harming the innocent. The people responsible for those attacks are either dead or facing trial."

The newspaper also chronicled that other opponents to the attacks were philanthropists who at times built bigger and better homes for the bombed-out families. This action negated the punishment administered by the government.

After lengthy discussions of last night's unsettling blast with arguments on both sides, we boarded our bus for Bethany, the home of Lazarus and his sisters, Mary and Martha, on the southeast slopes of Mount Olive. Jesus often stayed there when visiting Jerusalem. According to the Bible, He ascended into heaven at this site. The chapel of the Ascension commemorates the happening (Luke 24:24-53).

Next, Shafik drove us to the Lions' Gate entrance to the Old City. We said farewell to him with grateful hugs. From this point on we would be walking or hailing cabs. Our last visit as a group was to St. Anne's Church in the Muslim quarter of the Old City. As Caesarea Maritime had impressed me as the most memorable Roman ruin, this church settled into my memory. It became my most repeated story on my return home.

The Romanesque church completed in 1138 was built near the remains of a Byzantine basilica and over a grotto thought by the Crusaders to be the birthplace of the Virgin Mary. According to tradition Anna and Joachim, Mary's parents, lived there. The church had three aisles, extremely high cross-vaulted ceilings, pillars, and clear, clean lines with an unadorned interior. The altar displayed five sculptures: on the far left was Saint Anne teaching her daughter Mary; next left, was the Nativity; in the center was Jesus' Descent from the Cross; to the right was the Annunciation; and at the far right was Mary's presentation at the temple.

Saint Anne's Church possesses acoustics renowned throughout the world. The sounds move across the open space and up from the grotto. Soloists and choirs travel to Jerusalem for the purpose of singing in the cavernous interior.

Sculpture of Saint Anne
and the young child Mary
in St. Anne's Church

At all our previous Masses, our group had sung hymns led by one of our members from the Chicago area. We had no accompaniment. We had no rehearsals. We had no score, only the words to the hymns. Predictability, our renditions were tentative, muffled, and off key. Father Don kept encouraging us and predicting a musical miracle. At our final "concert" he promised we would sound like the Mormon Tabernacle Choir. We were skeptical. This morning we were ready to test Father Don's improbable prediction.

After viewing the sculptures and artifacts in the church, our choir mistress gathered us together in pews near the front of the church. Since we didn't have our song sheets, she suggested we sing a familiar Christmas carol. We settled on "Silent Night." She gave us the pitch.

"Silent night. Holy night. All is calm. All is bright. Round yon Virgin, Mother and Child...," we began singing. We looked around at each other with disbelieving eyes. And disbelieving ears. We sounded good. We sang like a rehearsed choir. The music surrounded us.

While we were singing a smaller tour group filed into the church and sat in pews across the aisle from us. One of their group stayed standing and waited for us to finish our carol. She applauded our efforts.

In perfect English, she asked, "Would you join us in singing a selection? We are a church choir from Düsseldorf, Germany. I am the choir director."

We agreed.

We chose "Hark the Herald Angels Sing." Our two groups began singing. Now the sound was louder, more melodious, and more forceful. We were all enjoying our voices producing beautiful music while watching the hand movements of our German maestro. Then, as we approached the end of the lyrics, she raised both arms high in the air and quickly lowered them. We stopped singing. A miracle! Our voices continued to fill the air without our singing a single note!

As we left the sanctuary, we shook hands with the Fräulein and thanked her for demonstrating the wonder of St. Anne's acoustics.

When we filed out into the courtyard, Sister Luna, the Catholic nun from Iraq, awaited us. Father Don had invited her to meet with us to say farewell.

Father Don dismissed us. We were on our own to eat lunch, to return to the Mount Zion Hotel, and to board the transport bus to the Ben Gurion Airport at our appointed time later that afternoon.

Anne Marie at the left, Sister Luna, Father Don, and our group saying farewell in the courtyard of Saint Anne's Church

Father Don had not forgotten his promise to me. He sought me out and gave me directions to the pomegranate shop. Two other members of our group joined Nancy and me in pursuit of the shop. After a few hesitant turns and thirty minutes of walking we reached the Armenian Ceramics Center just inside the New Gate in the Old City.

The owner, George Sandrouni, proudly showed us through his shop and indicated his ability to ship merchandise to the United States or anywhere in the world. Items emblazoned with pomegranates filled the shop. I searched the shelves for either juice glasses or coffee cups decorated with pomegranates. No luck. I wanted to buy small items that I could fit into my personal luggage as I did not want to ship the gifts. Eventually, I chose three gifts, two for me and one for Connie.

For Connie, I bought a small catchall, shaped like a pomegranate in dark, lustrous red. Connie could use it on his desk to hold paper clips or other such items. For me, I chose a unique bowl for serving olives, divided into two sections. The large side for the olives and the small side for their pits. Plus, I chose a small, decorative tile decorated with the seven species of Israeli agricultural products, emblematic of the fruits God bestowed on the Jews in their promised land: olives, wheat, barley, pomegranates, grapes, figs, and dates (Deuteronomy 8:8).

The other shoppers, including Nancy, bought much larger pieces, spent lots of shekels, and shipped their purchases home.

Our pomegranate hunt over, Nancy and I decided to eat lunch at the highly recommended King David Hotel, the most famous and legendary

Pomegranate gifts: decorative tile at top, small pomegranate-shaped catchall at left, and divided olive bowl

hotel in Jerusalem. We set out for the destination, but never found it. A cab hailed us. In desperation, with aching feet and growling stomachs, we climbed in and instructed the driver to take us to the Mount Zion Hotel. Upon arriving, we gave the cabby all of our remaining shekels. To this day, we are not sure if we overpaid or underpaid our Palestinian savior.

At the hotel bar, we ordered a glass of wine and an American turkey club sandwich, minus bacon and ham. From the window overlooking the hills of Jerusalem, we saw the surveillance apparatus for the ever present Iron Dome, Israeli's mobile all-weather air defense system. Since its inception in 2011, it had intercepted over 1,200 rockets by late October 2014.

As we sipped our wine, we two college sorority sisters in our seventies, one a practicing Roman Catholic and one questioning her

Israeli's Iron Dome apparatus circling in the sky

atheism, reflected on the significance of our trip to the Holy Land. For Nancy, she fulfilled her dream to visit Jerusalem, the Galilee, and Petra to strengthen her faith and to walk in the footsteps of Jesus. For me, I filled the gap in my biblical knowledge and encountered the power of spiritual feelings when viewing the actual or designated historical settings where the Bible stories and the birth of Christianity and Judaism occurred. Would the sites and history and commitment of my companions prove that God existed? Or would the inconsistencies and lack of concrete evidence foster my continued adherence to atheism? In the final chapters and epilogue I consider and weigh all the information I have learned from my studies and field excursions. When my memory needs a jolt, I refer to my black with white polka dots notebook. It is my tangible miracle.

Chapter Twenty-Eight

In the Very Beginning

The Holy Land Pilgrimage was over. I returned home to ponder the mystery of the creation of the universe. Can anyone ever know the truth? Is the truth as unattainable as the meaning of *forever* to the little girl Judy? Unlike my younger self so many years ago, who could only speculate on an unending universe, as an adult I researched the origins of many religions, studied the findings of eminent scientists, and traveled to Jerusalem in a search for the truth. In these final two chapters I satisfy myself. For many, it will not be enough, but for me, my search is over. Reason is my faith.

***

"In the beginning God created the heaven and the earth" (Genesis1:1). So begins the Bible's account of our creation in the first verse of Genesis.

Then, in (Genesis 2-27), God creates the entire universe in six days. On the first day God made light and darkness, and day and night. On the second day God made Heaven. On the third day God made the seas and the land and called the land Earth. And on the land God made vegetation. On the fourth day God made the sun, the moon, and the stars. On the fifth day God made birds and sea creatures. On the sixth day God made land creatures and humans in his own image.

"So God created man in his *own* image, in the image of God created he him; male and female created he them" (Genesis1:27). Then, at the beginning of Chapter 2, on the seventh day God ended his work and rested.

Biblical scholars set the date for the creation of the universe as the same date for the creation of Adam and Eve at about 6,000 years ago. How did they reach that conclusion? They added the 4,000 years of Adam and Eve's genealogy tree, as recorded in the Bible, to the approximate 2,000 years from Jesus' birth to the present. From this calculation, they concluded God created the universe about 6,000 years ago.

On the other side of the debate, anthropologists credit evolution for the creation of *Homo sapiens* and set the date for the first appearance of our ancestors or hominins at about seven million years ago. At that time they believe members of the *Family Hominidae* evolved. How did scientists establish this date in the prehistoric time line of Earth's birth?

The Bible names two distinct individuals as our progenitors, Adam and Eve. Evolution postulates that there was no identifiable single first person. Nor first rabbit, nor first shark, nor first chicken, nor any first single member of a species. I guess you could say each species blurred into an eventual new species from its originating species. Like the well-known, fanciful riddle: Which came first the chicken or the egg? Or the parent, or the offspring? To an evolutionary biologist, the answer is obvious. The chicken came first, as each species had to have parents. Below is a quick 101 course in chicken-species evolution.

Many millennia ago, a hen-like bird mated with a rooster-like bird. When the sperm and egg combined, the chicken-like egg mutated slightly. After many more generations, the chicken-like offspring from the chicken-like egg became noticeably different looking. Voilá, a new species—a recognizable chicken. Thus, the riddle is answered. The new chicken species, composed of true hens and of true roosters, lays true chicken eggs that become true chickens. First the chicken, then the chicken egg!

Another easily understood explanation for evolution and the absence of an actual first person ancestor stems from my favorite evolutionary biologist and author Richard Dawkins. His book, *The Magic of Reality*, written for youngsters ages eight through thirteen, but also an informative read for adults, contains a chapter entitled, "Who Was the First Person?" He asks us to play a mind game in order to comprehend the unseen variations and enormous amount of time required for evolution.

Dawkins tells his reader to imagine his own, or his sibling's, or his parents', or any person's lifespan. From birth to death, our journey comprises designated stages: infant, baby, toddler, youngster, child, juvenile, pubescent, adolescent, young adult, adult, middle-aged, and elderly. There is no one set day when the individual changes from one life cycle to the next. We morph indistinguishably from one stage into another without any exact date to mark on the calendar highlighting the occurrence.

Then, Dawkins asks us to transfer the phenomenon of this same rationale to the birth of a new species. The offspring, like the chicken-like species, has a parent which looks very much like itself, but each offspring may continue to vary slightly from its parent throughout eons of time. Then, one day the species has changed into a new species. This enormity of time needed for evolution to occur is one of the greatest difficulties in grasping its concept.

In comparing the literal, biblical account of our ancestry to the scientific theory of our ancestry, keep in mind if religious theologians and scientists wish to entertain both versions, they are able to meld the two ideas with a concept called theistic evolution.

Today, the majority of mainline Protestant churches and the Catholic church have adopted a view of scientific evolution called theistic evolution. The American Scientific Affiliation of Christians, a Christian organization of scientists, offers this explanation of evolution that includes a theory for God's roll in the process of evolution. This theory of theistic evolution (TE)—also called evolutionary creation—proposes that God's method of creation was to cleverly design a universe in which everything would naturally evolve.

Even Charles Darwin, the father of the theory of evolution, revised his words to placate the theologians of his era. The first edition of his classic book *On the Origin of Species* ended with this much quoted statement: "There is grandeur in this view of life, with its several powers, having been originally breathed into a few forms or into one; and that, whilst the planet has gone cycling on according to the fixed law of gravity, from so simple a beginning endless forms most beautiful and most wonderful have been, and are being, evolved."

In response to criticism from religious sources and most notably from his deeply religious wife Emma, in the second edition, published only a few months after the first edition, Darwin added "by the Creator" at the end of the closing sentence.

A recent poll of Americans in 2015 from the Pew Research Center reported that 98 percent of scientists believe humans evolved over time as compared to 65 percent of the public. Although this poll indicates almost all scientists believe in evolution, that is not to say that they don't believe in God or embrace a religious faith. Thus, this religious versus evolutionary conflict continues to rage in the twenty-first century among educated thinkers. In writing this book, I present *my* beliefs as to the creation of my ancestors. Were they Adam and Eve, or were they unidentified hominins who began to roam the world about seven million years ago?

For clarification, below are listed the two most recent scientific definitions used in referring to our numerous extinct and extant ancestors.

> <u>Homonid</u>: the group consisting of all modern and extinct Great Apes (that is, modern humans, chaimpanzees, gorillas and orangutans plus all their modern ancestors). <u>Hominim</u>: the group consisting of modern humans, extinct human species and all our immediate ancestors (including members of the genera *Homo, Australopithecus, Paranthropus,* and *Ardipithecus).*

Now that I have suggested to you that evolution can be portrayed to enlist God's or a higher power's hand in its intricacies, why do the creationist/intelligent design proponents persist in the belief that evidence of evolution is a myth with no possibility of fact, while at the same time, declaring their version is not a myth, but a fact? I conclude it is because they have not read scientific findings or considered and weighed the preponderance of available evidence. Whereas, on the other hand, most evolutionists have read the Bible, or at least are familiar with the creation story of Adam and Eve. In fact, myriad creation myths or stories are found in almost every culture and every age, going back to the Paleolithic or Stone Age.

Now, I propose a mind game. Imagine you live in the Stone Age. You have no stone tablets, or parchments, or cave drawings to explain your existence or environment to you. Where would you look for the answers? I suggest you would use your senses to try to interpret the world around you. You see and feel the sun; you experience darkness, the moon, and the stars above you. You see lightning and hear the thunder that follows. Would you connect the two? You see plants and trees bearing fruit. Would you wonder where they came from? Would you understand how seeds from the fruit of a plant produce another plant? You see rivers, lakes, and oceans. Perhaps you see a volcano erupting. You see many varieties of animals, birds, and fish. You observe birth and death. How would you explain the existence of all this?

If I were that imaginary cave woman, with no knowledge of history or conception of the future to guide me, I think I would assign powers beyond my understanding and control to be the cause of all the miracles in my world. Events with no known cause are considered supernatural. Eventually, I would have invented powerful Gods as an explanation. And that is exactly what happened.

One of the attributes which makes us human is our ability to imagine and think in the abstract. We want to know where we came from. What happens when we die. This manner of thought led to our creation stories and beliefs.

Let's peruse a few creation stories from the Stone Age and from around the world. We will find they are different in detail but alike in the belief that mysticism, the occult, magic, or the power of unseen Gods are the theoretical reasons for the unknown mysteries of nature.

At the time of this writing, the earliest evidence of man's awareness of the afterlife was documented to be during the Middle Paleolithic Period, from 120,000 to 35,000 BCE. In 1908, a Neanderthal burial site was discovered at La Chapelle-aux-Saints, France. Bodies were buried with food and tools, thought to be for use in the afterlife.

Shamans were nearly universal throughout all cultures worldwide. Dated at 20,000 BCE, the earliest shaman image was painted on a cave wall in the Ariège region of southwestern France.

Painting of a shaman at Les Trois-Frères cave in France

My favorite artifact from the Paleolithic Period, dated at 24,000 BCE, is the palm-sized statue, named the Venus of Willendorf. The very chubby fertility figurine was carved from limestone and tinted with red, thought to be a symbol of menstrual blood. In 1908, a workman discovered the relic at a paleolithic dig at Willendorf, Austria. Similar statues have been found in other locations

Let's jump ahead in history and survey, in brief, a few of the traditional and revered creation stories from around the world.

GREEK: First came chaos, then Eurynome, Goddess of
                    All Things, evolved and mated with the north
                    wind or some legends say a snake and begat
                    Eros, God of Love. Then earth and sky begat
                    the Titans who begat the Greek gods with Zeus
                    being the youngest son.

NORSE: First chasm, somewhat like Greek chaos, of fire
                    and ice. The two combined and produced a giant,
                    Ymir, and then a cow, Audumla, who nourished
                    Ymir.

INDIAN: Hinduism teaches the universe always has been,
                    always will be, but is always in flux.

CHINESE: Heaven and Earth were in chaos or in a cosmic
                    egg for 18,000 years, then broke apart and
                    formed P'an-ku that grew for another 18,000
                    years before becoming earth, sky, moon,
                    mountains, rivers and soil. Parasites feeding on
                    P'an-ku's body, impregnated by the wind, became
                    human beings.

EGYPTIAN: The Chaos Goose and the Chaos Gander
                    produced an egg that was the sun, Re. The
                    Gander was Ged, the earth god.

ZOROASTRIAN: In the beginning goodness fought evil, until evil
                    was worn out. Then goodness created the cosmic
                    egg. A cosmic man escaped, became a plant
                    on earth, and a man grew from one side and a
                    woman from the other.

Now that we have surveyed some of the creation stories replete with supernatural explanations for our creation, let's consider the scientific version for our origin. Anthropologists believe hominids first appeared in the evolutionary record 200,000 years ago, a minuscule dot in time in relation to the age of the earth. In order to understand the scientific premise for our birth, it is necessary to outline the time line for the formation of the earth. Science contends Earth formed approximately 4.5 billion years ago (BYA) in the period named the Hadeon Eon, from the Greek

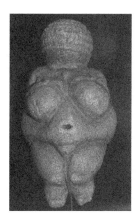

*Venus of Willendorf displayed at
the Naturhistorisches Museum in Vienna, Austria*

word *Hades* or hell. (It seems the "chaotic" creation stories had the right idea.) During the first 700 million years of Earth's formation, icy comets bombarded the earth causing oceans, atmosphere, and rain. As the crust cooled, rocks and continental plates formed. The first life appeared in the Precambrian Eon, 3.8 BYA with the emergence of simple life, in the form of prokaryotic cells. These unicellular organisms lack a nuclear membrane, do not develop or differentiate into multicellular forms, and are capable of living in deep oceans, hot springs, or currently almost anywhere in or on our bodies, as bacteria.

For two billion years, the earth underwent "earth-changing" conditions: strata multiplied accumulating as large land masses in the seas; oxygen developed in the earth's atmosphere; several glaciation periods appeared, one of them labeled the "Snowball Earth" as some geologists hypothesized that the earth was completely frozen. Importantly, for our lineage, during this time, advanced single-celled and multi-celled life evolved.

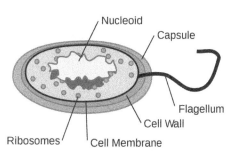

*Graphic of a simple prokaryotic cell
(magnification: 18,300x)*

Then, beginning roughly 550 MYA (million years ago), our current eon, named the Phanerozoic Eon (from the Greek *fanéros* visible and *zoí* life) began. The beginning of this eon was named the Cambrian Period, 543 MYA to 490 MYA. This prolific period was christened the Cambrian Explosion. Most of the major groups of animals first appeared in the fossil record, including mollusks, crustaceans, spiders, insects, and animals with spinal cords that eventually evolved to us, *Homo sapiens*.

In the Triassic Period, roughly 200 MYA, the first mammal appeared. Although controversial, with its exact classification still in flux among paleontologists and taxonomists in scientific circles, most of them consider the *Ecozostrodon* to be the first mammal species. This three-inch long, shrew-like creature laid eggs, but fed its young on mother's milk.

Artist's depiction of an Ecozostrodon

Now we jump ahead another 200 million years to the Paleocene Epoch, sixty-five MYA, to chart the appearance of the first primate, classified in taxonomy in the *Order Primates,* eventually to include us *Homo sapiens*. The scientists seem to have followed the theologians who claim we were made in God's image, by naming ourselves *Primates* or *first* in the Class Mammalia—not in the sense of first evolved, but in the sense of first in importance.

The candidate for the earliest fossil primate is of the genus *Teilhardina*. Several species belonging to the genus have been identified. The small one-ounce mammal lived in Europe, Asia, and North America about 47 to 56 MYA, during the Early Eocene Epoch.

Traditional taxonomists classified primates into two major groups: prosimians (lemur-like in form) or anthropoids (manlike in form). In the 1950s, a German entomologist suggested a new method of classifying organisms. The new system called cladism grouped species not by physical similarities, but by evolutionary descent, often resulting in a more accurate pinpointing of the common ancestor.

Extinct fossil primate Teilhardina, *exhibited at the Museé d'Histoire Naturelle Brussels*

Primates evolved from ancestors who lived in the trees of subtropical forests. Extant primates live in the tropical forests of Asia, Africa, and the Americas, except for humans who live on all continents but Antarctica. Primates range in size from the mouse lemur weighing one ounce to gorillas weighing more than 400 pounds.

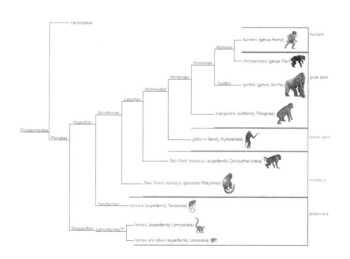

A cladagram illustrating possible classification of living primates [1]

The right side of the above cladogram lists the common names for each group of primates. The prosimians include lorises, lemurs, and tarsiers. All the other primates are anthropoids. The monkeys split into New World monkeys and Old World monkeys when continental drift separated North and South America from Asia, Europe, and Africa during the Eocene Epoch, 54 to 33 MYA. Gibbons comprise the group named lesser apes, while orangutans and gorillas are considered great apes. Chimpanzees and humans are grouped together as one family, *Hominini*, but occupy separate genera.

Unlike the Bible's unequivocal assertion that God created humans 6,000 years ago in the Garden of Eden, now thought to be the country of Iraq, anthropologists admit the story of our beginnings is incomplete. They continue studying, researching, excavating, analyzing, and reconstructing at digs, universities, and labs all over the world in order to update, and increase their knowledge of the human story. According to science, the story of our hominin ancestors began seven MYA and ended approximately 50,000 years ago with the evolution of true modern humans, *Homo sapiens*. The chart below lists a plethora of extinct hominin species or the possible "missing links" who are candidates for our progenitors.

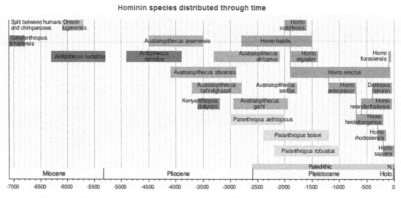

Millions of years, Hominin species distributed through time [2]

The journey began in the Early Piocene Epoch, about seven MYA, thought to be the time of the split between chimpanzee and human ancestors. A small partial cranium and a few pieces of jaw bone were found in the central African country of Chad in 2001. Scientists classified the fossil in the hominin family of the genus *Sahelanthropus* (from *Sahel*, a region in Chad plus *anthropus*, the Greek word for human), and named the species *tchadensis* (from *tchad*, the location of the fossil find plus *ensis*, Latin for "pertaining to"). They nicknamed the skull Toumaï which means "hope of life" in the local language and calculated the date of the fossil to be about seven MYA. Debate continues as to whether the specimen was bipedal or not.

Another separate genus with a single species listed on the chart was classified as genus *Orrorin* (meaning "original man" in the Tugen language) and species *tugensis* (meaning found in the Tugen hills of Kenya). This early species found in 2000 is dated to 5.1 to 6.2 MYA. It differed from the later genera of *Ardipithecus* and *Australopithecus* by having smaller teeth and thicker enamel on its teeth. The femur bone suggested the species was bipedal.

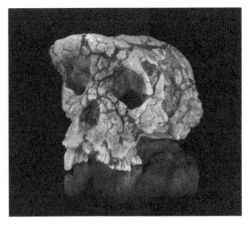

Cast of a Sahelanthropus tchadensis *skull, nicknamed Toumaï*

The next genus chronicled in the time line was *Ardipithecus* (from *ardi* meaning "ground" in Arabic and *pithecus* meaning "ape" in Greek), so an ape who lived on the ground, not in trees. Two species were assigned to this genus: *kadabba* (meaning "oldest ancestor" in the Afar language of the Rift Valley of Ethiopia) and *ramida* (meaning "root" in the Afar language). These early half-ape and half-human ancestors lived 5.6 to 4.4 MYA.

The *Ardipithecus ramidus* fossil was discovered in 1994. Its discovery was not formally announced until 2009. The small female hominin was nicknamed "Ardi." Note how it took fifteen years of study, analysis, and reconstruction before the paleontologists exhibited their discovery.

The next genus represented on the chart is *Australopithecus* (from the Latin *australis* meaning "southern" and the Greek *pithecus* meaning "ape"). At this writing, seven species comprise this genus. They lived from roughly 4.5 to 2.5 MYA and overlapped both the genus *Ardipithecus,* which was dying out, and our genus *Homo* which was evolving.

The most famous single fossil find among the genus *Australopithecus* was the fossil nicknamed "Lucy." In 1974, after searching for fossils all morning, Donald Johanson, an American paleoanthropologist, along with a graduate student, stumbled upon a cache of bones from one individual. When they arrived back at camp with news of their remarkable discovery, the Beatles' song, "Lucy in the Sky with Diamonds" was blaring on the radio. In celebration, the group named their find, Lucy.

After careful study and reassembly of the many fragments, Dr. Johanson realized they had discovered a new species, which lived 3.9 to 2.9 MYA and named it *Australopithecus afarensis,* after the Afar region in Ethiopia where the fossils were found. The skeleton was determined to be of a young female, between twenty or thirty years old, three and a half feet tall, and weighing barely sixty pounds. Most importantly, she walked upright, determined from how the thigh bone connected to the hip bone.

In 2007, *Lucy's Legacy: The Hidden Treasures of Ethiopia,* a public exhibit, embarked on a six-year tour of the United States. Due to possible damage to the fragile fossils, she was returned to Ethiopia in 2013. Now she is only portrayed by casts of her skeleton.

Skeleton and restoration model of Lucy (Australopithecus afarensis) *in exhibit at the National Museum of Nature and Science, Tokyo, Japan.*

Another famous fossil from the *Australopithecus* genus was the Taung child. The skull was found in 1924 at a limestone quarry near Taung, South Africa. Raymond Dart, head of the Anatomy Department at Witwatersrand University in Johannesburg, South Africa, noted that the ape-like skull displayed human traits. The eye orbit, the teeth arrangement, and how the base of the skull attached to the spinal column suggested the creature was bipedal. He named the specimen *Australopithecus africanus,* or Southern African ape.

This was the first time, the word *pithecus,* as we know already as the word for "ape" in Greek, had been assigned to a possible hominin ancestor. The claim was met with skepticism. At that time, the scientific community thought a large brain would have come before bipedalism. By the slow and thorough method of scientific investigation, it was thirty years before the Taung child was accepted as a hominin ancestor and not an ape ancestor.

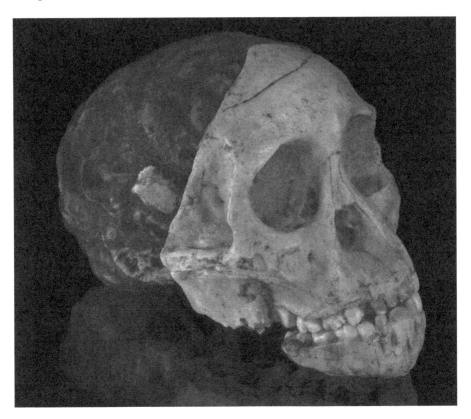

Cast of the Taung child

From the find in 1924 and up to a recent find in 2008, paleontologists continue to discover and add new species to the genus *Australopithecus.* Six skeletons consisting of a male, a female, a juvenile male, and three infants, discovered at the Malapa Fossil site at the Cradle of Humankind World Heritage Site in South Africa, were identified as a new species *Australopithecus sediba,* (the species name from the Sotho African language meaning "natural spring " or "well"). The remains were dated to roughly 2 MYA, overlapping the time when fossils assigned to the *Homo* genus lived. Thus, some scientists have suggested the species as a direct ancestor of the *Homo* lineage.

Near the bottom of the chart is a seemingly detached genus which lived from 2.5 to a million years ago. Scientists determined it not to be *Australopithecus* or *Homo,* but a different genus *Paranthropus* (from the Greek *para* "beside" and *ánthropos* "human"). As the name suggests, most anthropologists do not think this genus was a direct ancestor of humans, but lived at the same time and beside our evolving progenitors.

Replica of the Black Skull

At this writing, the genus *Paranthropus* consists of three species. This branch of the hominin family tree continues to baffle the scientists. Few specimen fossils have been found. Some consider it a subtribe of the *Australopithecus*. Members of this genus *Paranthropus* have gorilla-like sagittal cranial crest and broad, grinding herbivorous teeth.

The oldest dated *Paranthropus* genus is the species *Paranthropus aethiopicus*. In 1985, in Kenya near to Ethiopia, Richard Leakey and Alan Walker discovered a "black skull," so called due to the dark coloration from manganese. They named it as a new species, *aethiopicus,* in the genus *Paranthropus* and dated the find to 2.5 MYA. Little is known of the species due to lack of collaborating fossils.

Artist Reconstruction of a Paranthropus boisei

The species *Paranthropus boisei* (named for Charles Boise who financed the discovery team of the fossil) is considered the largest of the *Paranthropus* genus and lived for about one million years, from roughly 2 MYA to 1 MYA in Eastern Africa. The anthropologist Mary Leakey discovered the first member of this species in 1959 in Tanzania. Its characteristics were similar to the subtribe *robust australopithecus*. Its brain volume was slightly larger than *Australopithecus africnus* and *Australopithecus afarensis* and near the size of a modern day chimpanzee.

In scientific circles, the species gained fame after Mary Leakey's son, Richard Leakey, suggested from nearby artifacts that *Paranthropus boisei* was the first hominin to use stone tools.

The third member of this genus is *Paranthropus robustus*. The time span for this species dates from 2.0 to 1.2 MYA. After Raymond Dart's discovery of *Australopithecus africanus* in 1925, in 1938 Robert Broom, a seventy-year old scientist, prospecting in Kromdraii, South Africa, discovered some bones quite different from those of an *Australopithecus africanus*. He was convinced the fossils represented a new species of hominin and named it *Paranthropus robustus*. In a cave in the area, fragments from 130 individuals were unearthed. Examination of the fossils confirmed the individuals only lived to age seventeen. The *Paranthropus robustus* species has only been found in South Africa. The other two members of the genus were found at later dates and in other parts of Africa.

In the next chapter in the long journey of evolution we meet our genus, *Homo,* derived from the Latin word which means "man." The *Homo* genus lived at the same time as the *Australopithecus* and the *Paranthropus* genera. The first species in the *Homo* genus lived 2.8 MYA.

1. https://en.wikipedia.org/wiki/Primate (Accessed July 6, 2017)
2. https://en.wikipedia.org/wiki/Human_evolution (Accessed July 6, 2017)

Chapter Twenty-Nine

The Very First of the Homo Species

I can say one thing with certainty. There is no one *very* first ancestor of *Homo sapiens*. Paleontologists can say with certainty that they will leave no stone unturned as they study our ancient ancestry. New digs, new methods, new insights are always advancing or revising our knowledge so that no fact is written in stone or all facts are written in stone.

When I began my study of science in high school in the 1950s, my reference guide was the *Field Book of Natural History,* published in 1949. The now outdated information listed only five progenitors of our genus, one of whom was proven to be a fraud four years later in 1953. In 2010 and 2012 in their high school biology classes my grandchildren studied seven *Homo* species from a textbook published in 2004. A Wikipedia chart in 2016 listed six *Homo* fossils as possible candidates for the "missing links" in our lineage. Since I began researching this book, paleontologists announced the discovery of three more *Homo* species. It appears evolutionary evidence explodes exponentially as paleontologists keep digging until they unearth the truth about our forebears by discarding and adding to their knowledge.

Although my mini-encyclopedia of natural history, published in the mid-twentieth century, contains correct information about the solar system and constellations, rocks and minerals, and plants and animals, after seventy years, some of the information has become obsolete and much of it has been supplemented. The field book listed five members of the human family tree: Piltdown Man, Java Man, Cro-Magnon Man, Neanderthal Man, and Modern Man—and one, Piltdown Man, was a hoax.

The disingenuous story of the Piltdown Man occurred due to racism and nationalism, both concepts prevalent in the early twentieth century. Europeans wished to prove man originated in Europe, not in Africa. In 1908, a workman found a partial skull in a gravel pit at Piltdown, East Essex, England and gave it to Charles Dawson, a local amateur paleontologist. Dawson reconstructed the skull and attached a jawbone to it. In December, 1912 he exhibited the skull at a meeting of the Geological Society of London, claiming a workman had given it to him four years earlier. Dawson suggested it was the "missing link" to the *Homo* species and named the new species *Eoanthropus dawsoni* or "Dawson's dawn-man." Although the finding did engender controversy at the time, it was not until forty-five years later in 1953, that the British Natural History Museum declared the composite was a forgery, cobbled together from a mixture of a small modern human skull, an orangutan jaw, and some chimpanzee teeth.

Besides the embarrassment to scientific prestige, hoaxes can lead science down a blind alley and delay the discovery of the truth. In this instance, it had led scientists to rethink their hypotheses as to the development of mankind. The large skull with apelike mandible seemed to indicate that the brain expanded before the jaw adapted to chewing more nutritious food. When, as initially thought and now accepted as the more probable fact, the ability to eat and chew protein-fueled animal products caused the expansion of the brain. Thus, the "discovery" of the Piltdown Man rebutted the conventional theory for almost fifty years.

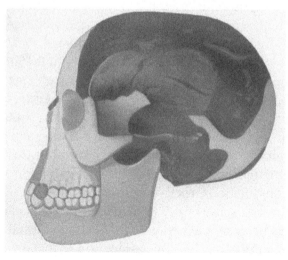

The reconstructed skull of the Piltdown Man

Unlike specious Piltdown Man, Java Man and Cro-Magnon Man are common names for actual hominins. Besides the Latin name given to a new species in accordance with Linnaen taxonomy, scientists often assigned a nickname to fossils. Java Man, and also Peking Man (although not mentioned in the field book) were examples of familiar names for the species known as *Homo erectus,* or "upright man." This *Homo* species was thought to be the first to leave Africa.

Cro-Magnon Man, sometimes called *Homo sapiens sapiens,* was the name given to early modern man, who was first discovered in 1868 in France on property owned by Monsieur Magnon. Once a commonly used term for any early humans, current scientific language prefers European Early Modern Human or EEMH in place of Cro-Magnon. The earliest EEMH remains are carbon dated to 43,000 to 45,000 years ago.

Most of us are familiar with the name Neanderthal, thought to be the last, except for us, among hominin descendants to go extinct. Although fossils found in 1829 and 1848 were later identified as Neanderthal skulls, the species name derives from the 1856 discovery of a fossil in the Neanderthal Valley in what is now Germany. A point of clarification, some scientific journals spell Neanderthal as Neandertal to correspond to the renaming of the German site where the fossil was first discovered. In this book I use the more common spelling, Neanderthal. The official Latin taxonomical name of *Homo neanderthalansis* can never be changed as the laws governing biological nomenclature forbid changing the spelling of any genus.

Scientists believe Neanderthals and *Homo sapiens* were the last two survivors in the *Homo* lineage. From the DNA comparison of Neanderthals and *Homo sapiens,* geneticists determined the two species diverged from a common ancestor, probably *Homo erectus,* between 350,000 and 400,000 years ago. *Homo erectus* originated roughly from 2,000,000 years ago and lived until 200,000 years ago. They ranged over the three continents of Africa, Europe, and Asia.

At about 350,000 to 400,000 years ago, the African branch began evolving as modern humans, while the Eurasian branch evolved as Neanderthals. The African prototype expanded beyond Africa about 200,000 years ago and reached the Middle East about 100,000 years ago. The Neanderthals had been living there at least 100,000 years before that. The two species probably co-existed in what are now Israel, Lebanon, Syria, and Turkey for around 50,000 years using similar tools and practicing a similar culture.

What happened about 50,000 years ago to wipe out the Neanderthals is the unsolved evolutionary mystery. Was it genocide by modern man, or conversely, assimilation by modern man; gradual inability to adapt after climate change at the end of the Ice Age; or losing the competition in the human evolution race due to poorer hunting skills or lesser intelligence that doomed the Neanderthals?

One theory which seems plausible to me is that the Neanderthals lived in extended families, not in larger units as did the descendants of modern man. Hunting was a prime activity for the Neanderthals. Women and children joined in the hunt. The result was more injuries to vulnerable family members, creating a shrinking gene pool. Scientists have many hypothesis but they do not know for certain why the Neanderthals went extinct an estimated 30,000 to 24,000 years ago.

As I researched the scientific and speculative information amassed on the subject of the Neanderthals and their demise, I learned to admire them and mourn their extinction. Their bad press stemmed from the poorly reconstructed skeleton of the "Old Man of La Chapelle." In 1908 scientists discovered an almost intact skeleton buried in a limestone cave at La Chapell-aux-Saints, France. They estimated he was quite old at the time of his death as he had lost several teeth and bone had regrown along the gums.

Enter French geologist and paleontologist Pierre Marcellin Boule, the villain in this scientific hoax. He had a preconceived perception of Neanderthals as unintelligent, clumsy brutes more similar to gorillas than humans. With this prejudicial mindset, he reconstructed the Neanderthal bones to portray a stooped figure with bent knees, jutting head, and even an opposable toe, thus perpetuating the cultural stereotype of an ancestor more akin to apes than humans.

In the 1950s a reanalysis of the skeleton of the man from La Chapelle indicated that the aged man probably suffered from osteoarthritis and the disease was the reason for his stooped posture. Then, in 1985 anthropologist Erik Trinkaus examined the skeleton and confirmed that Neanderthals did indeed walk upright and the joint deformity discovered in the 1950s would not have prevented upright bipedalism. He suggested that Boulon had intentionally constructed the skeleton in the stooped position due to his own false predilection.

In the twenty-first century Neanderthals continue to fascinate paleontologists and laymen alike. For historical fiction novels of Neanderthals and early modern men I suggest reading Jean Auel's

Earth Children Series, a group of historical fiction novels of Neanderthals and early modern men. In the first book, *The Clan of the Cave Bear,* Ayla, the protagonist, is a child of "the others" or modern man, but is raised by a Neanderthal clan after an accident separates her from her tribe. For a scientific but also informal, readable account, read *Humans Who Went Extinct* by Clive Finlayson, paleoanthropologist and director of the Gibraltar Museum. With fascinating detail he compares the history of the Neanderthals to modern men and suggests their extinction and our survival was a matter of luck. For an actual scientific comparison of the genes of Neanderthals

Display at le musée de l'Homme de Néanderthal, La Chapelle-aux-Saints

and *Homo sapiens,* I recommend accessing the Smithsonian National Museum of Natural History web site under sub-heading Ancient DNA and Neanderthals. DNA cannot be denied. The salient fact is that non-African *Homo sapiens* share 1 to 4 percent of their DNA with Neanderthals.

Archaeologists, paleoanthropologists, and geologists working together strive to unlock the mystery of our extinct cousins. In fact, some scientists consider them a sub-species of *Homo sapiens.* Since the first Neanderthal fossils were identified, over four hundred specimens have been found ranging across Europe, the Middle East, and Asia from arctic Siberia to temporal, sunny Spain.

They have a robust frame, a low, flat skull, pronounced brow, and almost no chin, but a brain slightly larger than ours. Some were fair-skinned with blue eyes and red hair.

Now let's consider why there were seven species mentioned in the high school biology text while only six were listed at a later date on the internet. The six species noted in both sites were aligned in the same descending and sometimes overlapping order in the same geological eras. Please refer back to Chapter Twenty-Eight, page 284 to review the evolutionary chart. In order of appearance from the first named *Homo* species to us on the evolutionary tree are *Homo habillis* "handyman," *Homo ergaster* "working man," *Homo erectus* "upright man," *Homo heidelbergensis,* first found in Heidelberg, Germany so "Heidelberg man," *Homo neanderthalensis,* named for skull found in the Neanderthal Valley, Germany, so "Neanderthal man," and last but definitely not least, *Homo sapiens* "wise man."

The 2004 biology text book added the species *Homo* antecessor "explorer man" between *Homo erectus* and *Homo heidelbergensis.* As palaeontology is not an exact science some researchers do not believe

Skeleton and restoration model of Neanderthal in Exhibit at the National Museum of Nature and Science in Tokyo, Japan.

Homo antecessor should be considered as a separate species. They dispute categorizing the bones as a new species and believe them to be *Homo ergaster.*

In the 1990s in the Atapuerca Mountains of Northern Spain a Spanish research team found eighty fossils belonging to six individuals. The specimens were dated to 800,000 years ago. The teeth were primitive and similar to those of *Homo erectus* but the facial bones seemed to belong to a more modern man. This led the researchers to believe they had discovered a new species, a possible "missing link" between Neanderthals and *Homo sapiens* and named it *Homo antecessor.* Later analysis determined the fossils were from juveniles and that might have explained the facial contours that don't change until after puberty. Until more fossils are found, evidence of a new species is not confirmed.

From the charts *Homo habilis* has the honor of oldest discovered *Homo* species to date. When did the *Homo* genus split from the *Australopithecus* genus to become a new genus? Scientists placed our earliest *Homo* ancestor at near the end of the Pliocene era, roughly 2.7 or 2.8 million years ago (MYA).

What did the first *Homo* ancestor look like? Our first ancestor looked more like an ape than a human with fur on its body, long arms, and short legs. However, it exhibited two defining characteristics of a *Homo*—increased brain size and tool-making ability. The average cranial capacity was 650 cubic centimeters, compared to 1,350 cubic centimeters for the average modern man or 500 cubic centimeters for an *Australopithecus.* Their height ranged from three feet, five inches to four feet, five inches. Their weight averaged seventy pounds.

The first *Homo habilis* fossil was discovered in 1960 by the husband and wife team of Louis and Mary Leaky at Olduvai Gorge, Tanzania, near where Louis Leakey unearthed many crude, stone tools. The scientific

Forensic facial reconstruction of Homo habilis

community continues to debate its placement in the human lineage. At least five other fossil finds have been found and cataloged in the *habilis* species in Kenya and Tanzania.

Another possible human ancestor whom I have not mentioned previously is *Homo rudolfensis*. Richard Leaky, son of Mary and Louis Leaky, discovered a skull in 1986 near Lake Rudolf in Kenya and suggested he had found a new species. Since scientists have not reached a consensus as to whether this fossil is in the genus *Australopithecus* or in the genus H*omo,* I have not included this debated specimen in our lineage.

The next human ancestor in chronological order on the time line is *Homo ergaster* who lived about two million years ago and died out maybe 500,000 years later. Co-existing with *ergaster* was *Homo erectus* who appeared in the record at about the same time but possibly lived as recently as 70,000 years ago, to earn it the longest-surviving *Homo* species award. Many anthropologists consider the two to be of the same species. Many researchers divided the two species by location. Fossils found in Africa were classified as *ergaster* while those in Asia as *erectus*.

Model of the face of an adult Homo erectus, *displayed at the Smithsonian Natural History Museum*

These two species were the first to look more human than simian. Body proportions were similar to modern humans with long legs and shorter arms, a long lower cranium, larger brain cavity, and projecting nasal aperture. The height ranged from five feet to six feet and the weight from eighty-five pounds to one hundred fifty pounds. The species had no body hair, dark skin, and the whites of the eyes were visible.

What caused the difference in anatomy between *habilis* in the Pliocene era and *ergaster/erectus* in the Pleistocene era? The main reason was climate change that caused environmental change. The Pleistocene geological epoch occurring roughly from 2,500,000 to 11,700 years ago produced recurring glacial periods. This fluctuating climate caused a change in the ecosystem of Northeast Africa. Over time the tropical forests were replaced by the African savannah—a grassland with small or dispersed trees and a seasonal rainfall. Species had to adapt or go extinct.

During this long period of climatic fluctuation, our ancestors adapted. Instead of living in trees they had to venture out into the open grassland to hunt for food. They had to develop different skills, such as speed, cunning, cooperation, and tool making in order to compete in the open and vast environment. Since large, dangerous predators slept during the hottest part of the day, our human ancestors did their hunting in the heat of the day. Many anthropologists credit this hunting strategy as one possible reason for the loss of body hair. Body fur is a protection against the sun but it also retains heat. By natural selection, humans without body hair were able to sweat and regulate their body temperature through skin pores rather than by panting as in the case of most mammals. This mutation proved successful. The skin also produced more melatonin and turned darker to protect from the sun's harmful rays. Another suggested theory for hair loss was to rid the body of lice. Our primate cousins spent a large percentage of their social time in grooming sessions.

In order for the *Homo ergaster/erectus* to increase its efficiency in long distance running the rib cage increased while the pelvis narrowed. For the female, this anatomical change produced two effects. First, a trade off in evolutionary development occurred. While a chimpanzee is born with their brain almost fully mature, a human baby is born with a small, underdeveloped brain in order to fit through the tight birth canal. Thus, the infant was dependent on its mother for nourishment and care for a much longer time as the brain grew.

The second effect, in response to the longer need for infancy care, was perhaps the origin of female/male bonding. In order for the mother to nurse and care for her offspring, she became more dependent on her mate. Experts believe this was the beginning of cooperation between male and female and the beginning of modern human values and the nuclear family.

Another advancement among our ancestors was the improvement in tool making. The *habilis* and early *ergaster/erectus* made primitive Oldowan tools, found in the Olduvai Gorge in Tanzania, barely more than a rock with a chipped edge. But by 1.6 MYA *ergaster/erectus* invented the more sophisticated heart-shaped hand axes, known as Achulean bifaces, named after their first discovery in Saint-Achuel, France. This became the tool of choice for nearly all early human history until 100,000 years ago.

*Examples of primitive Oldowan chipped tool
versus Achulean hand axes*

As *erectus* emigrated out of Africa and east toward the Indonesian Island of Java, the terrain and vegetation changed and again *erectus* adapted. Instead of stone tools our ancestors fashioned spears and clubs from bamboo stalks. They shared the bamboo forests with pigs, native elephants and the giant vegetarian ape, the largest extinct primate *Gigantopithecus* or giant ape. A large tooth from this creature was first found in 1935 by an anthropologist in a Chinese apothecary shop, where the fossilized teeth were ground up to be used in medicines.

Since then, in China and Southeast Asia scientists have discovered enough teeth and mandibles to infer the probability of a new, extinct genus of primates consisting of three species. They lived in the bamboo forests from nine million years ago to as late as 100,000 years ago and coexisted with our ancestors. The largest of the new genus was *Gigantopithecus blacki* at a height of nine feet and about 1,200 pounds—a true to life Big Foot.

Many fossils representing *Homo ergaster/erectus* have been found and are still being found in sites in North, East, and West Africa and East and West Asia. A Dutch surgeon found the first Asian fossil in 1891 in Indonesia. In the 1920s more *erectus* fossils were found in China in what is now called the Peking Man Site. In 1984, near Lake Turkana, Kenya a member of the Richard Leakey team found an almost intact fossil skeleton of an *ergaster/erectus* boy which dated to 1.5 to 1.6 million years ago. The specimen consisted of 108 bones, the most complete human skeleton ever discovered. Researchers estimated the age at death between eight and thirteen years. The skull was low and sloping with no chin, but the nose projected, not flat as seen in apes.

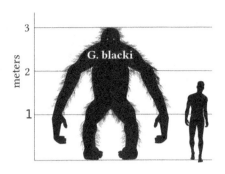

Comparison of a 1.8 meter human to a Gigantopithecus blacki

The next hominin species listed on the chart is *Homo heidelbergensis* who lived approximately 600,000 to 200,000 years ago. The placement of this specimen in the taxon of human lineage has been so perplexing to paleontologists that the dilemma has been nicknamed the "muddle of the middle." Some scientists believe *Homo ergaster/erectus* morphed into Neanderthals and modern man without another named species to bridge the gap. Others push to recognize *Homo heidelbergensisis* as a new and distinct species and that it should be characterized as such.

Much of the conflict is being resolved as more and more fossils considered to be *Homo heidelbergensis* have been found in the last thirty years. In 1907, in Germany a workman found a large mandible in a sandpit. He turned it over to a professor at the University of Heidelberg, who determined it to be a new species, the first *Homo heidelbergensis* fossil. Since then, researchers have discovered many fossil remains believed to be from the species *Homo heidelbergensis.*

The simplest explanations to the controversy seems to be that H*omo ergaster/erectus* evolved into a species with a bigger brain and migrated out of Africa approximately 400,000 years ago into Germany, France, England, and also West Asia. Eventually this species evolved into Neanderthals. Some anthropologists preferred to skip

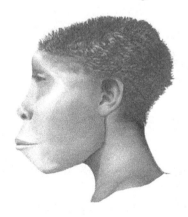

Reconstruction of Turkana Boy or Nariokotoma Boy, Homo erectus *1.6 MYA*

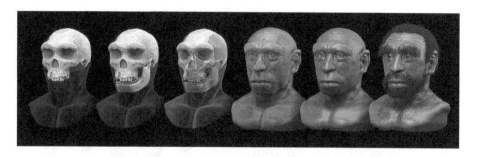

Forensic facial reconstruction of Homo heidelbergensis

the *Homo heidelbergensis* designation and called the fossils "archaic modern man." Their life style was similar to early Homo sapiens. They built shelters out of wood and rock, used fire, and communicated with "words" and gesture.

Before we examine the very first *Homo sapiens,* I want to mention three hominin species discovered within the last fifteen years: *Homo floresiensis* in 2004, *Homo denisova* in 2010, and *Homo naledi* in 2013. These three species, or subspecies, as well as our cousins the Neanderthals, lived contemporaneously with us *Homo sapiens.*

Homo floresiensis, affectionately nicknamed Hobbits, due to their small statue at 3.5 feet, after the characters in J.R.R. Tolkien's epic novel, *The Hobbits.* Paleontologists discovered the remains of nine individuals in a cave on Flores, an island in Indonesia. Theories abound as to their placement in the taxon and the reason for their diminutive size.

Cave on Flores Island where Homo floresiensis *were discovered*

At this writing, current data supports they arrived on the island as *Homo ergtaster/erectus* about one million years ago and obtained their dwarf size about 700,000 years ago due to insular dwarfism. This is a condition where large animals reduce in size over several generations when confined to a limited environment like on an island. It is thought this species died out about 50,000 years ago.

It is amazing to think that from the pinkie finger bone of a child and one adult molar found in the Denisova cave in southern Siberia in 2010 paleontologists announced the discovery of a new human species. They extracted DNA from the pinkie bone and compared it to the genomes of modern humans and Neanderthals. The studies proved the little girl was closely related to Neanderthals but distinct enough to merit the classification of a separate species.

Scientists continue to debate the relationship between archaic humans. Were we all one species or subspecies? DNA analysis proved we interbred, so by definition we were one species.

Homo naledi is literally the most recent "star" in our hominin lineage, as *Naledi* means "star" in the Sotho language. In 2013 an amazing treasure trove of over fifteen individuals were discovered by spelunkers in the Rising Star Cave system at The Cradle of Humankind World Heritage Site in South Africa. As yet, the fossils have not been chronometrically dated, but scientists estimate their age to be one million to two million years old. Their find caused anthropologists to rethink the meaning of becoming human. The current hypothesis contends the bodies were deposited into the cave at the time of death. Was it a ritual burial or just a means to depose of the bodies?

I recommend that you read the twenty-six page spread on our newly discovered ancestor for yourself in the October 2015 edition of the *National Geographic* under the title "Almost Human: A New Ancestor Shakes Up Our Family Tree."

To me, the evidence is incontrovertibly true. There were no *very* first *Homo sapiens*. The scientific community continues to study the evolving story of our beginnings. Paleontologists tentatively agreed archaic man became anatomically indistinguishable from modern man about 250,000 to 200,000 years ago, while anthropologists tentatively conclude that behavioral modernity of language and culture began about 50,000 years ago.

For you and your children I recommend viewing the BBC television Series *Walking with Cavemen* available through Netflix. The African landscape and the live-action scenes bring the story of our ancestors to life.

EPILOGUE

I hope this memoir of my journey back to stardust interested you, informed you, and awakened your curiosity as I searched for our beginnings, our end, and the meaning of "forever." The original plan for the book was a triptych covering my life, world religions, and Darwinian evolution. Much of the research on the latter two subjects has been done and I hope to publish my findings in the future. I owe thanks to my Venice Writers' Group who kept pushing me to write three books, not one large book. I heeded their advice and wrote this memoir.

After forty-five years as an atheist, would a thirteen-day tour of the Holy Land change my mind? Would God speak to me or show me a sign? Would the belief and devotion of my fellow pilgrims convince me that God existed? Would I witness a miracle? Would I understand why so many people have faith in God?

Or, would I gain insight and compassion for such a troubled part of the world? Would I learn history from touching, seeing, and experiencing instead of from books? Would I marvel at ancient ruins and respect the past? Would I meet new people with different views from mine?

In my mind, the answers to the first set of questions are "no." The answers to the second set of questions are "yes."

No, I did not witness "miracles." In the text I called some of my experiences "miracles." I used the word with literary license in an attempt to add interest or suspense to my story. I believe none of the "miracles," met the orthodox definition of "miracle" in the sense of an event that is impossible to explain by known laws of nature and therefore must be attributed to a supernatural or transcendent agency. I ascribe my "miracles" to either "luck" or "coincidence."

Marilyn vos Savant, author of the column "Ask Marilyn" in the Sunday *Parade* magazine defines "luck" as a random occurrence that operates either for or against us. She defines "coincidence" as a random occurrence that brings two or more related incidents together.

My first chance for a supernatural "miracle" occurred in Bethlehem. We hiked up the hill to the Church of the Nativity while the church bells and the muezzin's chant intermingled in the early evening air. The setting breathed of "miracles" and spirituality. I looked skyward. Would God appear to me with a sign declaring His existence? I was receptive. But

I felt nothing other than the pleasure of my surroundings. Yes, I tingled with excitement at actually being in Bethlehem near the calendar date of Christmas. The memory of that enchanted evening lingers with me now, but God, or Baby Jesus, or the Holy Spirit did not reach out to touch my "soul."

In the text, my first declared "miracle" happened at the Jordan border when the two Jordanian young men returned my wallet. This was "luck" in the lexicon of Marilyn vos Savant, not a supernatural "miracle." Again, finding my notebook on our return to the Roman Colosseum at Bet Shean National Park was also "luck" not a "miracle." Also, locating my notebook in the Artzy bag after fearing it lost was definitely not a "miracle," only an act of perseverance. Perhaps my Muse of Zippori whispered to me, "Judith, look in the bag."

The glorious rendition of "Hark the Herald Angels Sing" came the closest to a spiritual "miracle." Our unrehearsed voices joined with the German singers and produced sound to rival the Mormon Tabernacle Choir. This was a "miracle" of coincidence. We were in the church, famed worldwide for its amazing acoustics, when the German conductor entered with her choir members. This coincidence combined to create the miraculous music.

The journey closes with a nod to a final "miracle"—my black with white polka dots notebook. Not a religious "miracle" but a literary "miracle." By constant reference to it for dates, facts, names, impressions, and most importantly my thoughts in real time, I relived the Israeli experience, as I wrote this book.

The trip did not change my view of God. On the secular side, I appreciated the beauty of the biblical verses and the power of the parables from Father Don's daily readings. I also reveled at being a witness to the history, beauty, ruins, and abundant religious sites in Israel. But for skeptics like me, these archaeological relics are not proof of an omnipotent, omnipresent, and omniscient God.

With an open mind, I had given God another chance—one sincere, final attempt on my part for a dose of faith to appear and challenge my atheism. I experienced no "miracles," or insights, or evidence of actual biblical events. Belief in God is only possible through faith, not by reason. I cannot abandon reason to accept God by faith alone. Faith is defined as a belief in something for which there is no proof or evidence. Reason is defined as the power of the mind to think and understand in a logical way.

To accept God by faith alone is a request I cannot honor. I respect the right of an individual to resolve the mysteries of God by faith. But please respect my right to add reason to the question of the existence or non-existence of God.

We atheists are moral, loving, thoughtful, caring, and lawful citizens who live among you. Our numbers continue to grow. In May 2015 the Pew Research Center conducted a poll of the religious affiliations of Americans. The number of unaffiliated (no named religion) grew from 16.1 percent in 2007 to 22.8 percent in 2014. The change occurred among all ages, all races, and all economic and educational levels. In a worldwide survey in 2015 atheists and the nonreligious were in the majority in Scandinavia, Germany, the Netherlands, East Asia, and China. In a personal survey most of the children among my friends and relatives do not attend church, except on major religious holidays.

Today many influential thinkers in the news are atheists. Among them are Woody Allen, Ayaan Hirst Ali, Jerry Coyne, Richard Dawkins, Sam Harris, Stephen Hawking, Bill Maher, Stephen Pinker, Phillip Roth, and Neil deGrasse Tyson.

From the past some of the most prominent thinkers, philosophers, poets, authors, scientists, and politicians were atheists:

- Lucretius, Roman poet and philosopher (99BCE to 55BCE) author *On the Nature of Things*

- Omar Khayyan, Persian astronomer and mathematician (1048-1131)

- Thomas Hobbes, English political philosopher (1588-1679) author of *Leviathan* on liberal social thought

- Benedict de Spinoza, Dutch Jewish philosopher (1632-1677) author of *Ethics* a work critical of the Bible and the Divine

- David Hume, Scottish philosopher and essayist (1711-1776) author of *Treatise of Human Nature* considered the most important work in Western philosophy

- Percy Bysshe Shelley, English romantic poet (1792-1811) known for his epic poetry, expelled from Oxford after writing *The Necessity of Atheism*

- John Stuart Mill, English philosopher and economist (1806-1873) wrote against slavery and for women suffrage

- Karl Marx, German economist and philosopher (1818-1883) author of *The Communist Manifesto*

- George Elliot, English novelist (1819-1890) author of seven novels including *Silas Marner*

- Charles Darwin, English naturalist and geologist (1809-1882) father of evolution and author of *On the Origin of the Species*

- Mark Twain, American humorist and novelist (1835-1910) author of *Tom Sawyer* and *Huckleberry Finn*

- Joseph Conrad, Polish-British writer (1857-1924) considered one of the best writers in the English language, famous for *Heart of Darkness* and *Lord Jim*

- Thomas Hardy, English novelist and poet (1840-1928) famous for *Far from the Maddening Crowd* and *Tess of the d'Urbuvilles*, and the poem "God's Funeral"

- H. L.Mencken, American journalist and satirist (1880-1956) remembered for his satirical reporting on the Scopes Trial which he dubbed the "Monkey Trial"

- Sigmund Freud, Austrian neurologist (1856-1939) founder of psychoanalysis

- Albert Enstein, German physicist (1879-1955) developed the theory of relativity

- George Orwell, English novelist (1903-1950,)famous for the novel *Nineteen Eighty-Four*

- Bertrand Russell, British philosopher (1872-1970) awarded the Nobel Prize in Literature in 1950

- Carl Sagan, American astronomer and astrophysicist (1939-1996) known for research on extra-celestial life

- Ayn Rand, Russian-American philosopher and novelist (1905-1982) author of *The Fountainhead* and *Atlas shrugged*

Even from this list of famous thinkers from today and yesteryear, no one has proven the existence or non-existence of God either by faith or the scientific method— the procedure for investigating phenomena in order to gain new knowledge or correct previous knowledge by empirical or measurable evidence subject to specific principles. This technique for gathering knowledge dates to the seventeenth century.

A scientist observes or considers a phenomenon from nature, his readings, or his thoughts. He/she forms a specific or broad conjecture or hypotheses to explain the happening. Then he/she tests his supposition by conducting experiments. One characteristic of a scientific theory or hypotheses is falsifiability or refutability. Or, in other words, the inherent possibility that it can be proved false. How does this apply to the existence or non-existence of God?

The statement "no black polar bear exists" is falsifiable because if a black polar bear is found the statement would not be true. The statement "no God exists" is also falsifiable for the same reason. If evidence of God is found, then the statement is not true. But in contrast, the statement "God exists" is not falsifiable. It cannot be proved that God does not exist. It is not a scientific theory. It can only be accepted on faith. It is the same as saying "unicorns, fairies, leprechauns, or the Loch Ness monster exist." It is probable that they don't exist, but it cannot be proven.

Therefore, factoring all the thoughts of prominent atheists past and present, my own observations, reason, and the scientific principle of falsifiability, I conclude God does not exist.

After I die, I have requested my descendants release this obituary, written in memory of the little girl, Judy, searching for the meaning of *forever*.

Rousseau, Judith Heaney

November 1, 1937 – (Month, Day, Year of Death) Judith Heaney Rousseau (age) of Venice, Florida, formerly of Marblehead and Swampscott, Massachusetts died on (date). She is survived by (names of relatives). She has returned to stardust whence she came. She lives on in the memories of her friends and in the memories and genes of her children, grandchildren, great-grandchildren, and beyond *forever*. In lieu of flowers, please donate to (name of a charity).

ACKNOWLEDGMENTS

As this book espouses, there is no one single, first *Homo sapiens*. For me, there is no one single person to thank for help in writing this memoir... there are many people.

I thank my mother for her persistence in saving all the family memorabilia over ninety-six years and through numerous moves. Without them, this book would not have been possible. Thank you, Mom!

I thank my husband, who while working in his office around the corner from my computer desk, always listened to my questions on spelling or grammatical uncertainties, confirmed or dismissed any unsure memory, and proofread each proffered chapter when "hot off the press." Thank you, Connie!

Thanks to two sorority sisters, Nancy Fitz-Gerald and Phyllis McGrath, who convened with me one weekend to collaborate over our college memories and share literary expertise. All three of us were English majors. Thank you, Nancy and Phyllis!

I also thank my immediate family members who answered my many email requests for opinions and suggestions. My youngest son, Bry, an editor at The New York Times, gave me advice on the cover composition and interior content. My older sons, Terry and Don, emailed their sincere opinions on the cover and content. My daughter-in-law, Cheryl, an executive coach, used her business acumen to edit and add flavor to some of my wording and helped finalize the title. My granddaughter, Ellie, a 2016 graduate of the University of Massachusetts, compared her contemporary college life to my college years at the same university, experienced over fifty years ago. My grandson, Conrad IV, a student at Boston University, thrilled at being a "consultant" on my work. Thank you Bry, Terry, Don, Cheryl, Ellie, and Conrad!

The chapters on my visit to Jerusalem were only possible due to the dedication of Father Donald Senior, C.P. (Congregation of the Passion of Jesus Christ) and his assistant Anne Marie Tirpak. Without their leadership the trip to the Holy Land would have been just another guided tour. Their pre-trip information and suggested readings prepared me for all the holy sites with comprehensive background material. And while on the adventure, their care and concern when I lost and misplaced my black and white polka dots journal, on more than one occasion, endeared them to me. Thank you Father Don and Anne Marie!

The Venice Writers' Group in Venice, Florida, my colleagues during ten years of twice monthly sessions, helped me ready the book for publication. They challenged, corrected, and changed many commas, words, dangling participles, and even entire paragraphs. Thank you Venice Writers' Group!

Two from the group deserve individual recognition for their invaluable help. Louise Reiter, former editor for The Palm Beach Post, taught me the importance of using The Chicago Manual of Style for reference. Her encyclopedic knowledge of this indispensable tome was legend among our group. Our ever persistent cry when confounded by a grammatical question was, "Ask Louise, she'll know." After countless and tireless corrections I think I learned the distinction between the relative pronouns which and that. At least I know to go "which hunting" after completing a chapter. Thank you, Louise!

Roger Sakowski, our computer guru, taught me how to navigate in Microsoft Word and Libre Office. He spent a day on my computer formatting my work in order for me to send it to my publisher. Thank you, Roger!

And an enormous word hug to my publisher, Barbara Dee, and her team at Suncoast Digital Press. As a first-time and inexperienced author, I spent many months searching for just the right publisher, one able to guide me but not overwhelm me. I also wanted to work "face-to-face," not strictly by email. Suncoast Digital Press met all my requirements. My husband, who was also my lawyer, and I met at her office in Sarasota, Florida and signed the contract that very day. I have been happy with her knowledge and professionalism, but most happy with her obvious, genuine joy in helping me publish my memoir. Thank you Barbara Dee and Suncoast Digital Press!

PHOTO ACKNOWLEDGMENTS

All photos, maps, and images are from my own personal albums, my own photography, by permission, or in the public domain except where noted below:

Page 56 - Ford Perfect courtesy of Jason Vogel
https://commons.wikimedia.org/wiki/File:1948_Ford_Prefect_E93A.jpg
(CC BY-SA 3.0) https://creativecommons.org/licenses/by-sa/3.0/

Page 111 – Photo of Professor Frank Prentice Rand courtesy of University of Massachusetts Archives

Page158 - Tunnels in Gaza courtesy of the Israeli Defense Forces
https://commons.wikimedia.org/wiki/File:IDF_Soldiers_Uncover_Tunnels_in_Gaza_(14513059999).jpg
(CC BY-SA 2.0) https://creativecommons.org/licenses/by-sa/2.0/

Page 159 - Ruins in Beit Hanoun courtesy of btselem
https://commons.wikimedia.org/wiki/File:20140805_beit_hanun7.jpg
(CC BY 4.0) https://creativecommons.org/licenses/by/4.0/

Page 188 - Monastery of the Temptation courtesy of Dmitrij Rodionov, DR
https://commons.wikimedia.org/wiki/File:Monastery_of_the_Temptation_(Jeriho).jpg
(CC BY-SA 3.0) https://creativecommons.org/licenses/by-sa/3.0/

Page251- Mona Lisa of the Galilee courtesy of Tomisti
https://commons.wikimedia.org/wiki/File:Mona_Lisa_of_the_Galilee_large.jpg
(CC BY-SA 3.0) https://creativecommons.org/licenses/by-sa/3.0/

Page 282 - Morganucodon watsoni courtesy of FunkMonk (Michael B. H.)
https://commons.wikimedia.org/wiki/File:Morganucodon.jpg
(CC BY-SA 3.0) https://creativecommons.org/licenses/by-sa/3.0/

Page 283 - Fossil of Teilhardina courtesy of Ghedoghedo
https://commons.wikimedia.org/wiki/File:Teilhardina_belgica.jpg
(CC BY-SA 3.0) https://creativecommons.org/licenses/by-sa/3.0/

Page 285 - Sahelanthropus tchadensis cast courtesy of Didier Descouens
https://commons.wikimedia.org/wiki/File:Sahelanthropus_tchadensis_-_TM_266-01-060-1.jpg
(CC BY-SA 4.0) https://creativecommons.org/licenses/by-sa/4.0/

Page 286 - Restoration model of Lucy courtesy of Momotarou2012
https://commons.wikimedia.org/wiki/File:Skeleton_and_restoration_model_of_Lucy.jpg
(CC BY-SA 3.0) https://creativecommons.org/licenses/by-sa/3.0/

BIBLIOGRAPHY

Ali, Ayaan Hirsi. *Infidel.* New York: Free Press, 2007.

Allen, E. A. *The Prehistoric World or Vanished Races.* Nashville TN: Central Publishing House, 1885.

Armstrong, Karen. *Jerusalem One City, Three Faiths.* New York; Alfred A. Knopf, Inc.
— *The Case for God.*

Auel, Jean. *The Clan of the Cave Bear.* New York: Bantam Books, 1983.
— *The Land of Painted Caves.* New York: Bantam Books, 2011.
— *The Mammoth Hunters.* New York: Bantam Books,1985.
— *The Plains of Passage.* New York: Bantam Books, 1991.
— *The Shelters of Stone.* New York: Bantam Books, 2010.
— *The Valley of Horses.* New York: Bantam Books, 1984.

Barbery, Muriel. *The Elegance of the Hedgehog.* Paris, France: A Gallic Book, 2006.

Barker, Dan. *Godless How an Evangelical Preacher Became One of America's Leading Atheists.* Berkeley, CA: Ulysses Press, 2008.

Bartlett, Anne. *The Aboriginal First Peoples of Australia.* Minneapolis,MI: Lerner Publications Company. 2002.

Bates, Ernest Sutherland. *The Bible Designed to be read as Living Literature.* New York: Simon and Schuster, 1936.

Beauman, Sally. *The Visitors.* New York: Harper Collins, 2014.

Bell, James Stuart and Campbell, Stan. *The Complete Idiot's Guide to the Bible.* New York: Alpha Books, 2005.

Betts, Robert Brenton. *The Druze.* New Haven: Yale University Press, 1988.

Blomberg, Mark B. *Basic Instinct The Genesis of Behavior.* New York: Avalon Publishing Group Inc., 2005.

Bock, David. *The diary of a Reluctant Atheist.* Austin, TX: Published by David Bock, 2015.

Bowker, John. *World Religions The Great Faiths Explored & Explained.* New York: DK publishing, Inc., 1997.

Brennert, Alan. *Moloka'i.* New York: St. Marin's Press; Reprint Edition, 2004.

Bridges, E. Lucas. *Uttermost Part of the Earth.* New York: E. P. Dutton and Company, INC., 1949.

Brooks, Geraldine. *Caleb's Crossing: A Novel*. New York: Penguin Books, 2011.

Brown, Charlotte Lewis. *After the Dinosaurs Mammoths and Fossil Mammals*. New York: Harper Collins Publishers, 2006.

Bryson, Bill. *A Short History of Nearly Everything*. New York: Broadway Books, 2003.

Burpo, Todd   *Heaven is for Real: A Little Boy's Astounding Trip to Heaven and Back*. New York: Harper Collins Publishing, 2011.

Burstein, Dan and deKeijzer, Arne. *Secrets of Angels and Demons*. London: Weidenfield & Nicolson, 2005.

Chacour, Elias. *Blood Brothers The Unforgettable Story of a Palestinian Christian Working for Peace in Israel*. Grand Rapids, Michigan: Chosen Books, 2003.

Chaucer, Geoffrey. *The Canterbury Tales*. Amazon Digital Services LLC, 2010.

Chewning, Emily Blair. *Anatomy Illustrated*. New York: Simon and Schuster, 1979.

Cochran, Gregory and Harpending, Henry. *The 10,000 Year Explosion How Civilization Accelerated Human Evolution*. New York: Basic Books, 2009.

Conway, D. J. *By Oak, Ash, & Thorn Modern Celtic Shamanism*. Woodbury, Minnesota: Llewellyn Publications, 1995.

Conwell, Russell H. *Acres of Diamonds*. Amazon Digital Services, LLC, 2010.

Coyne, Jerry A. *Why evolution is True*. New York: The Penguin Group, 2009.

Crace, Jim. *Being Dead, A Novel*. New York: Farrar, Straus, and Giroux, 2000.

Davis, Percival and Kenyon, Dean H. *Of Pandas and People The Central Question of Biological Origins*. Dallas, TX: Haughton Publishing Company, 1989.

Darwin, Charles. *The Autobiopgraphy of Charles Darwin*
— *Geological Observations in*
— *The Origin of Species*. New York: Banton Books, 1859.
— *The Voyage of the Beagle*. Amazon Digital Servises LLC, 2014.
— *What Darwin Saw*. New York: Weathervane Books, 1879.

Dawkins, Richard. *The Blind Watch Maker Why the Evidence of Evolution Reveals a Universe Without Design.* New York: W.W. Norton & Company, 1987.

—*The God Delusion.* New York: Houghton Mifflin Company, 2006.

—*The Greatest Show on Earth.* New York: Free Press Division of Simon and Schuster, 2009.

— *The Magic of Reality: How WeKnow What is Really True.* New York: Simon and Schuster   Digital Sales Inc., 2012

—*The Selfish Gene.* New York: Oxford University Press Inc., 1989.

—*Unweaving the Rainbow: Science, Delusion and the Appetite for Wonder.* New York: Mariner Books Reprint edition, 2000.

Dawood, N. J. *The Koran.* New York: Penguin Books, 1956.

De Botton, Alain. *Religion for Atheists: A Non-believer's Guide to the Uses of Religion.* Amazon Digital Vintage: Random House LLC, 20132

Dennett, Daniel C. *Breaking the Spell Religion as a Natural Phenomenon.* New York: Penguin Group, 2006.

—*Darwin's Dangerous Idea Evolution and the Meanings of Life.* New York: Simon and Schuster Paperbacks, 1995.

De Waal, Frans. *The Bonobo and the Atheist In Search of Humanism Among the Primates.* New York: W. W. Norton & Company, 2014.

Dowd, Michael. *Thank God for Evolution! How the Marriage of Science and Religion Will Transform Your Life and Our World.* San Framcisdco: Council Oak Books, 2007.

Eddy, Mary Baker. *Manual of the Mother Church—The First Church of Christ Scientist.* Boston: Allison V. Stewart, 1895.

Eyewitness Travel. *Jerusalem Israel,Petra & Sinai.* New York: Dorling Kindersley Limited, 2012.

Ehrenreich, Barbara. *Living with a Wild God.* New York: Hachette Book Group, 2014.

Farhan, Mohammad. *Petra The Art, The History and The Nature Petra By The Local.* Jordan: Book Rack, 2009.

Faulkner, Raymond O. *The Egyptian Book of the Dead.* San Francisco: Chronicle Books, 1994.

Finlayson, Clive. *The Humans Who Went Extinct.* New York: Oxford University Press, 2009.

George, Francis Cardinal. *Handbook for Today's Catholic Fully Indexed to the Catechism of the Catholic Church.* St. Louis, Missouri: Liguori Publications, 2004.

Gilbert, Elizabeth. *The Signature of All Things.* New York: Penguin Group, 2013.

Goldin, Barbara Diamond. *Journeys with Elijah.* New York: Harcourt Brace & Company, 1999.

Golding, William. *The Inheritors.* New York: Harcourt, Inc., 1955.

Goldstein, Rebecca Newbergere. *36 Arguments for the Existence of God. A Work of Fiction.* New York: Pantheon Books, 2010.

Gonzalez- Wippler, Migene. *TheComplete Book of Amulets & Talismans.* St. Paul, Minnesota: Llewellyn Publications, 1991.

Gould, Stephen Jay. *The Book of Life An Illustrated History of the Evolution of Life and Earth.*New York: W. W. Norton & Company, 2001.
—*Wonderful Life The Burgess Shale and the Nature of History.* New York: W. W. Norton & Company, 1989. 2014.

Griffith, Ralph H. T. *The Rig Veda.* Amazon Digital Services: Vakya Books, 2015.

Gunderson, Cory. *Religions of the Middle East.* Edna Minnesota: ABDO Publishing Company, 2004.

Haines, Tim. *Walking with Dinosaurs A natural History.*New York: Doring Kindersley Publishing Inc., 1999.

Hamer, Dean. *The God Gene.* New York: Anchor Books, 2004.

Harris, Sam. *Lying.* Amazon Digital: Four Elephants Press, 2013.

Hastings, Selina. *The Children's Illustrated Bible.* New York: DK Publishing, Inc., 2005.

Hawking, Stephen. *A Brief History of Time.* New York: Bantam Books, 1988.
—*The Grand Design.* New York: Bantam Books, 2010.

Hazelwood, Nick. *Savage The Life and Times of Jemmy Button.* New York: St. Martin's Press. 2000.

Hitchens, Christopher. *The Portable Atheist Selected Readings for the Nonbeliever.* Boston: Da Carpo Press, 2007.

Hoffman, Alice. *The Dovekeepers: A Novel.* New York: Scribner, 2011.

Holy Bible. *Authorized King James Version.* London: Collins' Clear-type Press.

The Holy Land The Land of Jesus. Herzlia, Israel: Palphot Ltd.

Howells, William. *The Heathens Primitive Man and His Religions*. Salem, Wisconsin: Sheffield Publishing Company, 1986.

Hubbard, L. Ron. *A Description of Scientolgy*. Ontario: L. Ron Hubbard Library, 1994.

Huntford, Roland. *The Last Place on Earth*. New York: Random House Inc., 1999.

Hume, David. *Dialogues Concerning Natural Natural Religion*. Amazon Digital Services LLC, 2012.

Inman, Nick and Mcdonald, Ferdie. *Jerusalem, Israel,Petra, and Sinai*. New York: Dorling Kindersley Limited, 2012.

Jaffe, Nina. *The Mysterious visitor Stories of the Prophet Elijah*. New York: Scholastic Press. 1997.

James, William. *Varieties of Religious Experience: A Study in Human Nature*. Amazon Digital Press: Herkalion Press. 2014.

Jessup, Peter. *The Complete History of New Zealand*. Amazon Digital Services LLC, 2013

Johnson, Linda. *Complete Idiot's Guide to Hinduism*. New York: Penquin Group, 2009.

Joyner, Rick. *The World Aflame The Welsh Revival and Its Lessons For Our Time*. Charlotte, NC: Morning Star Publications, 1993.

Kahneman, Daniel. *Thinking Fast and Slow*. New York: Farrar, Straus and Giroux, 2011.

Kalita, Mark F. *7 Day Bodhi*. Charlesyon, SC: 2013.

Kent, Hannah. *Burial Rites.*New York: Little, Brown & Company, 2013.

Khan, Maulana Wahiduddin. *The Quran (Translation)*. New Delhi: Goodword Books, 2009.

Kidd, Sue Monk. *The Invention of Wings*. New York: Penguin Books Reprint Edtion, 2014.

King, Lily. *Euphoria*. New York: Atlantic Monthly Press, 2014.

Kingsolver, Barbara. *Flight Behavior: A Novel*. New York: Harper Reprint Edtion, 2012.

Kipling, Rudyard. *Just So Stories*. Amazon Digital Services LLC. 2012.

Krauss, Lawrence, M. *A Universe from Nothing*. New York: Free Press, 2012.

Kurzwell, Arthur. *The Torah for Dummies*. Hoboken, NJ: Wiley Publishing, Inc., 2008.

Lyell, Charles. *Principles of Geology*. Amazon: Penguin; Abridged Ed edition, 2005.

Lynch, John and Barrett, Louise. *Walking with Cavemen Eye-To-Eye with Your Ancestors*. London: Headline Book Publishing, 2002.

Malthus, Thomas. *An Essay on the Principles of Population*. Amazon Digital Services LLC. 2013.

Michener, James A. *The Source*. Greenwich, CN: Fawcett publications, Inc., 1965.

Miller, James. *Examined Lives from Socrates to Nietzsche*. New York: Farrar, Straus and Giroux, 2011.

Miller, Kenneth R. and Levine, Joseph. *Biology*. Upper Saddle River, NJ: Pearson Prentice Hall, 2004.

Miller, Kenneth R. *Finding Darwin's God*. New York; Harper Perennial, 1999.

Moriarty, Liane. *What Alice Forgot*. New York: Berkley Books, 2009.

Moring, Gary F. *The Complete Idiot's Guide to Theories of the Universe*. New York: Penguin Group, 2002.

Murphey-O'Connor, Jerome. *The Holy Land An Oxford Archaeological Guide*. New York: Oxford University Press, 2008.

Nouwen, Henri J. M. *Life of the Beloved Spiritual Living in a Secular World*. New York: The Crossroad Publishing Company: 1992.

O'Reilly, Bill and Dugard, Martin. *Killing Jesus.*New York: Henry Holt and Company, LLC, 2013.

Orloff, Sandra. *God is Santa Claus for Grown-ups*

Osborn, Kevin and Burgess, Dana L. *The Complete Idiot's Guide to Classical Mythology.*New York: The Penguin Group, 2004.

Otsuka. Julie. *The Budda in the Attic*. New York: Random House LLC, 2011.

Paul, Richard. *A Handbook to the Universe*. Chicago: Chicago Review Press, 1948.

Paine, Thomas. *Common Sense and Rights of Man*. New York: Signet Classics, 1969.

Pallen, Mark. *The Rough Guide to Evolution*. New York: Penguin Group, 2009.

Pascal, Théophile. *Reincarnation A study in Human Evolution*. Amazon Digital Service: HardPress, 2015.

Penczak, Christopher. *The Inner temple Witchvraft Magick, Meditation and Psychic Development*. Woodbury, Minnesota: Llewellyn Publications, 2011.

Pfeiffer, Ida. *A Woman's Journey Around the World*. Amazon Digital Services LLC, 2012.

Philips, Doug. *The Bad People Stole My God*. Amazon Digital Services LLC, 2013.

Pinker, Steven. *The Blank Slate The Modern Denial of Human Nature*. New York: Penguin Putman, Inc., 2002.
— *How the Mind Works*. New York: W. W. Norton & Company, 1997.

Pritchard, James and Page, Nick. *Atlas of Bible History*. New York: Harper Collins Publishers, 2008.

Readers Digest History of Man. *The Last Two Million Years*. New York: The Reader's Digest   Association, 1979.

Robinson, Gerda Hartwich. *The Inner War My Journey from Pain to peace*. Lulu Publishing: 2013.

Robinson, Tara Rodden. *Genetics for Dummies*. Hoboken, NJ: Wiley Publishing, Inc., 2005.

Robisheaux, Thomas. *The Last Witch of Langenburg Murder in a German Village*. New York: W. W. Norton & Company, 2009.

Rose, Petra. *Everything Scattered will be Gathered Emerging from Patriarchal Fundamentalism*. Sarasota, Florida: Suncoast Digital Press, 2015.

Russell, Gerard. *Heirs to Forgotten Kingdoms*. New York: Basic Books, 2014.

Saint Augustine. *The Confessions of Saint Augustine*. New York: Random House LLC, 2011.

Salzman, Mark. *Lying Awake. A Novel About Devotion and Doubt*. New York: Vintage Books, 2000.

Schrödinger, Erwin. *What is Life? with Mind and Matter*. Cambridge: Cambridge University Press, 1067.

Shubin, Neil. *Your Inner Fish A Journey Into the 3.5-Billion-Year History of the Human Body*. New York: Random House, 2008.

Skybreak, Ardea. *The Science of Evolution and The Myth of Creationism Knowing What's Real and Why It Matters*. Chicago: Insight Press, 2006.

Sloan, Christopher. *The Human Story Our Evolution from Prehistoric Ancestors to Today*. Washington, D.C.: National Geographic Society, 2004.

Smith, Joseph. *The Book of Mormon*. Salt Lake City, Utah: The church of Jesus Christ of latter Day Saints, 1981.

Smith, Laura S. *The Illustrated Timeline of Religion A Crash Course in Words & Pictures*. New York: Sterling, 2007.

Stace, Alexa. *The Atlas of the World*. London: Z-Publishing Ltd., 2001.

Stanley, Steven M. *Children of the Ice Age How a Global Catastrophe Allowed Humans to Evolve*. New York: W. H. Freeman and Company, 1998.

Stevenson, Robert Louis. *A Child's Garden of Verses*. Amazon Digital Services LLC, 2016.

Stout, Martha. *The Sociopath Next Door*. New York: Random House Inc., 2006.

Studium Biblicum Franciscanum. *The Holy Land*. Herzlia, Israel: Palphot Ltd.,

Sultan, Sohaib. *The Koran for Dummies*. Hoboken, NJ: Wiley Publishing, Inc., 2004.

Sutherland, Alexander. *History of Australia and New Zealand*. Amazon Digital Services LLC, 2014.

Swindoll, Charles R. *Ellijah A Man of Heroism and Humility*. Nashville,TN: Thomas Nelson, 2009.

Teilhard de Chardin, Pierre. *The Phenomenon of Man*. New York: Harper Row/Harper Touch Book; 2nd edition, 1965.

Thimmesh, Catherine. *Lucy Long Ago Uncovering the Mystery of Where We Came From*. New York: Houghton Mifflin Harcourt Publishing Company, 2009.

Tolle, Eckhart. *The Power of Now A Guide to Spiritual Enlightenment*. Novato, CA: Namaste Publishing, 1999.

Toporov, Brandon and Buckles, Father Luke. *The Complete Idiot's Guide to World Religions*. New York: Alpha Books, 2004.

Trollope, Anthony. *Barchester Twoers*. Amazon Digital Services LLC. 2016.

Van Rose, Susanna. *Eyewitness Earth*. New York: DK Publishing, 2013.

Voltaire. *Candide*. Amazon: Dover Publications; Reprint Edition, 2012.

Walker, Barbara A. *Man Made God*. Seattle, WA: Stellar House Publishing, 2010.

Wallace,Lewis. *Ben-Hur, A Tale of the Christ*. Amazon Digital Services LLC, 2014.

Watson, James D. *The Double Helix*. New York: The Penguin Group, 1969.

Warren, Rick. *The Purpose Driven Life What on Earth Am I here For?* Grand Rapids, Michigan: Zondervan, 2002.

Williams, D, Eric. *Heaven is for Real, This Book Isn't An Astounding Refutation of a Story About a Trip to Heaven and Back.* Amazon Digital Services LLC, 2011.

Winston, Robert. *The Moral Animal Why We Are the Way We are: The New Science of Evolutionary Psychology.* New York: Vintagre Books, 1994.

—*Human Instinct How our Primeval Instincts Shape our Modern Lives.* New York: Bantam Books, 2011.

Woods, Len. *Handbook of World Religions.* Uhrichsville, Ohio: Barbour Publishing, Inc., 1973.

Wright, Fred and Wight, Sharon. *World's Greatest Revivals.* Amazon Digital Services LLC: Destiny Images, 2011.

Wright, Robert. *The Evolution of God.* New York: Little, Brown and Company, 2009.

—*Nonzero The Logic of Human Destiny.* New York: Vintage books, 2001.

Yoon, Carol Kaesuk. *Naming Nature The Clash Between Instinct and Nature.* New York: W. W. Norton & Company, 2009.